高等院校物流管理专业系列教材 · 物流企业岗位培训系列教材

物流英语

（第2版）

卢亚丽　赵　伟◎主　编
李战国　杨　萌◎副主编

清华大学出版社

北　京

内容简介

本书根据经济全球化的快速发展,结合物流英语教学改革的新特点,系统介绍物流管理、仓储、包装、采购、运输、配送、物流信息系统以及供应链管理等物流专业英语基本知识,并通过强化实训,培养提高读者的应用能力。

本书具有知识系统、案例丰富、注重创新、集理论和实践于一体的特点,因而既可以作为普通高等院校本科物流管理、国际贸易、电子商务等专业的首选教材,同时兼顾高职高专、应用型大学的教学;也可作为物流和外贸企业从业者的培训教材,并为广大社会学习物流专业英语的人员提供有益的参考和借鉴。

图书在版编目(CIP)数据

物流英语/卢亚丽,赵伟主编. —2 版. —北京:清华大学出版社,2017 (2025.1重印)
(高等院校物流管理专业系列教材 物流企业岗位培训系列教材)
ISBN 978-7-302-49108-8

Ⅰ.①物… Ⅱ.①卢…②赵… Ⅲ.①物流 – 英语 – 高等学校 – 教材 Ⅳ.①F25

中国版本图书馆 CIP 数据核字(2017)第 301363 号

责任编辑:贺 岩
封面设计:汉风唐韵
责任校对:王荣静
责任印制:丛怀宇

出版发行:清华大学出版社
  网 址:https://www.tup.com.cn, https://www.wqxuetang.com
  地 址:北京清华大学学研大厦 A 座   邮 编:100084
  社 总 机:010-83470000   邮 购:010-62786544
  投稿与读者服务:010-62776969,c-service@tup.tsinghua.edu.cn
  质量反馈:010-62772015,zhiliang@tup.tsinghua.edu.cn
印 装 者:三河市君旺印务有限公司
经 销:全国新华书店
开 本:185mm×230mm 印 张:15.25   字 数:295 千字
版 次:2012 年 6 月第 1 版 2017年12月第 2 版 印 次:2025 年 1 月第 4 次印刷
定 价:38.00 元

产品编号:075021-02

编审委员会

主　任

　　牟惟仲　　中国物流技术协会理事长、教授级高级工程师

副主任

　　翁心刚　　北京物资学院副院长、教授

　　冀俊杰　　中国物资信息中心原副主任、总工程师

　　张昌连　　中国商业信息中心原主任、总工程师

　　吴　明　　中国物流技术协会副理事长兼秘书长、高级工程师

　　李大军　　中国物流技术协会副秘书长、中国计算机协会市场
　　　　　　　发展分会秘书长

委　员

吴江江	林　征	车亚军	张建国	孙　军	梁　露
刘徐方	田振中	张劲珊	李爱华	刘阳威	郑秀恋
王　艳	罗佩华	李　青	刘　华	林玲玲	梁　旭
王海文	刘丽艳	李耀华	卢亚丽	丁玉书	温卫娟
张淑谦	林南南	李秀华	刘文歌	朱凤仙	任　斐
崔　娜	李战国	雷　燕	耿　燕	罗松涛	于汶艳

总　编

　　李大军

副总编

　　刘徐方　　王海文　　李爱华　　田振中　　卢亚丽　　孙　军

　　物流是国民经济的重要组成部分，也是我国经济发展新的增长点，加快我国现代物流发展，对于调整经济结构、促进产业升级、优化资源配置、改善投资环境、增强综合国力和企业竞争能力、提高经济运行质量与效益、实现可持续发展战略、推进我国经济体制与经济增长方式的根本性转变，具有非常重要而深远的意义。

　　为推动我国现代物流业的健康快速发展，国务院陆续下发《国务院关于印发物流业调整和振兴规划的通知》（国发〔2009〕8 号）、《国务院办公厅关于促进物流业健康发展政策措施的意见》（国办发〔2011〕38 号）、《国务院办公厅关于促进内贸流通健康发展的若干意见》（国办发〔2014〕51 号）等多个文件，制定和完善相关配套政策措施，以有序实施促进物流企业加大整合、改造、提升、转型的力度，并逐步实现转型发展、集约发展、联动发展、融合发展，通过物流的组织创新、技术创新、服务创新，在保证我国物流总量平稳较快增长的同时，加快供需结构、地区结构、行业结构、人力资源结构、企业组织结构的调整步伐，创新服务模式，提高服务能力，努力满足经济建设与社会发展的需要。

　　2015 年 3 月，经国务院授权，国家发展和改革委员会、外交部、商务部联合发布《推动共建丝绸之路经济带和 21 世纪海上丝绸之路的愿景与行动》，随着我国改革开放和社会主义市场经济的加速推进，随着国家"一带一路、互联互通"倡议的制定和实施，我国迅速融入全球经济一体化的进程中，中国市场国际化的特征越发凸显。

　　物流既涉及国际贸易、国际商务活动等外向型经济领域，也涉及交通运输、仓储配送、通关报检等多个业务环节。 面对当前世界经济的迅猛发展和国际市场激烈竞争的压力，加强物流科技知识的推广应用、加速物流专业技能型应用人才的培养，已成为我国经济转型发展亟待解决的问题。

需求促进专业建设，市场驱动人才培养，针对我国高等职业教育院校已沿用多年的物流教材陈旧和知识老化而亟须更新的问题，为了适应国家经济发展和社会就业急需，为了满足物流行业规模发展对操作技能型人才的需求，在中国物流技术协会的支持下，我们组织北京物资学院、大连工业大学、北京城市学院、吉林工程技术师范学院、北京财贸职业学院、郑州大学、哈尔滨理工大学、燕山大学、浙江工业大学、河北理工大学、华北水利水电大学、江西财经大学、山东外贸职业学院、吉林财经大学、广东理工大学、辽宁中医药大学、郑州升达经贸管理学院等全国20多个省市高职高专院校及应用类大学物流管理专业的主讲教师和物流企业经理，共同精心编撰了此套教材，旨在迅速提高高等院校物流管理专业学生和物流行业从业者的专业技术素质，更好地服务于我国物流产业和物流经济。

本套教材作为普通高等教育院校物流管理专业的特色教材，融入了物流运营管理的最新实践教学理念，坚持以科学发展观为统领，力求严谨，注重与时俱进，根据物流业发展的新形势和新特点，依照物流活动的基本过程和规律，全面贯彻国家"十二五"教育发展规划，按照物流企业对人才的需求模式，结合学生就业加强实践能力训练，注重校企结合、贴近物流企业业务实际，注重新设施设备操作技术的掌握，强化实践技能与岗位应用培养训练，并注重教学内容和教材结构的创新。

本套教材根据高等教育院校"物流管理"专业教学大纲和课程设置，各教材的出版对强化物流从业人员教育培训、提高经营管理能力，对帮助学生尽快熟悉物流操作规程与业务管理、毕业后能够顺利走上社会就业具有特殊意义，因而既可作为本科高职院校物流管理专业教学的首选教材，也可作为物流、商务贸易等企业在职员工的培训用书。

中国物流技术协会理事长　牟惟仲

2017 年 5 月于北京

Preface

　　全球经济一体化进程加快，世界各国之间的贸易交往日益密切，随着我国加入 WTO,我国流通市场已经对外全面开放，中国市场国际化的趋势已在形成，为我国物流企业参与国际物流市场竞争提供了良好的发展契机。

　　当前，随着国家"一带一路、互联互通"总体发展战略的制定和实施，面对物流市场国际化的迅速发展与激烈竞争，对从事国际物流运营人员素质的要求越来越高，社会物资流通和物流产业发展急需大量具有物流英语知识与应用技能的复合型专门人才。

　　英语是工具，也是一把打开世界门窗的钥匙，具有加强沟通、扩大交流范围的功能。 物流英语已成为我国物流企业进军国际物流市场所必须掌握的关键技能；尽快提高我国涉外物流企业从业人员的英语水平已成为目前亟待解决的问题。

　　《物流英语》一书正是为培养大量国际物流专门人才，解决物流企业发展对既懂物流专业知识，又熟练掌握物流英语及实际业务运作技能型人才的急需而编写的。 本书严格按照国家教育部关于"加强职业教育、注重实践教学、强化应用技能培养"等教育教学改革精神和要求，由长期从事物流英语教学的主讲教师及具有丰富经验的企业人士共同编写，本书的出版对提高从业人员的英语水平、提升物流企业的服务质量、促进我国外向型物流业的健康发展具有十分重要的意义。

　　本书自 2012 年出版以来，因写作质量高、突出应用能力培养，深受全国各高等院校广大师生的欢迎。 目前已是第 4 次重印。 此次再版，作者审慎地对原教材进行了反复论证、精心设计，包括结构调整、压缩篇幅、补充新知识、增加技能训练等相应修改，以使其更贴近现代物流业发展实际，更好地为国家物流经济和教学服务。

　　本书作为普通高等教育物流管理专业的特色教材，共 11 章，以学习者应用能力培养为主线，坚持科学发展观，根据现代物流业的快速发展，围绕物流运作所涉及的领域和业务，结合物流英语教学改革的新特点，系统介绍物流管理、仓储、包装、采购、运输、配送、物流信息系统以及供应链管理等物流专业英语基本知识，并通过强化实训，培养提高读者的应用能力。

本书融入了物流英语最新的实践教学理念，力求严谨，注重与时俱进，具有知识系统、案例丰富、注重创新、实用性强等特点。它既可以作为普通高等院校本科物流管理、国际贸易、电子商务等相关专业物流英语教学的首选教材，同时兼顾高职高专、应用型大学的教学；也可作为物流和外贸从业者的培训教材，并为广大社会学习物流专业英语的人员提供有益的参考和借鉴。

本教材由李大军筹划并具体组织，卢亚丽和赵伟主编，卢亚丽统改稿，李战国、杨萌为副主编，由物流英语专家王艳教授审订。作者编写分工：牟惟仲(序言)，卢亚丽(第1章、第2章)，赵伟(第3章、第4章)，李战国(第5章、第6章)，刘丽艳、李青、张淑谦(第7章)，杨萌(第8章)；华燕萍(文字修改、版式调整)，李晓新(制作教学课件)。

在本教材再版过程中，我们参考借鉴了国内外有关物流英语的最新书刊、网站资料，并得到编委会和物流协会有关专家教授的具体指导，在此一并致谢。为配合本书使用，我们提供配套电子教学课件，读者可以从清华大学出版社网站(www.tup.com.cn)免费下载。因作者水平有限，书中难免有疏漏和不足，恳请同行和读者批评指正。

编　者

2017 年 11 月

····· *Contents* ·····

Part Two　Extra-curricular Readings

Part One

Texts

Chapter 1

Overview of Logistics

Learning Objectives

- Understand the definition of logistics
- Understand some interpretations of logistics
- Understand why companies can get competitive advantages through logistics

Lesson 1.1　Origin and Definition

The *Oxford English Dictionary* defines logistics as "the branch of military science relating to procuring, maintaining and transporting material, personnel and facilities". However, the *New Oxford American Dictionary* defines logistics as "the detailed coordination of a complex operation involving many people, facilities, or supplies", and the Oxford Dictionary on-line defines it as "the detailed organization and implementation of a complex operation". As such, logistics is commonly seen as a branch of engineering that creates "people systems" rather than "machine systems".

In an effort to avoid potential misunderstanding about the meaning of logistics, this book adopts the current definition promulgated by the Council of Logistics Management (CLM), one of the world's most prominent organizations for logistics professionals. According to the CLM, "Logistics is a part of the supply chain process that plans, implements, and controls the efficient, effective forward and reverses flow and storage of goods, services, and related information between the point of origin and the point of consumption in order to meet customers' requirements."[1]

This definition needs to be analyzed in closer detail. First, The CLM definition indicates that the purpose of logistics is "to meet customers' requirements", so we maintain this firstly.

This is important for several reasons, with one being that logistics strategies and activities should be based upon customers' wants and needs rather than the wants, needs, and capabilities of other parties. The second reason for the importance of meeting customers' requirements is the notion that since different customers have different logistical needs and wants, a one-size-fits-all logistics approach (mass logistics) in which every customer gets the same type and level of logistics service will result in some customers being overserved and others being underserved.

Logistics is part of the supply chain process. The key point for now is that logistics is part of a bigger picture in the sense that the supply chain focuses on coordination among business functions (such as marketing, production, and finance) within and across organizations. The fact that logistics is explicitly recognized as a part of the supply chain process means that logistics has an impact on how well (or how poorly) an individual firm and its associated supply chain can achieve goals and objectives.

The CLM definition also indicates that logistics should be involved in all three activities—planning, implementing, controlling and not just one or two. Some suggest, however, that logistics is more involved in the implementation than in the planning of certain logistical policies.

Note that the CLM definition also refers to "efficient and effective forward and reverse flows and storage". Broadly speaking, effectiveness can be thought of as "how well a company does what they say they're going to do". [2] For example, a company promises that all orders will be shipped within 24 hours of receipt. In contrast, efficiency can be thought of as how well (or poorly) company resources are used to achieve what a company promises it can do. [3]

With respect to forward and reverse flows and storage, logistics has traditionally focused on forward flows and storage, that is, those directed toward the point of consumption. However, the logistics discipline has recognized the importance of reverse flows and storage (reverse logistics), which originate at the point consumption. Reverse logistics is also likely to gain additional attention in the future because online purchases tend to have higher return rates than other types of purchases.

Finally, the CLM definition also indicates that logistics involves the flow and storage of "goods, services, and related information". Indeed, in the contemporary business environment, logistics is as much about the flow and storage of information as it is about the flow and storage of goods. Advances in information technology make it increasingly easier and less costly for companies to substitute information for inventory. Consider the U. S.

Marine Corps which is in the midst of a decade-long strategy to improve its logistics. The Marines aim to replace inventory with information so that they won't have to stockpile tons of supplies near the battlefield. That's what the armed forces did during the Gulf War; only to find out they could not keep track of what was in containers and didn't even use many of the items.

New words and terms

Council of Logistics Management（CLM）		物流管理协会
the point of origin		起源地
the point of consumption		消费地
planning, implementing, controlling		计划、实施、控制
forward logistics		正向物流
reverse logistics		逆向物流
storage	*n.*	储存
inventory management		库存管理
warehousing	*n.*	仓储

Notes

1. Logistics is a part of the supply chain process that plans, implements, and controls the efficient, effective forward and reverse flow and storage of goods, services, and related information between the point of origin and the point of consumption in order to meet customers' requirements.
   物流是供应链运作过程中，以满足顾客需求为目的，对货物、服务和相关信息在产出地和消费地之间实现高效率、高效益的正向和反向流通及存储所进行的计划、执行和控制过程。
2. Broadly speaking, effectiveness can be thought of as "how well a company does what they say they're going to do".
   广义来说，效益被认为是"企业做其曾经承诺过未来将要做的事情所取得的效果"。
3. In contrast, efficiency can be thought of as how well (or poorly) company resources are used to achieve what a company promises it can do.
   反之，效率则被认为是企业在实现其工作目标的过程中资源利用的好坏。

Lesson 1. 2   Some Interpretation to Logistics

1. 6R Philosophy of Logistics

- Logistics is getting the right product or service
- To the right place
- At the right time
- In the right quantity
- For the right price
- In order to make the right customer satisfied

2. The Core Concept of Logistics

As the evolution of logistics concepts and practice, the world's developed countries and regions demonstrated the development of logistics customer service is the core concept of modern logistics. [1]

After more than 20 years of development, when the core concept of enterprise management changed from product manufacturing to sales and then turned to marketing and customer service, people's understanding of the logistics enterprises themselves from the functional activities rose to in order to meet customer demand for the purpose of the planning, execution and control of the management process. Therefore, logistics is service, and it is managed.

Clearly, the process of enterprise's logistics operation—whether the operation of the enterprise itself, or outsourced to third-party logistics company's operations, is customer service process. Logistics management, whether the enterprise self-management, or appointed third-party logistics company's management, is on the customer service process management. Therefore, the so-called modern logistics is customer service.

In addition, because the logistics function of the system goal is to satisfy customer needs. Therefore, from a customer service point of view, logistics is defined by scholars as: to the right cost and the right conditions, to ensure the right customer at the right time and right place, for the right product for availability, namely, the concept of logistics 6Rs. The so-called product availability, that is, the customers want to get products may face time and space distance issues. In fact, product availability is not only a functional assessment of the logistics system, the primary indicators, but also the main objective of the logistics system optimization.

3. The Importance of Logistics

Many businesses that deal with supply of goods or services have their own logistics department.[2] For example, a company supplying photocopying paper around the world will have a logistics team. The manager will oversee or delegate to his staff the process from the point of origin. The team will deal with the acquisition of paper from the paper supplier all the way to the customer who requests the paper. The supplier and buyer may be located in different countries.

A recent study found that logistics costs account for almost 10% of the Gross Domestic Product. The process itself covers a diverse number of functional areas. Involved in logistics are transportation and traffic, as well as shipping and receiving. It also covers storage and import/export operations.

Logistics plays a major role in the U. S. economy. In fact, the 15th Annual State of Logistics Report asserts that in 2003 logistics costs accounted for 8. 5 percent of the U. S. Gross Domestic Product. Not too shabby! As a piece of the corporate landscape, logistics covers a broad array of functional areas. At a bare minimum, the scope of logistics entails traffic/transportation, shipping and receiving, warehousing and import/export operations. Many times, the additional areas of inventory management, purchasing, production planning and customer service can fall under the umbrella of logistics as well.

New words and terms

evolution	*n.*	演变
assessment	*n.*	评估
acquisition	*n.*	获得物

Notes

1. As the evolution of logistics concepts and practice, the world's developed countries and regions demonstrated the development of logistics customer service is the core concept of modern logistics.
   随着物流概念和实践的演变,世界上发达国家和地区表明:物流客户服务的发展是现代物流的核心概念。

2. Many businesses that deal with supply of goods or services have their own logistics department.

许多专注于供给商品或服务的企业都有自己的物流部门。

Lesson 1.3　Competing through Logistics

There are many potentially conflicting demands on an organization today. All those unreasonable customers seem to want it yesterday, at no cost, and to be compensated of it goes wrong. Within a given supply chain, it is important that each organization understands how each group of products competes in the marketplace, and that it aligns its capabilities with those of its partners. It is impossible to be outstanding at everything, and supply chain partners need to give priority to capabilities that give each product group its competitive edge. These are the advantages where supply chain partners "dig in deep" by giving priority to investment by training and by focusing product development and marketing efforts. They need only match the industry average on other criteria. Let us look at the competitive priorities that can be delivered by logistics in the supply chain.

In the fierce commercial competition, when companies offer products in price, performance, quality, promotions, there is not much difference, then the customer service level that is, its beat his opponent, an important weapon to gain a competitive advantage. Because, products, prices and promotions can certainly offer customers value added, but the brutal competition makes products and prices, promotions easily imitated by competitors, and satisfactory customer service or good customer complaints resolved can be a clear difference between the two enterprises. Therefore, by providing outstanding customer service, modern logistics, enterprises gain a competitive advantage.

1. The Quality Advantage

The most fundamental objective—in that it is a foundation for the others—is to carry out all processes across the supply chain so that the end product does what it is supposed to do. Quality is the most visible aspect of supply chain performance. Defects and late deliveries are symptoms of quality problems in supply chain processes that are all too apparent to the end-customer. Such problems negatively influence the customer's loyalty.

2. The Time Advantage

Time measures how long a customer has to wait in order to receive a given product or service. Volkswagen call this time the customer to customer lead time: that is, the time it takes from the moment a customer places and order to the moment that customer receives the car he or she specified. Such lead time can vary from zero (the product is immediately available, such as goods on a supermarket shelf) to months or years (such as the construction of a new building). Competing on time is about survival of the fastest.

The time advantage is variously described as speed or responsiveness in practice. Speeding up supply chain processes may help to improve freshness of the end product, or to reduce the risk of obsolete or over-aged stock in the system.

New words and terms

advantage	*n.*	优势，有利条件，利益
obsolescence	*n.*	荒废，退化，逐渐过时
available	*adj.*	可用到的，可利用的，有效的

Exercises 1

I. Pair work: Discuss the following questions.

1. What is logistics?
2. Why is logistics so important?
3. Is logistics something new? Why?
4. What is the logistics main function?
5. How do you understand the development of logistics management?

II. Fill in the blanks with the following words in the boxes, and change the forms if necessary.

route	location	movement	originate	importance
inventory	purchase	flow	storage	logistics

1. The aim of _____ management is to minimize the amount of material in stock.
2. _____ is a hot topic in China and the whole world.
3. If the ship had sailed along the recommended _____, it would have been able to avoid the heavy weather.
4. People generally consider logistics as the _____ of goods, it is partly right, but logistics is much more than that.

5. Logistics involves the _____ of goods, but also of people, as well as housing and feeding them.

6. The foreign company has to _____ 500 TEUs of garments from China every year.

7. The meaning of the word "logistics" firstly _____ from the military.

8. The _____ expenses will be for your account if you place an order of 100,000 tons of roll steel at a time. My workshop uses ten tons a month.

9. With the development of modern economy, people become more and more aware of the _____ of logistics.

10. Whether facilities are owned or rented, the _____ of warehouses is extremely important.

source	activity	success	cost	procurement
analysis	manager	business	alike	land

1. Transport can be done by sea, air, _____, rail and pipe.

2. Mr. Wang is an inventory _____ in a bonded warehouse(保税仓库) in Capital Airport.

3. Logistics managers pay more attention to inventory at present, because inventory management can effectively reduce logistics _____.

4. Information is the key to the _____ of logistics strategy.

5. Warehousing is not a new _____, but it has gained new functions in modern logistics.

6. In every company customer service is _____ of information for demand forecasting.

7. Every firm, large and small _____, needs logistics strategic planning for its development.

8. Packaging is one of the most important _____ which are included in logistics system.

9. _____ deals with the buying of goods and services that keep the organization functioning.

10. Could you give me a brief _____ of the present situation in relation to logistics in China?

Ⅲ. Translate the following sentences into Chinese.

1. Modern logistics is one of the most challenging and exciting jobs in the world.

2. Every company that sells products has to need the service of logistics.

3. Many experts hold the opinion that logistics is an iceberg, only the top of which is seen, what is unseen is much bigger.

4. As logistics manager's roles and value have grown, the need for well-educated, talented professionals with a diverse array of skills has emerged.

5. Logistics is a unique global "pipeline" that operates 24 hours a day, planning and coordinating the transport of products to customers the world over.

6. In the past decades, important changes have occurred with the role of purchasing in modern logistics system.

7. Package can have both a consumer package and logistics package.

8. To make efficient use of the warehouse space, you should decide how large your orders must be.

9. We should keep in mind that one logistics system does not fit all companies. The number of activities in a logistics system can vary from company to company.

10. The strategic placement of warehouses near the company's major markets can improve the customers service levels.

IV. Translate the following sentences into English.

1. 请为我们介绍一下当前中国的物流现状。
2. 物流活动是供应链的构成部分。
3. 在工业生产中,物流成为快速增长的利润源。
4. 发达国家的物流成本占国民生产总值的 10% 左右。
5. 物流活动的顺畅运转对于 2008 年北京奥运会有巨大的影响。
6. 过多的包装会增加物流成本,然而包装不足可能引起货物损坏。
7. 降低库存是为了全面有效地利用资金。
8. 采购对公司的效益有很大影响。
9. 正确的需求预测可以提高客户服务水平。
10. 物资搬运在降低库存和提高生产率方面发挥重要作用。

V. Answer the questions according to the text of this chapter.

1. What is logistics? Please try to say the conception of logistics.
2. Please give some examples about the interpretation of 6R philosophy of logistics.
3. How can enterprises compete through logistics in these days?

Logistics Situational Dialogues 1

Mr. Carol, a logistical company deputy in China, is having a talk with some students majoring in logistics who are taking part in a professional interview. Now, they are talking warmly.

Jim（**one of the students**）：Mr. Carol, can I take you up a few minutes? I wish to make logistics my life-long career, but I don't know how to start. Could you give me some information?

Carol：With pleasure. What is your qualification for going into logistics?

Jim：I specialize in accounting and foreign trade. And I am studying in Logistics Department of UIBE. Am I qualified?

Carol：Are you specialized in computer?

Jim：Computer science is my weakness. I know little about it.

Carlo：Really? Well, I think you are not quite qualified. If you wish to make logistics your lifetime career, you must know some information in that field.

Jim：That's exactly what I want to know. I was told that I could start from the very root of a supply chain.

Carol：Yes, such as distribution management in a retail center or a third-party logistics firm like China Shipping Logistics. As a matter of fact, there is no fixed pattern of career development. By the way, have you had any internship in any logistics position?

Jim：I worked in a tallying company for two months during my last term in the college, if that is internship.

Carol：I am sorry, that is only your experience, not your experience in logistics. In fact, I think you'd better start as an analyst, since you have learned accounting.

Jim：How would you chart my career?

Carol：Logistics is a unique global "pipeline" that operates 24 hours a day; seven days a week and 52 weeks a year, planning and coordinating the transport and delivery of products and service to customers the world over. The career for a specific person is as unpredictable as the weather in England. But from our investigation, we understand you will be familiar with the logistics activities if you work as an analyst in a logistics department for some time, say, two years. Then you may be promoted to the position of a logistics engineer.

Jim：Two years? That is too long a time!

Carol：But that is the least possible time necessary for anyone without any experience. After working on that position you may become a project manager. The next position you may hope for is business development director or operations site manager.

Jim：How long would it take before I am appointed as a business development director?

Carol：Well, that is even more difficult to predict than the English weather. Generally speaking, it depends on how diligent you are and how good the business is.

Jim: I know what a logistics analyst does. He does a lot of data analysis and provides support for the development of client proposals. But what does a logistics engineer do?

Carol: Well, he handles more complex aspects of proposals, developing materials, handling requirements, transportation routes and schedules and other process.

Jim: Do their responsibilities increase with the promotion?

Carol: Yes. They have to, as you will get higher pay with each promotion. For example, when you are promoted to the position of a project manager, you will lead a team of logistics engineers and analysts.

Jim: Is there any other career path? I don't want to assume such great responsibility.

Carol: Well, you can refuse the promotion and stay as an analyst all your life!

Jim: Oh, what a pity!

Dialog Exercise 1

Please design a dialog to discuss:

If we want to gain advantages during the competing with other companies, What should we do about logistics?

The dialog should include the content we have learned.

The useful words which you may need are as followed.

definition	定义
purpose	目的
core concept	核心概念
competing advantages	竞争优势

Case Study 1

General Motors De Mexico

Summary

Penske Logistics has been a supplier to General Motors (GM) for more than 75 years. With a reach that extends to more than 60 countries, logistics is no small challenge for GM. GMM is GM's Mexican subsidiary and a vital part of GM's North American operations. GMM selected Penske to be its lead logistics provider (LLP) to help drive efficiency throughout all aspects of its distribution network. Within the first six months of the partnership, transportation costs had already been significantly reduced. And, more improvements were underway, including the implementation of proprietary software to provide instant access to real-time updates from every supply chain participant.

Challenges

- To reduce costs and inefficiencies in General Motors de Mexico's (GMM) growing inbound transportation network
- To increase overall visibility throughout GMM's supply chain
- To establish accountability procedures and measures for GMM's suppliers and carriers

Solutions / Results

- Within six months, Penske had reduced transportation costs by 15 percent.
- Penske implemented its proprietary Logistics Management System software to provide instant access to real-time updates from every supply chain participant, enabling proactive resolution of supplier and carrier issues.
- Penske reduced GMM's carrier base from 100 carriers to 20 within the first year. The rate of on-time supplier pickups has increased to 98 percent, while delivery rates are at 99 percent.

Getting Started

GMM works with more than 1,700 suppliers that produce approximately 13,000 parts a day. From railcars to chartered planes, the company's transportation network is sophisticated and complex.

GMM selected Penske Logistics to be its lead logistics provider (LLP). The fit was a natural one. At the time, Penske Logistics had served as LLP for several of GM's U. S. operations and had managed border crossings in Laredo, Texas, for nearly two decades. With an acute understanding of the Mexican culture and GMM's operating principles, Penske Logistics had a head start on helping GMM drive efficiency throughout all aspects of its distribution network.

Creating Collaboration Across the Transportation Network

Previously, GMM internally managed its complex transportation network, which consisted of eight operations on three sites in Ramos, Toluca and Silao. As higher demands continued to be placed on GMM's production and distribution operations, its transportation network lacked collaboration. In effect, each operation was making individual logistics decisions, creating costly redundancies and inefficiencies throughout the supply chain.

As LLP, Penske was challenged with reducing costs and improving efficiency in GMM's inbound transportation operations. Penske would now manage the inbound transportation of materials to each of the plants, as well as manage GMM's carrier relationships.

Penske presented a three-phase plan to be implemented within the first year:

- **Phase 1—Benchmarking** (**90 days**): Penske would conduct a comprehensive study of GMM's inbound transportation operations, including processes, infrastructure and personnel
- **Phase 2—Process Design and Engineering** (**90 days**): New procedures would be developed based on inefficiencies and benchmarks discovered in Phase 1
- **Phase 3—Implementation** (**180 days**): Penske would implement these new procedures, ensuring full ramp-up in all three plants

During Phase 1, Penske closely studied every aspect of GMM's inbound transportation operations. From carrier negotiation to routing, each individual activity within the plants was process-mapped to identify inefficiencies.

The conclusion was two-fold. Penske determined GMM lacked overall supply chain visibility, as well as quality control measures. GMM could not accurately forecast inventory needs at plants or monitor carrier progress. Carriers lacked an efficient way to communicate the status of inbound shipments to plant operators. Plant operators were spending valuable time tediously tracking carrier status. Furthermore, there was no way to effectively identify low performers within the supply chain and hold them accountable.

With the benchmarking phase complete, Penske outlined its plan for operational improvement. Penske would implement its proprietary Logistics Management System (LMS) software to track supply chain activity. Concurrent to the implementation of its LMS software, Penske would implement new quality control processes at each step in the supply chain to achieve supply chain visibility and accountability. Penske would maximize GMM's trained labor force by hiring or transitioning the company's current personnel to help implement many of the new processes and systems.

During implementation, Penske hired and assigned approximately 120 staff to man GMM's improved inbound transportation operations. GMM's existing material follow-up personnel represented nearly 80 percent of this staff, thus avoiding displacement of GMM's labor force.

The implementation of Penske's technology and new inbound transportation processes delivered GMM a return on investment almost immediately. Within six months, transportation costs were down by an astounding 15 percent.

Supply Chain Accountability and Visibility Exceeds Expectations

The results of Penske's three-phase plan exceeded GMM's expectations. Penske substantially reduced GMM's transportation costs, decreased its inventory and premium freight costs, and virtually eliminated assembly line shutdowns. In addition, the delivery of damage-free parts increased by 20 percent.

The implementation and deployment of Penske's LMS software undoubtedly played the biggest role in improving GMM's inbound transportation efficiency. Using this software, Penske's system operators can provide carriers precise routing and scheduling information on a daily basis, while tracking exact part numbers and pick-up quantities. The LMS software was also the catalyst for new transportation processes that increase overall carrier accountability. Upon completion of each task, drivers are required to call their dispatchers, who then log the completed activity into the LMS Web site.

For the first time, Penske operators had instant access to real-time updates from every aspect of the supply chain. Penske's LMS software proactively alerts operators of any carrier delays, reducing the amount of follow-up time previously expended by operators. In turn, operators are able to evaluate alternatives, such as engaging another carrier or expediting freight, to ensure service windows are met using the most cost-effective methods.

Penske also provided GMM with the ability to track, measure and rate the performance of all parties involved in the supply chain. With greater visibility of all inbound transportation operations, supply chain foul-ups are easily identified and handled.

Every aspect of supplier and carrier performance is tracked on a scorecard, allowing Penske to weed out parties performing at sub-standard levels. Within the first year of implementation, Penske reduced GMM's carrier base from 100 carriers to 20. This level of accountability has dramatically improved supplier and carrier performance. Window times for supplier pickups are currently being met 98 percent of the time, while delivery window times are being met at a rate of 99 percent.

Looking Ahead: The Future of a Successful Relationship

Penske achieved success with GMM through a unique relationship with the company. With a commitment to exceed expectations under budget, Penske puts 10 percent of its management fee at risk, ensuring its dedication to achieving results. This commitment continues to present new opportunities for both GMM and Penske.

Currently, Penske and GMM are considering sharing its transportation infrastructure with other companies in Mexico that have similar product or material flows. This would enable GMM to realize additional revenue and cost savings within its transportation network.

Meanwhile, Penske will continue to deliver unprecedented value to GMM's supply chain operations.

Please answer the following questions after reading the case.

1. What kinds of challenge is GMM facing in its logistics?

2. How does Penske help GMM to improve its supply chain performance?

3. Describe the benefits GMM has gained from Penske's logistics solutions.

小贴士

物流小常识

物流的本质是服务的,为制造商的产品生产和营销提供服务,为最终用户的产品可得性提供服务,为供应链的组织协调提供服务等。对于一个服务行业的企业,特别是那些本身没有什么硬件设施的,就是我们所称的"虚拟物流"企业,客户的满意度至关重要,迫切需要营销理念的创新。而 CRM 及一对一营销等新理念的导入,正迎合了这种需要。供应链管理就是指对整个供应链系统进行计划、协调、操作、控制和优化的各种活动和过程,其目标是将顾客所需的正确的产品(right product)能够在正确的时间(right time),按照正确的数量(right quantity)、正确的质量(right quality)和正确的状态(right status)送到正确的地点(right place)——即"6R",并使总成本最小。

Supplementary Reading 1

Logistics Activities and Fields

Inbound logistics is one of the primary processes of logistics, concentrating on purchasing and arranging the inbound movement of materials, parts, and/or finished inventory from suppliers to manufacturing or assembly plants, warehouses, or retail stores.

Outbound logistics is the process related to the storage and movement of the final product and the related information flows from the end of the production line to the end user.

Procurement logistics consists of activities such as market research, requirements planning, make-or-buy decisions, supplier management, ordering, and order controlling. The targets in procurement logistics might be contradictory: maximizing efficiency by concentrating on core competences, outsourcing while maintaining the autonomy of the company, or minimizing procurement costs while maximizing security within the supply process.

Distribution logistics has, as main tasks, the delivery of the finished products to the customer. It consists of order processing, warehousing, and transportation. Distribution logistics is necessary because the time, place, and quantity of production differs with the time, place, and quantity of consumption.

Disposal logistics has as its main function to reduce logistics cost(s) and enhance service(s) related to the disposal of waste produced during the operation of a business.

Reverse logistics denotes all those operations related to the reuse of products and materials. The reverse logistics process includes the management and the sale of surpluses, as well as products being returned to vendors from buyers. Reverse logistics stands for all operations related to the reuse of products and materials. It is "the process of planning, implementing, and controlling the efficient, cost effective flow of raw materials, in-process inventory, finished goods and related information from the point of consumption to the point of origin for the purpose of recapturing value or proper disposal. More precisely, reverse logistics is the process of moving goods from their typical final destination for the purpose of capturing value, or proper disposal. The opposite of reverse logistics is **forward logistics**."

Green Logistics describes all attempts to measure and minimize the ecological impact of logistics activities. This includes all activities of the forward and reverse flows. This can be achieved through intermodal freight transport, path optimization, vehicle saturation and city logistics.

Asset Control Logistics: companies in the retail channels, both organized retailers and suppliers, often deploy assets required for the display, preservation, promotion of their products. Some examples are refrigerators, stands, display monitors, seasonal equipment, poster stands & frames.

Emergency Logistics (**or Humanitarian Logistics**) is a term used by the logistics, supply chain, and manufacturing industries to denote specific time-critical modes of transport used to move goods or objects rapidly in the event of an emergency. The reason for enlisting emergency logistics services could be a production delay or anticipated production delay, or an urgent need for specialized equipment to prevent events such as aircraft being grounded (also known as aircraft on ground—AOG), ships being delayed, or telecommunications failure. Humanitarian logistics involves governments, the military, aid agencies, donors, non-governmental organizations and emergency logistics services are typically sourced from a specialist provider.

Construction Logistics is known to mankind since ancient times. As the various human civilizations tried to build the best possible works of construction for living and protection. Now the construction logistics emerged as vital part of construction. In the past few years construction logistics has emerged as a different field of knowledge and study with in the subject of supply chain management and logistics.

Chapter ◆2

Warehousing Management and Inventory Control

Lesson 2.1   The Strategic Role of Warehousing in Logistics

The warehouse is a point in the logistics system where a firm stores or holds raw materials, semi-finished goods, or finished goods for varying periods of time. Holding goods in a warehouse stops or interrupts the flow of goods, adding cost to the product or products. [1] Some firms have viewed warehousing cost very negatively; in short, they sought to avoid it if at all possible. This view is changing due to the realization that warehousing can add more value than cost to a product. Other firms, particularly distributors or wholesalers, went to the opposite extreme and warehoused as many items as possible. Neither end of the spectrum is usually correct. Firms should hold or store items only if possible trade-offs exist in other areas.

The warehouse serves several value-adding roles in a logistics system. Companies will sometimes face less-than-truckload (LTL) shipments of raw materials and finished goods. Shipping goods long distances at LTL rates is more costly than shipping at full truckload or carload rates. By moving the LTL amounts relatively short distances to or from a warehouse, warehousing can allow a firm to consolidate smaller shipments into a large shipment (a carload or truckload) with significant transportation savings. For the inbound logistics system, the warehouse would consolidate different suppliers' LTL shipments and ship a volume shipment to the firm's plant. For the outbound logistics system, the warehouse would receive a consolidated volume shipment from various plants and ship LTL shipments to different markets.

The second function of warehousing may be, customer order product mixing. Companies frequently turn out a product line that contains thousands of "different" products, if we consider color, size, shape, and other variations. When placing orders, customers often want a product line mixture—for example, 5 dozen four-cup coffee pots, 6 dozen ten-cup coffee pots with blue trim and 10 dozen with red trim, and 3 dozen blue salad bowl sets. [2] Because companies often produce items at different plants, a company that did not warehouse goods would have to fill orders from several locations, causing differing arrival times and opportunity for mix-ups. Therefore, a product-mixing warehouse for a multiple-product line leads to efficient order filling. By developing new mixing warehouses near dense urban areas, firms can make pickups and deliveries in smaller vehicles and schedule these activities at more optimum times to avoid congestion.

In addition to product-mixing for customer orders, companies using raw materials or semi-finished goods (e. g. , auto manufacturers) commonly move carloads of items mixed from a physical supply warehouse to a plant. This strategy not only reduces transportation costs from consideration, but also allows the company to avoid using the plant as a warehouse. This strategy will become increasingly popular as a increased fuel expenses raise transport costs and firms increase the use of sophisticated strategies such as materials requirements planning (MRP) or just-in-time (JIT) systems.

Cross-docking is an operation that facilitates the product-mixing function. In across-docking operation, products from different suppliers arrive in truckload lots, but instead of being placed into storage for later picking, they are moved across the warehouse area to waiting trucks for movement to particular customers. [3] The incoming materials are picked from the delivering truck or from temporary strong locations to fill a specific order and moved across the dock to a truck destined for the customer. The whole process is completed in a matter of hours.

The third function of warehouse is to provide service. The importance of customer service is obvious. Having goods available in a warehouse when a customer places an order, particularly if the warehouse is in reasonable proximity to the customer usually leads to customer satisfaction and enhances future sales. Service may also be a factor for physical supply warehouses. However, production schedules, which a firm makes in advance, are easier to service than customers: while customer demand is often uncertain, physical supply stock-out costs sometimes seem infinite.

The fourth function of warehousing is protection against contingencies such as transportation delays, vendor stock-outs, or strikes. A potential trucker's strike will generally cause buyers to stock larger inventories than usual, for example. This particular function is very important for physical supply warehouses in that a delay in the delivery of raw materials can delay the production of finished goods. However, contingencies also occur with physical distribution warehouses—for example, goods damaged in transit can affect inventory levels and order filling.

The fifth function of warehousing is to smooth operations in the manufacturing process. Seasonal demand is an example of smoothing. In effect, this balancing strategy allows a company to reduce its manufacturing capacity investment.

As we can see, warehousing functions can make important contributions to logistics systems and company operations. However, we must also view warehousing in a trade-off context; that is, ware housing's contribution to profit must be greater than its cost.

The idioms can give good examples for the role of warehousing:

(1) We cannot make bricks without straw.

(2) We must repair the house before it rains, that means timely carbon in the snow.

(3) A kind of accumulating for the connection of production and consumption.

New words and terms

consolidate	*v.*	拼装
volume shipment		大量运输
customer order product mixing		组合客户订购的产品
cross-docking	*n.*	交叉收货
physical supply warehouse		物料供应仓库
physical distribution warehouse		物料配送仓库

Notes

1. The warehouse is a point in the logistics system where a firm stores or holds raw materials, semi-finished goods, or finished goods for varying periods of time. Holding goods in a warehouse stops or interrupts the flow of goods, adding cost to the product or

products.

仓储是物流系统中的一个点。在这里,企业在不同的时间内存储原材料、半成品或产成品。在仓库中存放产品中止或中断了产品流动,增加了生产或产品的成本。

2. Companies frequently turn out a product line that contains thousands of "different" products, if we consider color, size, shape, and other variations. When placing orders, customers often want a product line mixture—for example, 5 dozen four-cup coffee pots, 6 dozen ten-cup coffee pots with blue trim and 10 dozen with red trim, and 3 dozen blue salad bowl sets.

如果我们考虑产品的颜色、规格、形状和其他特征,企业的一条生产线上通常会生产成千上万种不同的产品。当顾客订货时,通常需要产品线上不同产品的组合,例如,5 打4 个茶杯的咖啡套壶、6 打 10 个茶杯的蓝色花边的咖啡套壶、10 打红色花边另加 3 打成套的蓝色色拉碗。

3. Cross-docking is an operation that facilitates the product-mixing function. In across-docking operation, products from different suppliers arrive in truckload lots, but instead of being placed into storage for later picking, they are moved across the warehouse area to waiting trucks for movement to particular customers. The incoming materials are picked from the delivering truck or from temporary strong locations to fill a specific order and moved across the dock to a truck destined for the customer.

交叉收货是为促进产品组合功能而进行的操作。在交叉收货的运作中,不同供货商的产品以整车的数量运到后,不是被储存起来等待分拣,而是越过仓库运到停好的货车上以便送到特定的客户手中。运进的物料从运货车上或者短期储存地挑选出来,按照具体的订单配备好并通过平台转移到即将发往客户那里的货车上。

Lesson 2.2   Warehouse Operations

Once a warehouse mission is determined, managerial attention focuses on establishing the operation. A typical warehouse contains materials, parts, and finished goods on the move. Warehouse operations consist of break-bulk, storage, and assembly procedures. The objective is to efficiently receive inventory, possibly store it until required by the market, assemble it into complete orders, and initiate movement to customer. This emphasis on product flow renders a modern warehouse as a mixing facility. As such, a great deal of managerial attention concerns how to perform storage to facilitate efficient materials handling.

1. Handling

The first consideration focuses on movement continuity and scale economies throughout the warehouse. Movement continuity means that it is better for a material handler with a piece of handling equipment to perform longer moves than to undertake a number of short handling to accomplish the same overall move. Exchanging the product between handlers or moving it from one piece of equipment to another wastes time and increases the potential for product damage. Thus, as a general rule, longer warehouse movements are preferred. Goods, once in motion, should be continuously moved until arrival at their final destination.

Scale economies justify moving the largest quantities or loads possible. Instead of moving individual cases, handling procedures should be designed to move cases grouped on pallets, slip-sheets, or containers. The overall objective of materials handling is to eventually sort inbound shipments into unique customer assortments. The three primary handling activities are receiving, in-storage handling, and shipping.

Receiving

Merchandise and material typically arrive at warehouses in large quantity shipments.

The first handling activity is unloading. At most warehouses, unloading is performed mechanically, using a combination of a lift truck and manual processes. [1] When freight is floor stacked on the transport vehicle, the typical procedure is to manually place products on pallets or to use a conveyor. When inbound product has been unitized on pallets or containers, lift trucks can be used in facilities receiving. A primary benefit of receiving unitized loads is the ability to turn inbound transportation equipment more rapidly. Receiving is usually the unloading of a relatively high volume of similar product,

In-storage Handling

In-storage handling consists of movements within the warehouse. Following receipt and movement to a staging location, product must be moved within the facility for storage or order selection. Finally, when an order is processed it is necessary to select the required products and move them to a shipping area. Theses two types of in-storage handing are typically referred to as transfer and selection.

There are at least two and sometimes three transfer movements in a typical warehouse. The merchandise is initially moved from the receiving area to a storage location. This movement is typically handled by a lift truck when pallets or slip-sheets are used or by other mechanical means for other types of unit loads. The second internal movement may be required prior to order assembly depending upon warehouse operating procedures. When unit loads have to be broken down for order selection, they are usually transferred from storage to an order selection or picking area. When products are large or bulky, such as appliance, this intermediate movement to a picking area may not be necessary. Such product is often selected from the storage area and moved directly to the shipping staging area. The shipping staging area is the area adjacent to the shipping dock. In order selection warehouses, the assembled customer order is transferred from the selection area to the shipping staging area. Characteristically, in-storage handing involves lower volume movements than receiving but still relatively similar products.

Order selection is one of the major activities within warehouses. The selection process requires that materials, parts, and products be grouped to facilitate order assembly. It is typically for one area of a warehouse to be designated as a selection or picking area to assemble orders. For each order, the combination of products must be selected and packaged to meet specific customer order requirements. The typical selection process is coordinated by a warehouse system.

Shipping

Shipping consists of order verification and transportation equipment loading. Similar to receiving, firms any use conveyors or unit load materials handling equipment such as lift trucks to move products from the staging area into the transportation vehicle. Relative to receiving, warehouse shipping must accommodate relatively low-volume movements of a mixture of product, thus reducing the potential for economies of sale. Shipping unit loads is becoming increasingly popular because considerable time can be saved in vehicle loading. A unit load consists of unitized or palletized product. To facilitate this loading and subsequent unloading upon delivery, many customers are requesting that suppliers provide mixed combinations of product within a unit. The alternative is to floor stack cases in the transportation vehicle. Shipment content verification is typically required when product changes ownership. Verification may be limited to a simple carton count or a piece-by-piece check for proper brand, size, and in some cases serial number to assure shipment accuracy.

2. Storage

The second consideration is that warehouse utilization should position products based upon individual characteristics. The most important product variables to consider in a storage plan are product volume, weight, and storage requirements.

Product volume or velocity is the major factor driving warehouse layout. High volume product should be positioned in the warehouse to minimize movement distance. For example, high-velocity products should be positioned near doors, primary aisles, and at lower levels in storage racks. Such positioning minimizes warehouse handling and reduces the need for frequent lifting. Conversely, products with low volume should be assigned locations more distant from primary aisles or higher up in storage racks.

Similarly, the storage plan should take into consideration product weight and special characteristics. Relatively heavy items should be assigned storage locations low to the ground to minimize lifting. Bulky or low-density product requires cubic space. Floor space along outside walls is ideal for such items. On the other hand, smaller items may require storage shelves, bins, or drawers. The integrated storage plan must consider the characteristics of individual products.

A typical warehouse is engaged in a combination of active and extended product storage alternatives. Warehouses that directly serve customers typically focus on active short-term storage. In contrast, warehouses use extended storage for speculative, seasonal, or obsolete inventory.

When controlling and measuring warehouse operations, it is important to differentiate the relative requirements and performance capabilities of active storage and extended storage.

Active Storage

Regardless of inventory velocity, most goods must be stored for at least a short time. Storage for basic inventory replenishment is referred to as active storage. Active storage must provide sufficient inventory to meet the periodic demands of the service area. The need for active storage is usually related to the capability to achieve transportation or handling economies of scale. For active storage, materials handling processes and technologies need to focus on quick movement and flexibility with relatively minimal consideration for extended and dense storage.

The active storage concept includes flow-through distribution, which uses warehouses for consolidation and assortment while maintaining minimal or no inventory in storage. The resulting need for reduced inventory favors flow-through and cross-docking techniques that emphasize movement and deemphasize storage. Flow-through distribution is most appropriate for high-volume, fast-moving products where quantities are reasonably predictable. While flow-through products place minimal demands on storage requirements, it does require that products are quickly unloaded, unitized, grouped and sequenced into customer assortments, and reloaded into transportation equipment. As a result, the materials handling puts emphasis on accurate information and directed quick movement.

Extended Storage

Extended storage, a somewhat misleading term, refers to inventory in excess of that required for normal replenishment of customer stocks. In some special situations, storage may be required for several months prior to customer shipment. Extended storage uses materials handling processes and technologies that focus on maximum space utilization with minimal need for quick access.

A warehouse may be used for extended storage for several other reasons. Some products, such as seasonal items, require storage to await demand or to spread supply across time. Other reasons for extended storage include erratic demand items, product conditioning, speculative purchases, and discount.

Product conditioning sometimes requires extended storage, such as to ripen bananas. Food warehouses typically have ripening rooms to hold products until they reach peak quality. Storage may also be necessary for extended quality checks.

Warehouses may also store goods on an extended basis when goods are purchased on a speculative basis. The magnitude of speculative buying depends upon the specific materials and industries involved, but it is very common in marketing of commodities and seasonal items. For example, if a price increase for an item is expected, it is not uncommon for a firm to buy ahead at the current price and warehouse the product for later use.

The warehouse may also be used to realize special discounts. Early purchase discounts may justify extended storage. The purchasing manager may be able to realize a substantial price reduction during a specific period of the year. Under such conditions the warehouse is expected to hold inventory in excess of active storage. Manufacturers of fertilizer, toys, and lawns furniture often attempt to shift the warehousing burden to customers by offering off-season warehouse storage allowance.

The working principles of WMS system are as figure 2.1. WMS system includes six parts, they are inbound management, shelf operation, storage management, pickout operation, quality inspection and outbound management, they should all serve for the ERP system, SCM system and CRM system.

New words and terms

shipping	*n.*	装货
receiving	*n.*	收货
handling	*n.*	搬运

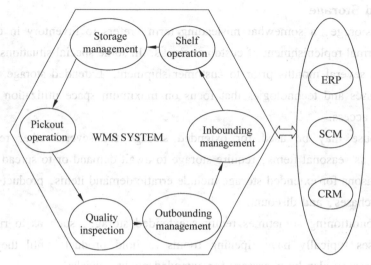

Figure 2.1   working principles of WMS system

Note

Receiving. Merchandise and material typically arrive at warehouses in large quantity shipments. The first handling activity is unloading. At most warehouses, unloading is performed mechanically, using a combination of a lift truck and manual processes.

产成品和原材料通常以很大的批量到达仓库。首先的搬运活动就是卸货。在大多数的仓库中,卸货一般是以叉车和人工相结合的方式进行操作的。

Lesson 2.3   Basic Inventory Concepts

There are many reasons why inventories are present in a supply channel. Just consider why a firm might want inventories at some level in their operations and they would also want to keep them at a minimum. Inventories are frequently found in such places as warehouses, yards, shop floors, transportation equipment, and on retail store shelves. Having these inventories on hand can cost between 20 and 40 percent of their value per year. Therefore, carefully managing inventory levels makes good economic sense. Even though many steps have been taken to reduce inventories through just in time, time compression, and quick responses practices applied throughout the supply channel, the annual investment in inventories by manufacturers, retailers, and merchant wholesalers (whose sales represent about 99 percent of Gross National Product) is about 13 percent of the U. S. Gross Domestic Product in 1996. Take care of the inventory and you take care of the cost.

Inventory refers to stocks of anything necessary to do business. Raw materials, goods in process and finished goods all represent various forms of inventory. Each type represents money tied up until the inventory leaves the organization and is paid for. For this reason it is undesirable to hold greater stocks than it necessary. [1] On the other hand, inadequate levels of stock create danger of production hold-ups or failure to meet customer demand.

Unless inventories are controlled they can be unreliable, inefficient, and costly. Inventory management involves the management of all aspects relating to stockholding, with the aim of providing the desired level of customer service at optimal cost.

The true costs of carrying inventory include the direct costs of storage, insurance, taxes, etc, but also the cost of money tied up in inventory. [2] Inventory ties up capital, so good inventory management improves customer service, increases sales, increases profit and increases working capital without having to borrow money.

Best practice inventory management involves simultaneously attempting to balance the costs of inventory with the benefits of inventory.

On the other hand, the interest accrues in the capital invested in the carrying inventory, which is in many cases, computed according to the prime interest. Usually, when business happens some kinds of tax are often levied on necessary inventory, and coupled with insurance cost and storage cost. Since the logistics cost can well amount to over 37% of the total cost, which result in the necessity of making plans for inventory. So that comes out the question of how to make a reasonable order. For example, when to order, how much to order and how to carry on inventory control procedures.

For the time being we are concerned only with the question of how much to order. The key to the problem is to balance the cost of maintaining inventories against the cost of ordering. The key to understanding the relationship is to remember that average inventory is equal to one-half the order quantity. The larger quantity ordered the fewer orders required per planning period and, consequently, the lower the total ordering cost.

The principles of inventory management and control are as figure 2. 2. There are three parameters in the model, they are order point, order quantity and order cycle. The three parameters are the most important parts in the purchasing management, these will affect the level of inventory management and control.

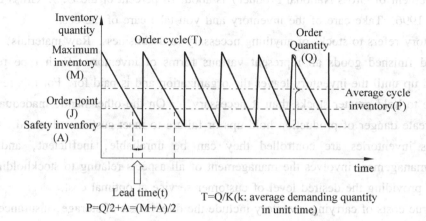

Figure 2.2　Inventory management and control

New words and terms

formulation	n.	制定,规划,构想,准备
inventory	n.	库存,盘点,详细目录,财产目录
unreliable	adj.	不可靠的
organization	n.	组织,结构团体
maintain	n.	维护维修,保留,坚持保养
hold-ups		库存积压
raw material		原材料

Notes

1. Each type represents money tied up until the inventory leaves the organization and is paid for. For this reason it is undesirable to hold greater stocks than it necessary.
   每一种库存代表着资金的占用,直到其离开存放处并被支付。因此,需要更大的库存是不受欢迎的。

2. The true costs of carrying inventory include the direct costs of storage, insurance, taxes, etc, but also the cost of money tied up in inventory.
   库存的真实成本包括直接储存成本、保险费和税金等,还包括库存的货币成本。

Lesson 2. 4   The Purpose of Inventory

There are five main purposes for inventory within the firm. Formulation of an inventory policy requires an understanding of the role of inventory in production and marketing. Inventory serves five purposes within the firm.

Why Should We Have Inventory

The most important reason for having inventory is the convenience of having things available when required. What needs to be available will depend on the type of organization or industry but might include:

- production material (raw materials and components) to support manufacture
- spares and consumables for repair and maintenance activities
- finished products ready for delivery to the final customer

Another factor is the possibility of cost reduction by taking advantage of bulk discounts from suppliers. By buying in bulk we accept a relatively level of stocks in exchange for a reduction in the purchase price. [1] The same reasoning applies to when we buy more than we immediately need so as to achieve a minimum order quantity or so as to avoid an unexpected price increasing.

We may also hold stocks as a buffer against things going wrong. For example, we might hold a high level of finished goods so that we can guarantee to meet customer demand. Similarly, we might hold a high level of raw materials stock so as to avoid any hold-up in the production process.

Economics of Scale

Inventory is required if an organization is to realize economies of scale in purchasing, transportation, or manufacturing. [2] For example, ordering large quantities of raw materials or finished goods inventory allows the manufacturer to take advantage of the per unit price reductions associated with volume purchases. Purchased materials have a lower transportation cost per unit if ordered in large volumes. This lower per unit cost results because less handing is required: for example, an order of 1 unit usually requires the same administrative handling as 1,000 units, and truckload and full railcar shipments receive lower transportation rates than smaller shipments of less-than-truckload (LTL) or less-than-carload (LCL) quantities.

Finished goods inventory makes it possible to realize manufacturing economies. Plant utilization is greater and per unit manufacturing costs are lower if a firm schedules long production runs with few line changes. Manufacturing in small quantities leads to short production runs and high changeover costs.

The production of large quantities may require that some of the items be carried in inventory for a significant period of time before they can be sold. The production of large quantities also may prevent an organization from responding quickly to stockouts, since large production runs mean that items are produced less frequently. The cost of maintaining this inventory must be "traded off" against the production savings realized.

Although frequent production changeovers reduce the quantity of inventory that must be carried and shortened the lead time that is required in the event of a stockout, they require time that could be used for manufacturing a product. In addition, at the beginning of a production running, the line often operates less efficiently due to fine-tuning the process and equipment setting.

When a plant is operating at or near capacity, frequent line changes that create machines out of date may mean that contribution to profit is lost because there are not enough products to meet demand. In such situations, the costs of lost sales and changeovers must be compared to the increase in inventory carrying costs that would result from longer production runs. To respond to this, many companies, such as Honda of America Manufacturing, have made a major effort toward reducing changeover times. This allows production of small lots, eliminating the loss of higher setup costs.

Balancing Supply and Demand

Seasonal supply or demand may make it necessary for a firm to hold inventory. For example, a producer of a premium line of bowed chocolates experiences significant sales volume increases at Christmas, Valentine's Day, Easter, and Mother's Day. The cost of establishing production capacity to handle the volume at these peak periods would be substantial. In addition, substantial idle capacity and wide fluctuations in the workforce would result if the company were to produce at a somewhat constant level throughout the year creates significant inventory buildup at various times during the year, but at a lower total cost to the firm. The seasonal inventories are stored in a freezer warehouse that was built next to the plant.

On the other hand, demand for a product may be relatively stable throughout the year, but raw materials may be available only at certain times during the year (e. g. producers of canned fruits and vegetables). This makes it necessary to manufacture finished products in excess of current demand and hold them in inventory.

Specialization

Inventory makes it possible for each of a firm's plants to specialize in the products that it manufactures. The finished products can be shipped to field warehouses where they are mixed to fill customer orders. The economies that result from the longer production runs and from savings in transportation costs more than offset the costs of additional handling. Companies such as Whirlpool Corporation have found significant cost savings in the operation of consolidation warehouses that allow the firm to specialize manufacturing by plant location. The specialization by facility is known as focused factories.

Protection from Uncertainties

Inventory is held as protection from uncertainties; that is, to prevent a stockout in the case of variability in demand or variability in the replenishment cycle.

Raw materials inventories in excess of those required to support production can result from speculative purchases made because management expects a price increase or supply shortage, perhaps due to a potential strike. Another reason to hold raw materials inventories is to maintain a source of supply. Regardless of the reason for maintaining inventory, the costs of holding the inventory should be compared to the savings realized or costs avoided by holding it.

New words and terms

specialization	n.	专门化,特殊化
component	n.	零部件
changeover	n.	完全改变
economies of scale		规模经济
hold stocks as a buffer		把库存作为缓冲器
stockout	n.	缺货

Notes

1. By buying in bulk we accept a relatively level of stocks in exchange for a reduction in the purchase price.

   进行批量购买,使我们可以用相当水平的库存以换取价格的降低。

2. Inventory is required if an organization is to realize economies of scale in purchasing, transportation, or manufacturing.

   如果一个组织认识到了在购买、运输和生产方面的经济规模,就需要库存。

Exercises 2

Ⅰ. Pair work: Discuss the following questions.

1. Why is warehousing necessary?
2. How do you understand the role of the warehousing?
3. What are the basic components of warehousing?
4. What are the main types of warehousing?
5. If you are a manager, do you refer public warehouse to private warehouse?
6. Are you familiar with the warehousing activities?

Ⅱ. Fill in the blanks with the following words in the boxes, and change the forms if necessary.

verify	automated	proximity	order	bridge
moderate	temporary	desired	achieve	sufficient

1. General purpose warehouse provide _____ environment conditions and a wide range of products can be stored in this kind.
2. Usually, warehouses are typically viewed as a _____ place to store goods.
3. The cost of small _____ became expensive to transport.
4. Warehousing plays a vital role in providing a _____ level of customer service.
5. Customer service may be the deciding factor for warehouse site location, _____ to markets can improve its service level.
6. Distribution center is a large and highly _____ warehouse designed to receive goods from various plants and suppliers.
7. A warehouse can be viewed as a _____ between supply and demand.
8. In order to _____ the efficiency they may have to hold stock, but this is not their main role.
9. Retailers found it difficult to source in _____ quantity from a single supplier.
10. After the goods are unloaded from the transportation carrier, they should be _____ against cargo manifest.

cause	expand	warehouse	reorder	specialize
inventory	strategic	stocks	balance	decline

1. Managers must establish and implement inventory policies on the basis of _____ consideration.
2. When he adopted new strategy in inventory management, he lowered the cost while _____ the sales.
3. The aim of reducing _____ is to make better use of overall assets.
4. Inventory refers to _____ of anything necessary to do business.
5. To make efficient an effective of the _____ space, you should decide how large your order must be.
6. When the stock is near the safety stock level, materials have to be _____.
7. Raw materials, goods in process and finished goods all _____ various forms of inventory.
8. Buffer stock is adopted to maintain _____ in demand or supply.
9. The order cost is _____ with the increase of quantity.
10. Inventory makes it possible for each firm to _____ in the products that it manufactures.

Ⅲ. Translate the following sentences into Chinese.

1. Over the years, warehousing has developed from a relatively minor scale of a firm's logistics system to one of its most important functions.
2. We can define warehousing as that part of a firm's logistics system.
3. Warehouses and distribution centers have a primary aim, which is to facilitate the movement of goods from suppliers to customers, meeting demand in a timely manner.
4. Warehousing decision involves decision on number, location, size and type as well.
5. Warehouses are used to receive, handle, store and ship products or materials.
6. Inventory is spread throughout the supply chain from raw materials to work in process to finished goods that suppliers, manufacturers, distributors, and retailers hold.
7. Inventory exists in businesses because of a mismatch between supply and demand.
8. Firms must store additional stocks just in case to meet changing demand.
9. If demand is relatively constant but materials are seasonal, then finished inventory helps meet demand when the materials are no longer available.
10. You should pay for the storage cost whether you store your goods in public warehouse, rented private warehouse, or a warehouse of your own.

Ⅳ. Translate the following sentences into English.

1. 仓储是生产者与消费者之间的纽带。

2. 仓库储存所有产品,配送中心以最低库存满足最大需求。

3. 商品的数量越多,所需仓库的规模也就越大。

4. 近年来,仓库的设施设备技术发展很快。

5. 产品必须储存,以便日后使用和消费。

6. 持有库存的主要原因是补偿需求的不确定性。

7. 频繁缺货会让客户寻求其他供应商。

8. 库存被认为是增值的一种手段。

9. 库存过量不仅增加仓储的费用,也增加其他方面的费用。

10. 并不是库存越小,企业的竞争能力就越小。

V. Answer the questions according to the text of this chapter.

1. What are the strategic roles of warehousing in logistics?

2. Please try to describe the main processing about warehousing operation.

3. How many parameters are there in the processing of purchasing in inventory control and what are they?

4. Please try to say the principles of inventory control.

5. What is the purpose of inventory management?

6. How do you understand the inventory?

7. Is inventory necessary to every company?

8. What is the primary goal in inventory?

9. Why is inventory used as a buffer?

10. Why is inventory so important to a firm?

11. How many functions of inventory are there?

12. As an inventory manager, how do you achieve inventory goal?

13. As an inventory manager, how do you make inventory decision?

Logistics Situational Dialogues 2

The following is a dialogue happened between a manufacturer and manger of inventory.

Huang (H), vice-president of operations in a manufacturing company, is meeting with Wang (W), supervisor of inventory. They are discussing inventory strategies to minimize the cost of a product needed for production.

H: Good morning, Wang. I would like to consult your practices in managing inventory.

You've been doing a great job, but we've got a big product project problem.

W: So I've heard. The machines are going to be running night and day for a long while.

H: We need to keep our costs as low as possible; I'm sure you can understand that.

W: Oh, yes, don't worry, I'm looking forward to getting your advice on any points on the view of practice. You know, it's hard to see the forest for the trees.

H: We'll be resetting our machinery the first of the month to handle the order we've received for engine model 280. We must try to get the most efficient in the production line.

W: What support from inventory do you need?

H: My primary concern is the deterioration of the oil that's needed for the machines. According to my idea the most important thing is to ensure the efficient supply. You have to place quite an order that will require a long run of the machines. We need to do everything we can to keep up supplies for several months.

H: That's what has made me worried. Manager, and I will have to work closely together on a local oil supplier.

W: I'm glad you're looking ahead. What is the market for on that-oil these days?

H: Well, it is in badly need within these days, and the price goes up rapidly since the heavy shortage in the world market.

W: So you must take a prompt action, time is efficiency. Nothing is impossible to a willing heart.

H: Thanks a lot for your enlightening me.

W: My great pleasure.

Dialog Exercise 2

Clothing production is an industry of having high quality requirements in inventory management. Because the VMI strategy is very popular in logistics times, after analysis and research between a clothing company and its supplier, they decide outsourcing for the operation of warehousing and inventory management. Tom is the purchasing manager of the clothing company, and Jack is the sales manager of the supplier company. They visit together to a large distribution center called Metro-Centre. The manager of distribution center, Kate first led them to visit their warehouse, and then they began to negotiate about the cooperation. Please try to finish this dialog. The useful words you may need are as followed.

strategic partner	战略合作伙伴
annual rent	年租金

rapid replenishment	快速补货
stockout rate	缺货率
warehousing management integration	仓储管理一体化
intelligent inventory control system	智能化的库存控制系统
Expect good cooperation!	期待愉快的合作!

Case Study 2

Specialist Wire and Rope Manufacturer Stock—Accuracy and Leakage Reduction

Challenge

Store issue processes were not being adhered with many engineers failing to record their requisitions of stocked products at the point of issue.

Consequently IESA's perpetual cycle counting routines were revealing a stock accuracy reading 70% or lower, compared to the benchmark target, IESA's average achievement across open access storerooms, of 95% or higher. The value of shrinkage—un—booked items—had a monthly average run rate of £ 8,000. The primary impacts were the loss of budgeting data to plan and manage the maintenance department, together with the risk of items becoming potential stock outs and effecting downtime in production.

This resulted in a high proportion of the monthly issues being costed as stock losses, leading to a lack of visibility. Furthermore, anecdotal evidence suggested potential downtime impacts due to unavailable parts.

Solution

IESA engaged with the engineering department and their management team to devise and implement a bespoke set of published KPI measures.

The measures recorded and ranked individual engineers based on their propensity for correctly recording their stock item requisitions, the aim being to drive process compliance through a combination of visibility and management support.

Additionally, IESA increased the scope of the perpetual inventory checking procedures together with the frequency to eliminate any potential, residual inaccuracies so as to be able to accurately track improvements as they were achieved.

IESA also provided the site with a set of bespoke, highly visual KPIs, exclusively for the engineering department, and this information was shared with key stakeholders and compliance was monitored at an individual level.

The information was shared on a monthly basis at a prearranged review meeting, progress was tracked and targets amended once they had been achieved. IESA also ran a high profile communication campaign alongside the KPI graphs to reinforce the message of compliance.

Benefits

- IESA's data management facilities allowed us to trace, on behalf of our client, the improvements in stock accuracy and process performance on a continued basis.
- Through April and May 2013 the barcoded systems recorded a doubling in the volume of recorded issues.
- The value of un-recorded stock issues has also fallen significantly, to below the 75% reduction targeted. The net effect of these improvement measures has been improved budget data for the engineering management team, increased stock availability and reduced production downtime, allowing the client to plan and cost maintenance activities with traceability and accuracy.
- Within four months the stock accuracy, based on results from daily cycle counts, improved dramatically to 90%, and it is anticipated that the target of 95% will be passed during Q4 2013. The KPIs will continue to be compiled and assessed in order to avoid any retrograde movement.

Please answer the following questions after reading the case.

1. Describe the challenges the customer is facing in stock management.
2. What solutions has IESA provided to prove stock management?
3. What are the benefits achieved by IESA?

小贴士

物流小常识（1）

供应商管理库存（Vender Managed Inventory，VMI）的核心思想在于零售商放弃商品库存控制权，而由供应商掌握供应链上的商品库存动向，即由供应商依据零售商提供的每日商品销售资料和库存情况来集中管理库存，替零售商下订单或连续补货，从而实现对顾客需求变化的快速反应。VMI 作为一种目前国际上前沿的供应链库存管理模式对整个供应链的形成和发展都产生了影响。VMI 帮助供应商等上游企业通过信息手段掌握其下游客户的生产和库存信息，并对下游客户的库存调节做出快速反应，降低供需双方的库存成本。目前许多跨国巨头和国内知名制造企业都在拥抱VMI,并享受着由它带来的丰盛果实——提高库存周转率、降低库存成本、消灭库存冰山、实现供应链的整体优化。

小贴士

物流小常识(2)

格兰仕"零库存"的管理思想通过对生产计划和物料的系统规划,实现了材料和产品的库存都按照计划来流动,只保留少量的合理库存。"零库存"管理的核心在于尽快地采购最好的原材料、制造更好的产品,并通过反应迅速的营销体系以最快的速度传递到消费者手中。通过对金碟 K/3 和 Forgood ERP 系统的规划和运用,集团能够对库存进行数字化管理,具体到每个型号的产品在工厂有多少库存、经销商仓库里有多少台产品、每个时期的产品库存周转率,都有了准确的统计数据,决策层在调配资源、落实产供销平衡的问题上能够获得充分的依据。其实,"零库存"在应用过程中就是一种信息流的规划,通过这种规划,能够提高企业的资金周转率,很好地降低经营风险。

Supplementary Reading 2

Warehouse Management System Features

A WMS uses a database configured to support warehouse operations, containing detail describing a variety of standard warehouse elements including:

1. Individual stock keeping units (SKUs) that are handled and stored, e. g., weight, dimensions, case pack, automatic ID labels (bar codes, etc.), and inventory by location with manufacture date, lot code, etc. SKUs may include basic materials, fabricated parts, assemblies, and industrial and consumer finished goods.

2. Warehouse storage locations, e. g., individual location number, picking sequence, type of use (picking, reserve storage, etc.), type of storage (each, case, pallet), location size or capacity, storage restriction (flammable, hazardous, high value materials, outdoor, etc.).

3. Dock doors, e. g., individual number.

4. Expected labor productivity rates by function or activity, e. g., cases picked per man-hour.

Daily management functions include

1. Planning—finalizing the daily plan for receiving dock activity, selecting the

workload/orders to be processed in the day or shift, (this may also be done by the business system), and calculating an estimate of the labor and vehicles required to pick and ship the orders to ensure the staffing is appropriate, and carriers are notified in time to meet the daily requirements.

2. Organizing—sequencing the orders to be picked. Organizing orders for picking can be accomplished in many ways, meeting the needs of the user. The primary objective is to be intentional, and not pick the orders in the sequence in which they were received unless the company wants to pay a carrier make sense for transportation and delivery. The initial way of organizing was called Wave Planning or Wave Picking, with two objectives, a. to minimize need for dock staging space, by having orders arrive at the shipping dock in trailer load sequence, and b. to create an order of flow that will support monitoring the progress through the day and eliminate/reduce last minute requests for overtime or delay of carrier departure, etc.

3. Staffing—assign staff to work functions and areas, by wave, to minimize staging.

4. Directing—ensuring the documented processes and procedures are embedded in the WMS and are consistently applied, used and appropriate for the nature of the work and service level intentions of the company [e. g., International Standards Organization 9000 (www. iso. org)]. This function may also be used to divide individual orders into logical work units and the ability to assign them to separate individuals for performance, consistent throughput requirements and physical layout, e. g., separating individual case picking from each unit picking, and individual pallet load picking, to improve productivity and supporting control.

5. Controlling—providing milestones for management to monitor progress through the day, providing the opportunity to respond to problems in a timely way, and report data for performance analysis.

Chapter 3

Transportation Management

Learning Objectives

- Understand the definition of containerization
- Understand the interpretation of intermodal transportation
- Understand the advantages and disadvantages of five transportation modes

Lesson 3.1   Railroad and Motor Carriers

1. Railroad

For the most part, railroads have not experienced the same intensity of price competition as airlines and motor carriers. This has enabled them to work on longer run operational improvement, such as making shorter, more frequent trips.

Railroads are investing in automated switching yards; lower cost fuels, including electric power from coal; and lighter weight cars. Also, they are using their research and development to improve productivity through improved track maintenance, automated inspection, and improved aerodynamics. Lighter weight aluminum cars and better intermodal vehicles are common.

Intermodal service, or trailer-on-flatcar (TOFC), has been a growth segment of railroad transportation. The double-stack train offers considerable cost savings to shippers, especially on international shipments. In addition, transit time is consistent and generally lower than via all rail and comparable to all truck. Recently, a marketing intermodal rail-truck service has been provided between the given origin-designation points. The use of intermodal marketing companies holds promise of increased intermodal business for the railroads.

Expanded globalization of business will have a positive impact on railroads. Shipments to and from the Pacific Rim countries are increasingly being moved to West Coast ports via piggyback. Similar developments are occurring with European Community shipments through East Coast ports. Finally as the U. S. , Mexico, and Canada finalize the North American Free Trade Agreement (NAFTA), the railroads stand to increase their share of shipments moving to and from Mexico because of the truck congestion at the Mexico border and the current requirement that only Mexican nationals can own and operate Mexican trucking companies.

In the opinion of some experts, mergers and the expansion of single-liner service are the key elements for successful market expansion for railroads. The mergers will give railroads additional opportunities to tailor services to meet shipper needs. The reduced reliance on interchange partners should enable them to better control the quality of their service.

The deregulated environment will allow railroads to continue to improve their techniques of industrial marketing by emphasizing segmentation of markets, bundled and unbundled services, and contracts. They will continue also to price flexibly, particularly on backhaul traffic. A key element in this flexibility is the complete deregulation of boxcar traffic and export coal traffic.

The railroads face some key challenges in this competitive marketplace from other carriers, especially motor carriers. A major factor to rail success is continued productivity. It is interesting in this era of deregulation that the old standard of the railroad industry, the boxcar, is a major concern. Boxcars are decreasing in demand and railroads are facing a real challenge to keep their boxcars in operation. TOFC is the fastest growing area for railroads and probably the most profitable. The railroads must decrease their costs and their prices on boxcar traffic in the future.

The Approach to Meet the Challenge

Railways will not be able to achieve new business objectives unless they can:

- Respond to new market opportunities arising from evolving social and economic needs regarding mobility;
- Develop more efficient and competitive services, which form an integrated part of an intermodal transport system;
- Support the reengineering of the supply chains (systems integrators, subsystems and component suppliers) and foster industrial collaboration to enhance:
  ➢ industrial efficiency;
  ➢ the competitive advantages of country's products in world railway markets.

The development of such a strategy requires consideration of the underlying political, regulatory, financial and technological issues. Against such a backcloth, research and development activities should play a supporting role. Wide consultation with organizations representing the main interests has identified the following as priority themes for research and development activities：

- the modular high-speed train；
- the urban rail network of the future；
- a nationwide system for integrated passenger/freight logistics；
- the "virtual factory"—a cooperative network for railway vehicle and assemblies production；
- the train cargo-liner—a contribution to integrated freight transport chains.

These themes were considered to offer the highest potential contribution to overall business, social and environmental objectives in the rail sector.

2. Motor Carriers

Motor carriers responded to the fuel increases with positive and oftentimes creative innovations.

The freedom of entry in the motor carrier industry has allowed the major carriers to fill in their service area gaps. With the increase in service areas, shippers have reduced the number of carriers with which they deal, with many shippers using fewer than 25 carries.

There will continue to be shakeouts as carriers restructure in the more competitive environment. As motor carriers broaden their services, increase the number of terminals, and compete for market share, it is likely that 10 – 12 carriers will dominate the long-distance LTL market.

The truckload picture is difficult to predict. It is likely that the intense competition will continue with lower prices. More common carriers will move to contract carrier status, in effect, and so will private carriers looking for backhauls to fill empty trailers. The net result will private carriers looking for backhauls to fill empty trailers. The net result will be more competition with generally lower prices but with more fluctuations related to supply and demand. It is likely that there will be additional instability associated with carriers coming and going. More shippers will forego private carrier service because of the low prices.

The general commodity truckload part of the motor carrier industry has become fragmented and intensely competitive. Leasing companies, truckload specialists, private carriers seeking backhauls, and former household goods movers have all entered this market. It is debatable whether the industry's overall financial health will return to previous levels associated with the regulated environment.

Two long-haul truckload carriers, JB Hunt and Schneider National, have announced strategic changes to the increased use of intermodal equipment. Both companies have committed to change their trailer fleet to a container fleet in the near future. The container will be picked up by the motor carrier, and the moved long-haul truckload carriers have become full-service intermodal marketing companies, providing pickup and delivery of the container.

New words and terms

railroads	n.	铁路运输
motor carriers	n.	汽车运输
intensity	n.	强度
car	n.	车厢
aerodynamics	n.	空气动力学，气体力学
aluminum	n.	铝
intermodal	adj.	联合运输的
segment	n.	段，节，片断
double-stack		双层
congestion	n.	交通堵塞
merger	n.	（两个以上的企业或公司的）合并；归并
reliance	n.	信任；信赖
bundle	n.	捆；束；包
backhaul	n.	（货运车的）回程（通常亦载货），回程运费
boxcar	n.	货车车厢
shakeout	n.	轻度经济衰退，股票市场震动
forego	vt.	（在位置时间或程度方面）走在……之前，居先
resultant	adj.	作为结果而发生的，合成的
turmoil	n.	混乱；骚乱，动乱
debatable	adj.	可争论的，可争辩的

Notes

trailer-on-flatcar	集装箱车架输送
automated switching yards	自动调车场，自动转换场
LTL	卡车零担（货物）

net result	最终结果
JB Hunt	美国 JB 亨特运输服务公司,世界物流企业 100 强之内
Schneider National	美国世能达物流公司

Lesson 3.2　Air Carriers, Water Carriers and Pipelines

1. Air Carriers

Labor, fuel, and capital costs have made making a profit difficult for air carriers. Shippers have been sensitive to high rates and this has made air carriers susceptible in spite of promised trade-off savings in inventory costs.

Fuel price increases have tended to moderate in the early 1990s, but other costs, including labor, parts, supplies, and capital, have continued to make it difficult for air carriers to make a profit. Airlines are likely to continue using trucks to complement their air service on the shorter (less than 500 miles) hauls. Ease of entry and the deregulated truck environment will enable this modal substitution to occur and will be advantageous to both the carriers and shippers.

In the deregulated climate of the 1990s, the larger airlines will closely evaluate marginal business, redeploy equipment to more profitable passenger and air cargo routes. Competition in the form of rates and service will increase, especially in the parcel-size shipment (under 70 pounds) where Federal Express and UPS Air are locked in a competitive struggle. Heavy-lift (shipments weighting more than 70 pounds) air carriers are indirect competition with LTL motor carriers on rates on domestic moves and container ships on international moves, but only when time is not important.

A particular segment to watch is the air cargo container business. The 20-foot box in the all-cargo plane offers some real productivity benefits and has attracted renewed interest for many carriers. The carriers are publishing all kinds of commodities prices on those containers to help attract business. Ground equipment can still be a problem, but this should change thus allowing efficient handling of 20-foot containers at nearly all airports with scheduled service.

2. Air Freight Rates

Air cargo tariff is very complicated and difficult to understand, as apart from the general cargo rates (GCR), there are specific commodity rates (SCR) and class rates (CR), and GCR itself varies to a certain extent with the quantity offered for consignment. A vast network of airlines provides speedy transportation service to almost all the big cities in the world and even to remotest places on the earth, rendering the compilation of air cargo tariff like a dictionary, so to speak, rather than a chart or a table. A complex code system is adopted to facilitate identifying the applicable freight rate to a particular consignment of goods. 3-letter codes are used for big cities, e. g. SYD for Sydney, RIO for Rio de Janeiro, DKR for Dakar, etc. and 2-letter codes for airlines, e. g. SK for Scandinavian Airlines System, MH for Malaysian Airlines System, etc. 4-digit codes are used for the description of commodities, e. g. 1224 which represents "leather, leather goods (articles made mainly of leather), excluding wearing apparel". It requires some special training in order to be well acquainted with the procedures and the air cargo tariff. This may be one of the reasons why the air cargo agent or air freight forwarder plays a more important part in handling air traffic than the shipping and forwarding agent in ocean shipping.

Before one delves into the structure of air cargo tariff, it may be appropriate to know what IATA is. It is the abbreviation of the International Air Transport Association, a world organization of scheduled airlines. Through this organization, the IATA member airlines have been able to knit their individual routes into a world-wide public service system. Owing to its preponderant position, it behooves us to get a general idea about IATA air cargo tariff.

Chargeable Weight

The first step to compute the transportation charges to be paid is to ascertain the chargeable weight. In the case of cargo which is bulky in relation to its weight, such as woolen sweaters, the chargeable weight will be established on the basis of cubic volume rather than the gross weight, while for cargo such as wolfram the actual gross weight is used. The latter is called "high density cargo" weighing more than one kilogram per $7,000 \text{ cm}^3$ or more than one pound per 194 cubic inches. For instance, a case of leather shoes weights 15kg, while its dimensions are $100 \times 70 \times 25 = 175,000 \text{cm}^3$, by dividing it by $7,000$, the chargeable weight is 25kg.

Air freight rates and charges have evolved over a long period of time in answer to the increasing demand for air transportation. The underlying principle of formulating air cargo tariff is basically similar to that of railway freight tariff, i. e., charge what the traffic will bear and mean while take the operating cost into consideration. Specifically, the freight rates for various commodities are determined by the value of goods, competing means of transportation, amount of traffic, kinds and quantities of merchandise being imported and exported, special handling requirements, etc. The air cargo rates are not necessarily the same for both directions. The rates do not include additional charges for pick-up, export and import clearance, delivery and storage, etc.

Minimum Charge

For any consignment no charge less than this minimum charge shall be paid to the carrier. Theoretically speaking, it represents the level below which it would be uneconomical to transport a consignment, taking into account the fixed costs involved in handling even a small package. Therefore, no chargeable weight needs be indicated on an air waybill when the minimum charge is entered in the rate charge column. For instance, the minimum charge from Beijing to Toronto is RMB ￥39. 91, from Beijing to Venice RMB ￥41. 49 (CAAC December 10,1979). The minimum charge from Amsterdam, the Netherlands to Montreal, Canada is DFL 95. 04 (DFL = Dutch Guilder). It applies to a consignment of 1 to 5kg, depending upon local regulation.

Specific Commodity Rate (SCR)

Specific commodity rates are usually lower than general cargo rates and are published for particular specified commodities from a specified point of origin to a specified destination point. They are subject to a minimum weight which is published in connection with the rates. The chief purpose of specific commodity rates is to offer the general public competitive rates and thus make it economical to send their goods by air and consequently make optimum use of the airline transportation capacity. Specific commodity rates are usually made in response to demands or applications of the shippers whose business involves regular transportation of the same specific commodities on a certain route, or based on the field research which shows the necessity of developing traffic between certain areas. It should also be pointed out that the same specific commodity rates may not be available in both directions of a given traffic route.

The commodities for which a specific commodity rate is published are divided into main groups such as edible animal and vegetable products, live animal and inedible animal and vegetable products, textiles, etc. The main groups are sub-divided in series of 100, which give more precise definition of the commodities in each sub-group. For example:

1200—1299 Leather, leather goods, skin, rugs, artificial leather, mostly excluding wearing apparel.

Further detailed and more specific definitions of commodities are available in the description list, e. g.

Item No.　Description of commodities

1231　　Handbags, pocket books, wallets and purses

1295　　Bags, belts, billfolds, brushes, cases, wallets, fitted or unfitted

If a shipper consigns a shipment of 150kg of ladies' leather handbags, which is to be sent from Frankfurt to Montreal. First, it is established that the said commodity is classified under Main Group 1000—1999, and to be exact, in the Sub-Group 1200—1299, the next step is to find out if there are any specific commodity rates in this series from Frankfurt to Montreal. By consulting the description list, one can find out the detailed description of items Nos. 1231 and 1295 corresponding to the shipment of ladies' leather handbags.

The specific commodity rates published for these items in the FRA-YUL rate listing are:

SCR　　1231　　Dmk 2.70/kg min weight 500 kg
SCR　　1295　　Dmk 3.98/kg min weight 100 kg
　　　　　　　　Dmk 3.72/kg min weight 300 kg

In view of the weight of the shipment, i.e., 150 kg. SCR 1295 with a minimum weight of 100 kg must be applied.

$$150 \times Dmk\ 3.98 = Dmk\ 597.00$$

The choice of the specific commodity rate is in a large measure determined by the weight of the shipment.

3. Water Carriers

Water carriers have been hit by escalating fuel costs like other carriers, but they have tried to offset those costs with other economies. New propulsion systems are being investigated, as well as new ship designs. However, intense rate competition has made the situation bleak for deep-water carriers.

The inland waterway carriers, especially the barge lines, face similar problems to those being experienced by the truckload motor carriers. In addition severe overcapacity will keep their rate levels depressed in the near future.

The seeming reluctance of Congress to spend federal funds to improve the waterway system significantly will constrain productivity. The lack of any increased productivity will curtail cost reductions that could result in lower rates to spur demand.

4. Pipelines

The pipelines will continue to be a major component of the transportation system for the movement of bulk commodities or those commodities that can be made into liquid form by the addition of water in what is then called "slurry". However, the lack of growth in demand for the movement of oil will continue to affect pipelines.

The major hope for growth in the pipeline industry continues to be the possibility of the development of coal slurry pipelines. The development of coal slurry pipelines is tied closely to the possibility of using federally approved eminent domain legislation.

The Slurry Transportation Association believes that more than 10,000 miles of such pipeline would be constructed if the enabling eminent domain legislation were approved. Approval probably will not be granted in the near future. However, if railroads raise rates on coal. Significantly, pressure may be brought to bear upon Congress to change its position on the eminent domain issue.

5. The Strengths and Weaknesses of Different Modes of Transportation

The various modes of transportation include air, water, rail, motor, pipeline, and intermodal (which will be discussed later in this chapter).

Rail transport is used for heavy and huge tons over long land hauls without paying great charges. The advantages include greater dependability, low-cost assurance, constancy and are not influences by traffic conditions and the weather. The main disadvantages are inflexibility and particular routes between fixed terminals. What's more, rail transport do not stop at intermediate points and there are some damages result from maintenance; cleaning and fueling rail car.

The most commonly used mode is road transportation. It is a door-to-door form transportation. The advantages of this transportation are the flexibility and the capability to get hardy places. On the other side, the disadvantages are weight limitations, fuel expenses and high maintenance. Besides, create air, water and soil pollution.

Compared with rail and road transportation, water transportation is an important part of international trade, also it is not restricted to land utilize. River and canals, coastal shipping and ocean transport are the basic kinds of water transportation. The ability to transport large amounts of bulk freights, liquids and containerized freights by ships is the most obvious benefit of water transportation. But, the disadvantages of this mode include transit times are long, damage risk is high, and hard to find appropriate ports. In addition, fueling are harmful for water.

Air transportation is best suited for high-demand of speed. However, aircraft operations cause noise, and waste disposal problems.

Generally speaking, water is typically the least expensive mode but is also the slowest, on the contrast, air is the most expensive however the fastest. Rail and water are best suited for large shipment, low-value, and loose time. Whereas air is best suited for small, high-value, emergency shipments. The characteristics of different transportation modes see Table 3.1.

Table 3.1   Transportation Characteristics

Mode	Service Features
Rail	Long distances; Low unit cost; High capability; Mass movement; Extensive coverage
Motor	Suits all types of goods; Door-to-door service; Intensive geographical coverage; Speed; Flexibility and frequency
Water	Mass movement of bulk commodities at the lowest cost; High capability; Advanced technology of loading and unloading
Air	Premium service; Reduced packaging and handling requirements Reduced costs for other logistics components
Pipeline	Mass movement of liquid and gaseous materials at vary low cost; High capability; Greatest dependability; Pricing flexibility

The comparison of different transportation modes is as figure 3.1.

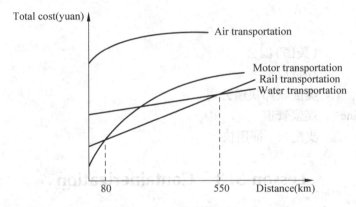

Figure 3.1   The comparison of different transportation mode

New words and terms

air carriers		航空运输
water carriers		水路运输
pipelines	*n.*	管道运输
slurry	*n.*	泥浆，浆状物
susceptible	*adj.*	易受影响的，容许……的
part	*n.*	零件
haul	*n.*	用力拖拉,拖运距离
substitution	*n.*	代替，取代作用，置换

evaluate	vt.	评价，估计
cargo	n.	（车、船、飞机等运输的）货物
route	n.	路线，路程，通道
parcel	n.	小包，包裹
escalate	v.	逐步升高，逐步增强
offset	n.	抵销，弥补
propulsion	n.	推进，推进力
bleak	adj.	没有指望的；令人沮丧的
barge	n.	驳船，游艇
constrain	vt.	强迫，抑制，拘束
spur	n./v.	鞭策，刺激
bulk	n.	大批，散装

Notes

Congress	（美国）国会
inventory costs	存货成本
Federal Express	美国联邦快递公司
coal slurry pipeline	煤浆管道
eminent domain	支配权，征用权

Lesson 3.3   Containerization

1. General Introduction

Containers are essential big boxes into which firms place small loads. Once commodities are loaded into a container, the individual items are not handled again until final delivery. The container permits economic and efficient transfer of unitized loads among different modes of transportation.

Containers come in a variety of sizes, generally in lengths of 20, 40 feet for international shipments. The cargo container is usually weatherproof, permitting storage outside or transport in open-top railcars or on a ship's deck. The container's construction is rugged enough for movement by mechanical means such as forklifts or cranes and for interchange between or among modes.

The container has gained wide acceptance in the international movement of manufactured goods. Railroads and motor carriers have joined forces to provide through movement of containers from the interior of the United States to foreign countries. Special double stack railcars are used to transport two containers per car. The use of double-stack trains has greatly increased the economic viability of containerized shipments.

On the domestic front, a number of long-haul trucking companies, J. B. Hunt and Schneider National, for example, began using domestic containers for long distance (greater than 800 miles) moves. The trucking companies bring a domestic container to the shipper's dock for loading, then transport the container to the railroad for a long-haul, intercity move. At the destination, the trucking company delivers the container to the consignee.

Very simply, containers are attractive to users because of reduced cost. Containerization reduces transportation cost, handling cost, loss and damage, inventory cost, and packaging cost.

2. Advantages of Containerization

The use of container, though an improvement over the conventional mode, does not dispense with the individual packing required for the cargo, and the cost of packing remains unreduced. This mode of carriage does not minimize the exposure to various risks in the course of transit, which include theft and pilferage. However, the saving in the operation cost is substantial when the carriage involves sea voyage only.

Use of this efficient process can be made even in situations where full container-load is not possible. In such cases, individual shipments coming to berths as breakbulk cargo, i. e. , traditionally packed cargo can be loaded into containers before being hoisted aboard the ship. At destination port the containers can be opened and the cargo stored for customs clearance and subsequent delivery to the consignee. Ships can be loaded and unloaded by cranes in a fraction of time needed for handling the general breakbulk cargo.

This mode of transportation provides the shipper with seagoing strong vans which not only protect shipments from damage and theft, but also can be used repeatedly, thus reducing the expense of export packaging.

Tankers and ore carriers are now highly mechanized in both loading and unloading and thus involve fewer hands. But conventional cargo ship place reliance on manual labor in the handling of cargo, including stacking, loading, stowing and unloading. This process oftentimes costs a ship of, say, 10,000 tons approximately one-third of her time in a trading year, leaving her only about 200 days at sea. This slow turnover in trading implies higher cost and less freight income.

However, a different picture will present itself in the case of container ships. A rough comparison will bear this out. On a conventional cargo ship, the rate of loading by a gang of from 16 to 18 hands is approximately 35 tons an hour, while a total of twenty containers weighing 20 tons each can be lifted by one crane in an hour. In one shift lasting 21 hours, only 735 tons can be loaded by sling, while in the same shift one crane can life 410 containers weighing 8,400 tons. Besides, due to mechanized loading, the number of hands can be greatly reduced.

There is another case in point. When containerized traffic was first initiated in China, a trial trip was made by a Chinese ship from Shanghai to Japan, which carried a total of 30 containers. The loading was done by nine wharf workers only and completed in one hour, while the loading of the same consignment, if shipped as breakbulk cargo, would have taken around 16 hours by a team of 19 workers.

The above clearly shows that containerized traffic is far more efficient than the traditional mode of transportation. It achieves not only a saving in the time for operations, but also a saving in labor, thus greatly reducing the operational cost and enabling the ship to be put to better and more profitable use.

The other advantages derivable from containerized traffic comprise minimization of losses and simpler packaging.

Containers being weather proof metal vans are capable of withstanding most of the risks while in transit and the cargo packed therein is always much safer than when conveyed in separate packing. Damage to cargo in the course of handling can also be well avoided, and the risk of theft and pilferage can be reduced to a large extent. This will reduce the chance of claims on the carrier even though certain of the claims are not answerable due to the immunities conferred on him under the contract of carriage.

Since cargo is consolidated into containers which usually serve as sort of outer packing, the traditional packaging normally required for breakbulk cargo can be dispensed with. Simpler packaging connotes a saving in the packing cost which is definitely of benefit to the cargo owner.

The high efficiency of containerized traffic will contribute considerably to the substantial saving in the carrier's overheads, thus rendering it possible for him to fix the freight rate at a more attractive level.

On the other hand, the capital investment that will be required for the operation of containerized traffic will be quite substantial.

First, the carriage of containers necessitates specific accommodations in the ship. Whilst conventional cargo ships are not absolutely unfit for the carriage of containers, the broken space that will ensue in the stowage due to the dimension of the hold, will prove uneconomical to the carrier. Container ships are therefore designed with a view to making the best possible use of the container.

Second, the manufacture or purchase of containers involves a considerable sum of money, especially when the number required is taken into account. A container ship carrying 750 containers which sails once a week on a fixed route requires triple that number of containers. A 20 feet size container costs approximately USD 2,000 and 2,250 containers will cost USD 4,500,000. The more container ships are employed, the bigger the number of containers that will have to be made ready, though not in like proportion, and the cost for this item alone will be fairly considerable.

Third, to meet the specific requirements for container ships, a special type of terminal different from traditional berths is required. Such terminal normally calls for a space three to six times the traditional terminal for handling a similar volume of inward and outward cargo. Whilst fewer sheds and godowns are needed at such terminal because most containers, being constructed of metals, can withstand any climate, the foundation of the terminal is to be so built as to be capable of sustaining the weight of straddle carriers having a lifting capacity of 30 tons each and gantry cranes along the berths to lift containers onto or out of ships. Further, there are always a great number of containers at the container yard and the container freight station, if it is situated within the framework of the terminal. In addition, there are containers spread out at the marshalling yard and along the apron, the frontage of the berth, ready for loading. The higher standard required in the construction of this type of terminal will cost considerably more than the traditional berth for conventional cargo ship.

The foregoing would, at first sight, appear to be a deterrent in the way of growth of containerization, particularly in countries in the third world whose financial resources might not permit of such a gigantic project, but the whole world is now well cognizant of the advantages of this renovated mode of transportation, and a steady development can be expected.

3. Descriptions of Containers

Most containers are constructed of steel because this metal is durable and strong. But other materials have also been utilized, including aluminum, plywood, plastics, and laminated wood.

Different types of containers are available to suit different needs. They chiefly comprise:

Dry Cargo Container

This type is designed for various species of dry cargo, dry edibles, machines, precision instruments, medical apparatuses and valuable cargo, etc.

Refrigerated Container, Also Called Reefer Container

This type, being fitted with a refrigerating machine, is specifically designed for frozen meat, eggs and fruits to be preserved at low temperature, which is adjustable from 26℃ ~ 28℃, but is operative only on being supplied with electric current.

Open Top Container

This type is, as the term implies, opened at the top and is normally covered by waterproof canvas after it is filled up. The open top container is fit for bulky and weighty cargo including mineral ores, etc.

Tank Container

This type is designed for vegetable oils, industrial oil, alcohol and other liquid cargo in bulk.

Flat Rack Container

This type is devoid of side and top plates and, instead, grates are fitted at both sides. It is usually used for the carriage of livestock, fresh vegetables or certain types of machines.

There are also car container, livestock container, pen container, etc., but these are not yet used extensively.

At the outset, the size of containers was not standardized, but on the recommendation of the International Organization for Standardization, abbreviated to ISO, the following standardized dimensions seemed as table 3.2 are now universally accepted.

Table 3.2   the Standard Dimension of the Container

	Height	Width	Length	Maximum Weight
	1AA2.591m 8′	2.438m 8′	12.190m 40′	30.48m/t 30 1/t
GROUP 1	1AA2.438m 8′	2.438m 8′	12.190m 40′	30.48m/t 30 1/t
	1B2.438m 8′	2.438m 8′	9.125m 30′	25.4m/t 25 1/t
	1C2.438m 8′	2.438m 8′	6.058m 20′	20.32m/t 20 1/t

Continued

	Height	Width	Length	Maximum Weight
GROUP 2	1D 2.438m 8′	2.438m 8′	2.991m 10′	10.160m/t 10 1/t
	1E 2.438m 8′	2.438m 8′	1.968m 6-2/3′	7.11m/t 7 1/t
	1FC 2.438m 8′	2.438m 8′	1.460m 5′	5.08m/t 5 1/t
	2A 2.100m 6′11″	2.300m 7′07″	2.920m 9′07″	7.110m/t 7 1/t
	2B 2.100m 6′11″	2.100m 6′11″	2.400m 7′11″	7.110m/t 7 1/t
	2C 2.100m 6′11″	2.300m 7′07″	1.450m 4′09″	7.110m/t 7 1/t

Sizes 1AA, 1A and 1C in the above list are now in general use.

New words and terms

containerization	*n.*	货柜运输,集装箱化
container	*n.*	集装箱
commodity	*n.*	商品
unitized	*adj.*	组成的,成组的,组合的
mode	*n.*	方式,模式
weatherproof	*adj.*	防风雨的,不受天气影响的
railcar	*n.*	铁路车
deck	*n.*	甲板
rugged	*adj.*	高低不平的,粗糙的,有皱纹的
forklift	*n.*	叉式升降机,叉车
crane	*n.*	起重机
interior	*adj.*	内部的
double-stack	*n.*	内部,双层
viability	*n.*	生机,生存能力
long-haul		长距离拖运
dock	*n.*	码头
intercity	*adj.*	城市间的

consignee	*n.*	收件人，收货人
hail	*v.*	拥戴、受欢迎
accumulation	*n.*	积累，堆积
synergy（＝synergism）	*n.*	协同，配合
manipulate	*vt.*	（熟练地）操作，使用（机器等）
differentiate	*v.*	区别，区分

Notes

1. Containerization reduces transportation cost, handling cost, loss and damage, inventory cost, and packaging cost.

   集装箱化运输能够降低运输成本、装卸费用、损失和破坏、储存成本和包装成本。

2. Intermodal or multimodal transportation 联合运输或多式联运

3. TOFC＝Trailers on Flatcar（铁路）平板车装运载有集装箱的拖车数

4. APL 美国总统船公司

5. supercarriers or megacarriers 超级承运商

Lesson 3.4   Intermodal Transportation

Intermodal transport service refers to the use of two or more carriers of different modes in the through movement of a shipment. [1] Carriers offer such services to the public by publishing a rate from origin to destination for one carrier of each available mode. In other situations, the logistics manager, through routing, uses different modes to get a product to its final destination. [2]

The logistics manager often must utilize different transport modes to service a given link. While intermodal services are necessary for numerous reasons, the basic reasons are the various mode's service characteristics and costs. For example, the limited accessibility of air transportation requires coordination with a land carrier to make the pickups and deliveries. Similar inaccessibility applies to rail, water, and pipeline, but not to motor, which has a definite advantage here. By manipulating the modes, a logistics manager can overcome a given mode's service disadvantage and retain the mode's basic advantage, usually low cost. This is the primary motivation for combining rail and water to move coal or grain: the rail segment improves water transport's accessibility, and the water portion permits savings by providing low-cost service for the long-distance move.

Intermodal services maximize the primary advantages inherent in the combined modes and minimize their disadvantages. The combined services will have both the good and the bad aspects of the utilized modes. For example, the coordination of rail and water will have a lower total cost than an all-rail movement, but a higher cost than all-water. Likewise, the combined system's transit time will be lower than an all-water movement, but higher than all-rail. The decision to use combined modes must consider the effect on total logistics costs.

There are ten possible intermodal service combinations: (1) rail-truck (2) rail-water (3) rail-air (4) rail-pipeline (5) truck-air (6) truck-water (7) truck-pipeline (8) water-pipeline (9) water-air (10) air-pipeline. Not all of these combinations are practical. Some that are feasible have gained little acceptance. Only rail-truck, called piggyback, has seen widespread used. Truck-water combinations, referred to as fishyback, gaining acceptance, especially in the international movement of high valued goods. And birdyback, the combinations of air-truck are also common.

Birdyback, fishyback, and piggyback services are examples of coordination in which a carrier physically transfers the motor carrier trailer, with the cargo intact in another mode. Birdyback combines the accessibility of motor with the speed of the airline; fishyback couples motor accessibility with the low cost of water carriage and piggyback adds the truck's accessibility to the low cost of rail service. In each case, the combined service suffers the disadvantages of one of the modes involved, for example, birdyback has the disadvantage of air transport's high cost.

One substantial block to intermodal service is that carriers are reluctant to participate. The carriers coordinate willingly, even eagerly, to move a product that any one carrier could not transport in its entirety, but once one carrier can transport the commodity in the entire distance though its own lines, the carrier is still hesitant to coordinate with other carriers.

Another problem with intermodal services is the transfer of freight from one mode to another. This creates time delays and adds to transportation costs. Some forms of coordination eliminate this problem by transferring a motor carrier trailer to another transport mode. The motor carrier trailer's transferability is a special coordination from termed containerization, the trailer being a container.

New words and terms

intermodal transport service	多式联运服务
make the pickups and deliveries	集货和交货
birdyback service	鸟背运输(空背运输)
fishyback service	鱼背运输(船背运输)

piggyback service　　　　　　　　　　　背负式运输(驮背运输)
transferability　　　　　　　　　　　*n.*　可传递性

Notes

1. Intermodal transport service refers to the use of two or more carriers of different modes in the through movement of a shipment.

   多式联运服务是指在货物的整个运送过程中,使用两个或多个不同类型的承运人。

2. Carriers offer such services to the public by publishing a rate from origin to destination for one carrier of each available mode. In other situations, the logistics manager, through routing, uses different modes to get a product to its final destination.

   承运人通过公布每种可用运输模式从起点到终点的运费来为大众提供服务。其他情况下,物流经理根据路线使用不同的运输模式来将产品送达最终目的地。

Exercises 3

Ⅰ. Pair work：Discuss the following questions.

1. Why is transportation important to the world?
2. How many kinds of transportation modes do you know? What are they?
3. What are the advantages of road transportation?
4. What are the disadvantages of air transportation?
5. What is the advantage of maritime transportation?
6. What kinds of commodity can be transported by pipeline?

Ⅱ. Fill in the blanks with the following words in the boxes, and change the forms if necessary.

low	important	maritime	feature	door-to-door
unique	cheap	advantage	proportion	movement

1. Waterway transport is the _____ method of moving goods world wide.

2. In recent years air transport has played a _____ role in global logistics.

3. Waterway transport includes _____ and river transportation.

4. Transportation refers to the physical _____ of goods from a point to another point.

5. Each transportation mode has its own requirements and _____.

6. Railway is especially good for cargoes with high volume and _____ value.

7. Road transportation can provide _____ delivery service.

8. The nature of pipeline is _____ in comparison to all other modes of transport.

9. Air transport accounts for the smallest _____ of cargo transportation.

10. The major _____ of air freight is the speed of travel.

Ⅲ. Translate the following sentences into Chinese.

1. Pipelines operate on a twenty-four-hour basis, seven days per week, and only are limited by commodity changeover and maintenance.

2. Water carriage is particularly suited for movement of heavy, bulky, low-value-per-unit commodities.

3. The main disadvantages of water transport are the limited range of operation and speed.

4. The two sides finally reached an agreement on the mode of transportation.

5. Freight rates are based on three factors, namely, distance, shipment and competition.

Ⅳ. Translate the following sentences into English.

1. 水运的主要优点是低成本。

2. 航空运输具有速度上的优势。

3. 此批货物正在运输途中。

4. 运输费用占到总物流成本的三分之一。

5. 我们最大的问题是如何降低装运费用。

Ⅴ. Answer the questions according to the text of this chapter.

1. How many transportation modes in logistics system? Please try to compare the advantages and disadvantages of five modes of transportation.

2. Please try to write three common intermodal transportation modes and write their respective advantages.

3. What is containerization? And what is the main function of containerization which can realize?

Logistics Situational Dialogues 3

A manager of a medium-sized firm that makes mini-moter homes in Michigan. His company usually doesn't make the parts themselves. The following is a dialogue happened between a manager and his stuff at the meeting. Macon is key partner themselves, all of them are mainly purchased from outside venders. His colleagues all think it expensive and not inconvenient. At the meeting they ask their leader why. The following is a dialogue happened between a manufacturer and a manager of inventory.

M: I think it is necessary to hold this professional meeting to discuss the supply of our parts. Have you ever heard there is a new term called JIT?

S: It sounds familiar, but I don't know the exact meaning, can you explain it for me?

M: Yes, sure, the term of JIT systems was first come out from Toyota company over 45 years ago. The company successfully use the out-source supply to produce the cars efficiently. And in turn, they generalized a complementary approach to production, they involves: quality control, supplier relation, and distributor relationship.

S: But what is the exact meaning of JIT?

M: "Just-in Time" means to deliver the right product with the right quality to right place, in the right condition, at the right time, in the right quantity and with the right cost.

S: It sounds nice! I hear it will become a new speaking and a theory in the logistic field.

M: Yes, and in the recent years, its meaning has been of widely comprehend. It's also used in other kind of the field. For example, First Aid, it means some emergency organization can save and the injured person at the first time and at the right place timely before the other help comes.

S: It is very interesting! I'll make a good research on it.

M: That is, it is really worth doing! It is really a principle of making the service efficient and profitable!

Dialog Exercise 3

Mr. Huang is a manufacturer in light – industry products. He wants to export some of his finished goods. He really has some troubles about how to transport his goods to the foreign country since this is his first time to do foreign trade transaction. So he consults the expert of transportation Pro. Make a dialog to discuss the choice of transportation means. The useful words which may be involved in the dialog are as follows.

transportation means   运输方式

ocean freight   海洋运输

a cheap mode of transport for delivering large quantities of goods over long distance

一种适合于运大批量的货物及走长距离路线的价格便宜的运输方式

commodities   货物,商品

Case Study 3

Victoria's Secret for Success

Intimate brands, Inc., is a leading specialty retailer of intimate apparel and beauty and personal care products through the Victoria's Secret and Bath & Body Works brands. In 1999, net sales for the Victoria's Secret brand, including stores, catalog and E-commerce, were $ 2.9 billion. Catalog and E-commerce accounted for 18 percent of the business, or $ 799 million.

For shipments under one pound, about 33 percent to 35 percent, Victoria Secret ships via the U.S. Postal Service. With products including clothing, shoes, accessories, and bath and beauty products, in addition to lingerie, orders can vary from a few ounces for a single item to several pounds. "We've always used some form of postal service," Karvchuk says, "because they provide a good service at a good price and because of customer's requests or orders that go to post office boxes." Kravchuk continues, "the USPS offers us a cost benefit in certain areas, and we take advantage of that." "However, he says even though cost is always one consideration, it is not the primary one. Service to customers is always primary."

Although there are requests for expediter service, with which Victoria's Secret Complies, many customers are happy with the company's pledge to deliver orders in 7 to 10 business days. It works hard to say within that time frame and monitors performance on a weekly basis to ensure that service level. The majority of orders come in by phone but also faxes and mail, with increasing activity via http://www. Victoria's secret. com. Contrary to what might be expected, Kravchuk says customer's delivery requirements on internet orders closely mirror phone orders. He has not seen a dramatic surge in requests for expedited delivery of internet orders.

For the past three years, Victoria's Secret has used Global Logistics, a package expeditor to service its USPS shipments in the southeast. Bob Thatcher, Global Logistics president, makes the distribution himself between being a consolidator and an expeditor because he focuses more on service and performance than price. Global Logistics focuses on serving major catalogers that focus more on service and performance than price. His goal is to provide three-to-five day service from the time an order is shipped to the time it is delivered to the household. This obviously fits well with the Victoria's Secret promised delivery. Intimate brands provide linehaul from its Columbus, Ohio, distribution center to Global

Logistics' facility in Stone Mountain, Georgia. Global then, sorts, palletizes, and manifests loads for delivery. Victoria's Secret sends an average of one trailer every day, five days a week. This may increase two trailers a day during the peak holiday season in December, as well as a sales period in January.

Among the services Global Logistics offers is serving as its customers' eyes in the field. For example, Global logistics is always on the alert for area-specific issues that may affect delivery, such as weather or other events and determines which ZIP codes will be affected. Sharing this information with Victoria's Secret helps Global Logistics keep delivery schedules on track. According to Thatcher, "We look at every opportunity to reduce time, either in transit or in steps, to ensure quick delivery."

One of the timesaving techniques it uses is taking orders processed on Fridays and getting them to the post office on Sunday and Monday. This can cut up to a day off delivery times. In reducing steps, Global Logistics isn't over-labeling. The shipper is responsible for applying all marketing (including the postage indicia) on its label. As a result, when Global Logistics receives the shipment, it just scans the five-digit bar code, sorts, palletizes, and manifests.

All deliveries are palletized for ease of handling. Thatcher is quick to point out that all of Global Logistics' deliveries to the bulk mail centers are standing appointments and live unloads. The alternative, Thatcher says, is drop and pick. Where a trailer is dropped at the bulk mail center and the postal service personnel have up to 24 hours to unload it. Although it typically does not take the full 24 hours, it is a variable that Thatcher does not want in his schedule.

According to Kravchuk, visibility of products at this point does not play a role in their distribution. He would, however, like to work more closely with the USPS to get delivery information in real time. Because Victoria's Secret does not apply a tracking number, Global Logistics tracks performance through the postal system with an 8,125 (mailing form) to ensure proper service.

Please answer the questions after reading the case.

1. What is the secret of Victoria's Secret for success?
2. Which transportation modes does the company adopt and how about the effectiveness?

小贴士

物流小常识：世界十大物流公司

USPS(United States Postal Service)美国邮政署——亦称美国邮局或美国邮政服务，是美国联邦政府的独立机构。拥有218 684辆汽车，是全球最庞大的民用车队。每年处理177亿信件，占全球数量的四成。美国邮政署是少数在美国宪法中提及设立的机构。

DPWN(Deutsche Post DHL)德国邮政-敦豪丹莎海空——是德国的国家邮政局，也是欧洲地区领先的物流公司，划分为邮政、物流、速递和金融服务4个自主运营的部门。2016年9月以2.5亿英镑收购英国邮政集团。

FedEx(Federal Express)美国联邦快递——是一家环球运输、物流、电子商务和供应链管理供应商，公司通过各子公司的独立网络，向客户提供一体化的业务解决方案。2015年豪投44亿欧元收购荷兰快递公司TNT(TNT Express)从而超越UPS。

UPS(United Parcel Service)美国联合包裹服务——作为世界上最大的快递承运商与包裹递送公司，UPS同时也是专业的运输、物流、资本与电子商务服务的领导性的提供者。

Maersk(A. P. Moller-Maersk)丹麦马士基——是世界上最大的航运公司，拥有250艘船舶，其中包括集装箱船舶、散货船舶、供给和特殊用途船舶、油轮等。

La Poste法国邮政——是垄断全国邮政业务的国有部门，其前身是法国邮电部邮政总局，主要业务分为信函业务、包裹和物流业务、金融业务三大部分，其在全球拥有200家子公司，17 000个投递点。

Cosco中国远洋——China Ocean Shipping Company是中国大陆最大的航运企业，全球最大的海洋运输公司之一，是我国53家由中央直管的特大型国企之一。

Japan Post日本邮政——是一个自负盈亏的国有公共公司，目标是提供全面的、迅捷的函件和包裹寄递业务，简单、安全的储蓄业务和汇兑业务以及简易保险业务等。

Nippon Express日通——公司业务主要分为汽车运输、空运、仓库及其他，从地域上看，其经营收入有93%来自日本。

TPG(荷兰邮政集团)为全球超过200个国家和地区提供邮递、速递及物流服务，从运营利润看，邮递、速递和物流分别占76%、15%和9%。

Supplementary Reading 3

Deutsche Post DHL Acquires UK Mail

September 2016, Deutsche Post DHL has reached an agreement to buy UK Mail for approximately 242.7 million pounds, or 281.6 million euros. With the acquisition, DHL will further strengthen its position in the European postal market, while putting more pressure on competitor Royal Mail in the United Kingdom.

As the Guardian puts it, the acquisition comes after "a difficult period for UK Mail". The postal company had some problems at its automated sorting facility and saw its boss Guy Buswell leave a week after it issued a second profits warning in three months due to these problems.

UK Mail will benefit significantly.

"We have made good strategic progress in recent years, establishing leading positions in our key markets of parcels and mail, investing in additional capacity in our operations and in IT and product and service innovation", Peter Kane, Chairman of UK Mail said, "The board believes that UK Mail will benefit significantly from becoming part of Deutsche Post DHL and will be better positioned to continue to develop our parcels and mail businesses. Our customers will have direct access to Deutsche Post DHL's integrated global parcel network and comprehensive logistics capabilities. We will have opportunities to win additional business from Deutsche Post DHL's existing customer base."

The BBC reported the breaking news at mid-day. The purchase is part of a European expansion drive by Deutsche Post. "UK Mail is well-run and an established provider of quality delivery services in the UK. It offers a complementary fit with our integrated offering," said Deutsche board member Jurgen Gerdes. UK Mail directors said it believed the deal was "fair and reasonable". Shareholders have yet to agree but under the terms of the deal they would receive 440 pounds a share.

About UK Mail

UK Mail is one of the biggest mail and parcel operators in the UK, offering solutions both locally and worldwide. It has a national network of more than 50 sites and 2,400 vehicles.

Answer the following questions

1. When did DHL acquire UK Mail?
2. What's the price of DHL acquires UK Mail?
3. How much will the shareholders of UK mail get per share?
4. What's the reason behind acquisition?

Chapter 4

Logistics Packaging

Lesson 4.1 Function of Logistics Packaging

Packaging can be divided into industrial packaging (exterior packaging) and consumer packaging (interior packaging). Generally speaking, consumer packaging, which mainly aims at containing the goods, promoting the sale of it and facilitating use of it, is of little value to logistics operation. But industrial packaging has a significant impact on the cost and productivity of logistics. [1]

Industrial packaging should perform the following functions to meet integrated logistics requirements.

First, it should protect the goods from damage during handling, storing and transportation. Damage caused by vibration, impact, puncture or compression can happen whenever a package is being transported. Hence, package design and material must combine to achieve the desired level of protection without incurring the expense of over protection. It is possible to design a package that has the correct material content but does not provide a necessary protection. Arriving at a satisfactory solution involves defining the degree of allowable damage in terms of expected overall conditions (because in most cases, the cost of absolute protection will be prohibitive) and then isolating a combination of design and material capable of meeting those specifications.

Second, it should promote logistical efficiency. Packaging affects not only marketing and production, but also integrated logistics activities. For example, the size, shape and type of packaging material influence the type and amount of material handling equipment as well as how goods are stored in the warehouse. Likewise, package size and shape affects loading, unloading, and the transporting of a product. The easier it is to handle a product, the lower the transportation rate. Hence, if the package is designed for efficient logistical processing, overall system performance will benefit.

The third important logistical packaging function is communication or information transfer. [2] To identify package contents for receiving, order selection and shipment verification, etc. is the most obvious communication role of packaging. Typical information includes manufacturer, product, container type, count, and Universal Product Code (UPC) number. Ease of package tracking is also important. Effective internal operation and a growing number of customers require that product be tracked as it moves though the logistics channel. This can be realized by the extensive use of radio Frequency Identification, a computer chip embedded in the package, container, or vehicle to allow the container and contents to be scanned and verified as it passes checkpoints in the distribution facility and transportation gateway. The final communication role of logistics packaging is to provide instructions as to how to handle the cargo and how to prevent possible damage. For instance, if the product is potentially dangerous, such as fireworks and table tennis balls, the packaging or accompanying material should provide instructions for avoiding moisture, vibration and heating, etc., as the case may be.

New words and terms

industrial packaging	工业包装
consumer packaging	商业包装
exterior packaging	外部包装
interior packaging	内部包装

Notes

1. Packaging can be divided into industrial packaging (exterior packaging) and consumer packaging (interior packaging). Generally speaking, consumer packaging, which mainly aims at containing the goods, promoting the sale of it and facilitating use of it, is of little value to logistics operation. But industrial packaging has a significant impact on the cost and productivity of logistics.

包装可以分为工业包装(外部包装)和商业包装(内部包装)两种形式。一般地说,旨在容纳商品、促进销售和方便使用的商业包装对于物流业务没什么重要的价值。但是工业包装对于物流中的成本和生产率却有着重要的影响。

2. The third important logistical packaging function is communication or information transfer. 物流包装的第三大重要功能就是沟通或信息传递。

Lesson 4.2　Package Marking

For many years, semiconductor package marking commanded little attention and continued with little change. However, the increasing demand for smaller components means that the available marking area also is smaller. So, while the complexity of electronic technologies increases, so do the demands on device identification technology.

Recently, the names of technology companies have become more complex with some names exceeding 20 characters in one line. Standards include two and three lines of identification codes to be marked, as well as a company logo. Marking codes require more details to be available to customers, ensuring that the correct product is purchased for their applications. The marks on the device package are the link to the component's complete identification and its process history.

Traceability

Traceability is valuable when defective components, parts, assemblies or products may be discovered during or after production or sale. Full traceability can allow accurate tracking and permit a partial rather than full recall to be carried out if necessary.

Traceability is defined as "the ability to trace the history, application or location of an entity by means of recorded identifications". Marking is only one of many steps. Data capture, management and analysis also are necessary to track manufactured products properly. Standardization must be implemented so different manufacturing elements result in a seamless flow of required information, and so that data and information can be exchanged between user and supplier. This improves overall semiconductor manufacturing capabilities.

Commercial marking specifications of semiconductor components are an outgrowth of military applications. These marking methods ensure correct component identification. Military requirements include package index identifier, chip identification code, drawing designator, part identification, country of origin, device type and class, case outline, manufacturer's designation, and many others. Today, component manufacturers' codes are based on some of these same requirements.

Traditional Marking Processes

Generally, product and part identification quickly eliminate errors, valuable time and material waste expenditures, while helping to streamline production. Choosing the right marking system must be done carefully. Origin of manufacture, craftsmanship, service and support also should be considered because technical support may become an issue later.

Some current package marking methods are reviewed below:

Pad Printing

Basic steps in this process include the cliché step, in which the desired image to print is etched into a plate. This plate typically consists of hardened steel. Once placed on the printer, the cliché is inked by an open inkwell, a doctoring system (applying ink and scraping off the excess), or by an ink-cup sliding across the cliché. The second step is the transferring step where the pad picks up the inked image from the cliché and travels to the component to be marked. The pad then makes contact with the component using pressure to deliver the image.

Ink Marking

Inkjet printers use drop-on-demand technology. This means that the ink flow is turned on and off during the printing process to create patterns of ink droplets, resulting in an image. Thermal inkjet printing uses heat to vaporize ink expelled through the print nozzle as tiny droplets. The technology basis is to deflect and control a continuous inkjet droplet stream onto the printed media or into a gutter for recirculation by applying an electric field to previously charged inkjet droplets.

Electrolytic Marking

This procedure uses a unit to generate a low-voltage electric current (typically at 8V) that is applied for a specific time onto the product through a stencil. An electrolyte chemical aids electricity flow applied to the marking head. The current etches away the top layer using conductive chemical solvents, leaving the stencil design permanently marked onto the product. The marking is completed in approximately two to three seconds.

Laser Marking

With the ability to provide legible characters smaller than any other available process, laser marking can provide capabilities that are not available with other processes. Laser marking also can present many different configurations, systems and methods. This technology will continue to grow, and it is important to select the proper laser wavelength for the application(s). The variety of processing capabilities possible with laser marking can improve the overall cost effectiveness of the marking system.

The production environment and type of machinery used to produce the product also must be considered. In most applications, it is ideal to mark the part prior to the packaging operation so that if any other process fails or is deemed to be a reject, the marking would not occur. This mark would verify that the component passed all assembly and testing operations, signaling a good product. Additionally, if the part required serialized numbers, this method would be the best choice to keep all the numbers in sequence.

Other Marking Variables

In today's high-volume manufacturing environment, it may be ideal to perform the marking operation on the fly, that is, while the product is moving or indexing on a conveyor or in-line type of system. This method lends itself to the laser marking concept for two major reasons. The first is the speed of typical laser marking systems. Second, most laser marking software has the capacity to modify one axis of marking in relation to the feed of the conveyor and moving part via an external quadrate encoder that is located on the conveyor mechanism. The laser manufacturer will be able to determine what the maximum marking "window" will be in relation to the size of the part surface to be marked and the speed of the conveying system. Packages marked with a laser system have cradle-to-grave traceability, even in harsh environments.

There are lasers that can process with some forgiveness in irregular surfaces, but this capability should be evaluated for any such application before committing to a particular process or piece of equipment. Other laser systems have limits on their material processing abilities and should be identified early in the research stage.

Laser marking systems have become a popular method of marking electronic components. From the operator and technician standpoint, the low-maintenance tool with no moving parts outside of the marking head adds to its appeal. Keeping the final output lens clean is the only maintenance required to the system.

New words and terms

semiconductor	n.	半导体
traceability	n.	跟踪能力
pad printing		移动印刷
ink marking		墨水标记
electrolytic marking		电解标记
laser marking		激光标记
other marking variables		其他的标记变量

Exercises 4

Ⅰ. **Pair work: Discuss the following questions.**

1. What are the purposes of packing?
2. What is packaging?
3. What are the differences between packaging and packing?
4. What purpose is the consumer package designed to?
5. What is difference between the consumer package and the industrial package?
6. Which package do you often see in your daily life?

Ⅱ. **Fill in the blanks with the following words in the boxes, and change the forms if necessary.**

exterior	appealing	discard	widespread	confuse
insufficient	withstand	significance	fulfill	containers

1. I always _____ John with his brother; they are very much alike.
2. We are sure to _____ the task ahead of schedule if everyone bears down.
3. Many plastic _____ are disposed of as waste, although they are reusable.
4. You're supposed to keep your car _____ in good condition by cleaning it.
5. You can schedule a weekend to _____ some things that perhaps you don't actually need.
6. The idea of a holiday abroad is certainly _____.
7. That invention is of great commercial _____.
8. She is strong enough to _____ intellectual challenge.
9. In today's world, trade barriers in international trade are still _____.
10. The case was dismissed because of _____ evidence.

forbid	marketplace	residual	instill	standpoint
instill	oddly	dictate	reinforce	shun

1. We are now in a position to _____ our own demands to our employers.
2. We'll _____ the cease with iron strap.
3. These policies _____ strong feeling of loyalty in P & G employees.
4. The smell of food _____ the hungry children into the hut.

5. I can't figure out why he's been behaving so _____.

6. Consumers may also _____ firms that pollute the environment or engage in unethical practices by not buying their products.

7. What is the reaction to the new car in the _____?

8. It is thus clear that the _____ influences of clannishness must not be underestimated.

9. From the _____ of success, a good work ethic is no less important than an education.

10. More and more public places in the United States _____ smoking.

III. Translate the following sentences into Chinese.

1. Packaging is an important concern for warehousing and materials handling, one that receiving increased attention around the world.

2. No matter what environmental conditions are encountered, the package is expected to protect the product, keeping it in the condition intended for use until the product is delivered the ultimate consumer.

3. New materials and smarter protective packaging systems contribute to reducing the load on our environment.

4. Good packaging allows efficient utilization of storage space as well as transportation cube and weight constraints.

5. This package is discarded before the products are placed on the shelf, so customer may never see this material.

6. Over the past two years, the company has increased the investment for its packaging industry in order to meet its customer's need.

7. Good packaging can have a positive impact on layout, design, and overall warehouse productivity.

8. We'll pack them two dozen to one carton, gross weight around 25 kilos a carton.

9. We have especially reinforced our pacing in order to minimize the extent of any possible damage to the goods.

10. The real art of packing is to get the contents into a nice, compact shape that will stay that way during the roughest journey.

IV. Translate the following sentences into English.

1. 环境的挑战使包装成为焦点问题。

2. 包装在保护商品方面起着重要的作用。

3. 不同的商品需要不同的包装。

4. 消费品的包装要适宜并具有吸引力,这样能够增强公司在市场中的形象。

5. 包装必须十分坚固,以承受粗鲁的搬运。

6. 箱子里垫有泡沫塑料以免货物受压。

7. 在外包装上请标明"小心轻放"字样。

8. 醒目的包装有助于推销产品。

9. 这种商品包装必须防湿、防潮、防锈、防震。

10. 这些产品由于包装不好影响了销售。

Ⅴ. Answer the questions according to the text of this chapter.

1. How many kinds of package are there in logistics system? Could you tell the different functions of them?

2. What is the package marking? And what is the function of the package marking?

3. How about the Traditional Marking Processes in packaging system?

4. What are the main functions of packaging?

5. Are there any other benefits of packaging in addition to what is mentioned in the text? If yes, what are they?

6. Name three products that you consider to be packaged well.

7. Why should we use reusable containers?

8. If packaging cost is reduced, can costs in other aspects of the total logistical operation be cut down? Why?

9. What information can be provided in the package?

Logistics Situational Dialogues 4

(*Mr. Lin is a marketing manager of Tsingtao Brewery Group in China. Peter is a businessman from European Union. Now Mr. Lin is discussing the packaging of Beer with Peter*)

Peter: Mr. Lin, I'm very glad we've settled the terms for the transaction of 500 cases of Tsingtao beer in general, and I would like to know what your packing for transportation is.

Lin: As a rule, when packing these small bottles of beer, we pack them six bottles in one carton, and four cartons in one box. Besides, all these boxes should be lined with shockproof cardboard from inside and reinforced with straps from outside.

Peter: That's ok. But I still want to discuss the matter of packing the beer. Will you hear my comments?

Lin: Certainly. We warmly welcome your comments and suggestions.

Peter: Your present packing is in glass bottles of two sizes—large and small. One large bottles is too much for an ordinary person to consume at one time, while the small size seems just right.

Lin: This comment of yours is very good. We should consider the normal quantity that an ordinary person consumes at one time, when we decide on the size of the beer bottle.

Peter: I don't think glass-bottles are popular nowadays for liquids. The shortcomings are obvious: first, they are easily broken in transit even though you put 24 bottles in a well-lined box; second, glass-bottles are too heavy and it would increase the cost of freight; third, it is not convenient to consume the beer packed in bottles because you have to use a bottle-opener to open them.

Lin: Yes, all these shortcoming exist as a matter of fact. Do you have any good ideas?

Peter: Liquids are now packed in tins, which have been gaining popularity on the world market. Many leading companies of beverage, such as Coca Cola, they pack their liquids in tins. I think you could use similar packing and incorporate an opener on the top of each tin.

Lin: As far as you know, when we pack our export liquids in tins, it will greatly increase the cost of packing. Now we are making efforts to reduce the production cost of tins.

Peter: I can understand that. But I hope that you will speed up your efforts in that direction. In fact I've already seen some good results.

Lin: Is that so? What's that?

Peter: At the last Guangzhou Fair, I tasted black tea ready-made, and packed in paper cartons. That packing would greatly reduce the cost of the goods.

Lin: The paper tins can only be used to pack liquids like tea and milk, but not beer perhaps, because there is some gas as well as the pressure from inside of the container when the container is opened. So, I'm afraid paper tins cannot stand the pressure.

Peter: You are right. You see I've forgotten the difference between beer and soft drinks.

Lin: Your thoughts are very helpful. I'll transfer your valuable proposals mentioned today to our production department for study so as to improve our packing. Thank you very much.

Dialog Exercise 4

Mr. White, a businessman from Austria, is talking about the subject of packaging with Mr. Liu, the marketing manager of a company in China. Please try to practice this dialog with each other.

W: How is your condition now, Mr. Liu?

L: For the sake of god, it's okay. I'm busy with my packaging business recently.

W: Good. Recently, the surface and the wrapping of the article become more and more attractive to the consumers, which will certainly help push sales, so you should pay attention to the package of my goods.

L: Yes, it is true, as a manager in this field, I know that package means what. With keen competition from similar towel producers, the merchandise must not only be of nice quality, but also good looking.

W: Right. We'll see to it that the towels appeal to the eye as well as to the purse.

L: As far as packing towels for sea shipment. As a rule, we use polythene wrapper for each article, all ready for shelf selling.

W: What about the outer packing?

L: We will pack them six towels each with a different color in a bow, then boxes to a carton.

W: Can you use wooden cases instead?

L: Why wooden cases?

W: I am afraid the cardboard boxes are not strong enough for sea transportation.

L: No need to worry about that. The cartons lined with waterproof plastic sheets, and the cartons are made of cardboard. They shall be handled with care.

W: Ok, but I am concerned that in case of damage or pilferage, the insurance company will refuse compensation on the improper packing, or packing unsuitable for sea voyage.

L: Well, if you insist anyway, we will use wooden cases, but the charge for that kind of packing will be considerably higher, and it also slows down delivery.

W: Then, I will cable home immediately for the final confirmation on the matter.

L: Please do. I will be waiting for your soonest reply.

W: I will call you up tomorrow. Good-bye, Mr. Liu.

L: Good-by, Mr. White.

Case Study 4

Shall Fox Postpone Its Labeling and Packaging Process to the DC?

Foxcompany (Fox) Co. Ltd. was founded in 1974 in Taiwan as a manufacturer of electrical components for computers. With strong research and development efforts, by 2011, it had accumulated more than 25,000 patents granted worldwide. Fox is now one of the world's 500 biggest companies according to Fortune magazine. Its biggest production operation is located in Shenzhen Longlong Science & Technology Park, which covers more than 3 square km with 15 factories. Not only does Fox have dormitories, a hospital, and a fire brigade, but it also broadcasts its own TV channel within the park.

Fox is highly specialized in producing computer components and produces and packages private-label components for various famous brand names, including Acre, Apple, Dell, Hewlett-Packard. The components manufactured are basically identical but are labeled and packaged differently for the various customers. The Shenzhen manufacturing facility replenishes a distribution center (DC) in Taiwan where the lead time is nine weeks. Fox adopts a continuous review policy to manage the inventory at its DC and want to maintain a cycle service level of 95 percent for all orders.

The previous month had been challenging: Apple asked for 5,000 extra units than were available at the DC, whereas Acer and Dell ordered 3,500 units and 4,000 units fewer, respectively. Although there was sufficient inventory available at the DC in the form of basic product. Fox was not able to meet Apple's demand because the excess inventory available was labeled and packaged for Acer and Dell. As a result, Fox lost the extra business opportunity and surplus inventory because of the wrong labels and packaging.

Labeling and Packaging at the DC

To allow more flexibility for production to accept such additional orders from customers by simply switching the inventory, the senior logistics supply chain manager proposes to postpone the labeling and packaging work to the DC, where the lead time of manufacturing and transportation remains unchanged. As a consequence, Fox would be able to meet Apple's sudden additional order more readily if other customers (e.g. Acer) placed a smaller order.

However, the management at the DC worried about the additional labeling and packaging work. Moreover, a detailed study revealed that the postponement would cost $1 more per unit. In particular, the DC managers believed that those $1 increases in cost per unit would be held against them once the process was changed and they would be under pressure to lower costs. They also thought the added workload affect the overall service level of the DC.

Please answer the questions after reading the case.

1. What is your opinion about this?
2. How would the inventory cost change if postponement were implemented?

小贴士

物流小常识

包装是在物流过程中保护产品,方便储运,促进销售,按一定技术方法采用容器、材料及辅助物等将物品包封并予以适当的装饰和标志的工作总称。简言之,包装是包装物及包装操作的总称。在社会再生产过程中,包装处于生产过程的末尾和物流过程的开头,既是生产的终点,又是物流的始点。在现代物流观念形成以前,包装被天经地义地看成生产的终点。因而一直是生产领域的活动,包装的设计往往主要从生产终结的要求出发,因而常常不能满足流通的要求。物流的研究认为,包装与物流的关系,比之与生产的关系要密切得多,其作为物流始点的意义比之作为生产终点的意义要大得多。因此,包装应进入物流系统之中,这是现代物流的一个新观念。在物流系统中,包装成本与运输成本存在"效益背反"的关系。

Supplementary Reading 4

Development of Packaging

Prior to World War II, packaging was used primarily to surround and protect products during storage, transportation, and distribution. Some packages were designed with aesthetic appeal and even for ease-of-use by the end consumer, but package design was typically left to technicians. After World War II, however, companies became more interested in marketing and promotion as a means of enticing customers to purchase their products. As a result, more manufacturers began to view packaging as an integral element of overall business marketing strategies to lure buyers.

This increased attention to packaging coincided with socioeconomic changes taking place around the world. As consumers became better educated and more affluent, their expectations of products—and their reliance on them—increased as well. Consequently, consumers began to rely much more heavily on manufactured goods and processed food items. New technologies related to production, distribution, and preservatives led to a massive proliferation in the number and type of products and brands available in industrialized nations. Thus, packaging became a vital means of differentiating items and informing inundated consumers.

The importance of consumer packaging was elevated in the United States during the late 1970s and 1980s. Rapid post-war economic expansion and market growth waned during that period, forcing companies to focus increasingly on luring consumers to their product or brand at the expense of the competition. Package design became a marketing science. And, as a new corporate cost-consciousness developed in response to increased competition, companies began to alter packaging techniques as a way to cut production, storage, and distribution expenses. Furthermore, marketers began to view packaging as a tool to exploit existing product lines by adding new items and to pump new life into maturing products.

Today, good package design is regarded as an essential part of successful business practice. Since many potential customers first notice a new product after it has arrived on the shelves of a store, it is vital that the packaging provide consumers with the information they need and motivate them to make a purchase. But packaging decisions involve a number of tradeoffs. While making a product visible and distinctive may be the top priority, for example, businesses must also comply with a variety of laws regarding product labeling and safety. Protecting products during transport is important, but businesses also need to keep their shipping costs as low as possible.

Ⅰ. Answer the following questions

1. Prior to World War Ⅱ, what was packaging primarily used to?
2. After World War Ⅱ, what did manufacturers begin to view packaging as?
3. When was the importance of consumer packaging elevated in the United States?
4. During the late 1970s and 1980s, what happened to the economic environment?
5. Today, what is good package design regarded as?

Ⅱ. True or False

(   )1. Prior to World War Ⅱ, packaging became a vital means of differentiating items and informing inundated consumers.

(   )2. After World War Ⅱ, package design was typically left to technicians.

(   )3. During the late 1970s and 1980s, marketers began to view packaging as a tool to exploit existing product lines by adding new items and to pump new life into maturing products.

(　　)4. Today, good package design is regarded as an essential part of successful business practice.

(　　)5. Today, companies are free to design their own package, they don't have to comply with any laws.

Chapter 5

Distribution Management

Lesson 5.1   Channels of Distribution

In any society—industrialized or non-industrialized—goods must be physically moved or transported between the place they are produced and the place they are consumed. Except in very primitive cultures, where each family met its own household needs, the exchange process has become the cornerstone of economic activity. Exchange takes place when there is a discrepancy between the amount, type, and timing of goods available and the goods needed. If a number of individuals or organizations within the society have a surplus of goods that someone else needs, there is a basis for exchange. Channels of distribution develop when many exchanges take place between producers and consumers.

The extent to which a channel of distribution creates an efficient flow of products from the producer to the consumer is a major concern of management. [1] For example, manufacturers depend on the distribution channel for such functions as selling, transportation, warehousing, and physical handling. Consequently, the manufacturer's objective is to obtain optimum performance of these functions at minimum total cost. In order to successfully market its products, a manufacturer must: (a) select the appropriate channel structure; (b) choose the intermediaries to be used and establish policies regarding channel members; (c) devise information and control systems to ensure that performance objectives are met. Likewise wholesalers and retailers must select manufacturers' products in a way that will provide the best assortment for their customers and lead to the desired profitability for themselves.

Due to the dynamic nature of the business environment, management must monitor and evaluate the performance of the distribution channel regularly and frequently.[2] When the performance goals are not met, management must evaluate possible channel alternatives and implement changes. Channel management is particularly important in mature and declining markets when market growth cannot conceal inefficient practices. Nevertheless, the distribution channel has been recognized as "one of the least managed areas of marketing".

What Is a Channel of Distribution?

"A channel of distribution can be defined as the collection of organization units, either internal or external to the manufacturer, which performs the functions involved in product marketing." The marketing functions are pervasive: they include buying, selling, transporting, storing, grading, financing, bearing market risk, and providing marketing information. Any organization unit, institution, or agency that performs one or more of the marketing functions is a member of the channel of distribution.

The structure of a distribution channel is determined by marketing functions which are performed by specific organization. Some channel members perform single marketing functions—carriers transport products, and public warehouse holders store them. Others, such as wholesalers, perform multiple functions. Channel structure affects: (a) control over the performance of functions; (b) the speed of delivery and communication; (c) the cost of operations. While a direct manufacture-to-user channel usually gives management great control over the performance of marketing functions, distribution costs are higher, making it necessary for the firm to have substantial sales volume or market concentration. With indirect channels, the external institutions or agencies (warehouse holders, wholesalers, retailers) assume much of the cost burden and risk, but the manufacturer receives less revenue per unit.

Most distribution channels are loosely structured networks of vertically aligned firms. The specific structure depends to a large extent on the nature of product and the firm's target market.

There is no "best" channel structure for all firms producing similar products. Management must determine channel structure within the framework of the firm's corporate and marketing objectives, its operating philosophy, its strengths and weaknesses, and its infrastructure of manufacturing facilities and warehouse. If the firm has targeted multiple market segments, management may have to develop multiple channels to service these markets efficiently. For example, Whirlpool Corporation sells a major portion of its product through Sears, uses distributors and dealers for its Whirlpool Brand line, and also sells to original equipment manufacturers.

The Evolution of Marketing Channels

Marketing channels develop because intermediaries (wholesalers and retailers) make the marketing process more efficient by reducing the number of market contacts. For example, in primitive culture most household-needs are met by family members. However, many household-needs can be met more efficiently by exchange. Specialization in production creates efficiency, and for this reason it has become a way of life. A household must exchange goods and services in order to provide for all of its needs.

Consider a community in which there are five households specializing in the production of one product per family. The number of transactions necessary for decentralized exchange among these households is ten. However, a central market operated by a dealer reduces to five the number of transactions necessary for centralized exchange. In this case, the ratio of advantage of the centralized exchange through one intermediary is two.

The advantage of an intermediary becomes more evident as the number of specialized producer increases. For example, if there are 100 specialized producers, the number of decentralized transactions becomes 4,950 and the ratio of intermediary advantage become 49.5. If 10 customers purchase from four suppliers it results in 40 market contacts. If the suppliers sell to these customers through one intermediary, the number of required contacts is 14, a 65 percent reduction. This example clearly demonstrates that a manufacturer selling to low-volume customers could substantially reduce selling and logistics costs by using a wholesaler/distributor.

New words and terms

cornerstone	n.	建筑物的基石
discrepancy	n.	不同,不符合
surplus	n.	剩余,过剩
minimum	n./adj.	最小量(的),最低限度(的)
intermediary	n.	中间人
devise	n.	想出,计划,设计,发明
assortment	n.	属于一类或数类的各色物品之集合
dynamic	adj.	动态的
monitor	v.	检查,控制
evaluate	v.	评价,估价

slowdown	*n.*	降低生产
conceal	*v.*	隐藏,隐瞒
pervasive	*adj.*	蔓延的,遍布的,渗透的
network	*n.*	网络
vertically	*adv.*	直立地,垂直地
align	*v.*	使一致,使密切合作
infrastructure	*n.*	基础设施
segment	*n.*	区分,部分
decentralize	*v.*	分散
centralize	*v.*	集中
ratio	*n.*	比,比率
evident	*adj.*	明显的,显然的

Notes

1. The extent to which a channel of distribution creates an efficient flow of products from the producer to the consumer is a major concern of management.

   配送渠道能否有效地将货物自生产地运输到消费地是管理者们所关心的主要问题。

2. Due to the dynamic nature of the business environment, management must monitor and evaluate the performance of the distribution channel regularly and frequently.

   由于商业环境的动态本质,管理部门必须定期对配送渠道的功能进行检查和评估。

Lesson 5.2 Distribution Centers

The Function of Distribution Centers

Distribution centers are used to store goods for short amounts of time during their journeys between points of production and to wholesale or retail outlets. [1] A distribution center is also a warehouse that emphasizes the rapid movement of goods.

Inventory analysis can help individual retailers determine whether they should stock all the items in question. Analysis may also show that, if the items in question are stocked only at the factories where they are manufactured, customer service levels may be inadequate because it takes too long to supply customers. Therefore, distribution warehouses represent a compromise. They are justified on the basis of cost analysis that a specified level of customer service can be achieved at minimum cost by locating inventories at intermediate locations. [2]

Distribution centers and warehouses in the supply chain perform the sorting function, meaning that they are the point at which goods are concentrated, and from this concentration a new and different assortment of goods is selected and moves forward to be dispersed to the next level. Storage and sorting features are unique to these facilities. Storage is a somewhat passive function. The sorting function is more dynamic and gets to the basics of logistics and supply chain thinking. [3] In how many places and at what locations should goods be concentrated so that new and different selections can be assembled and shipped to the next receiver?

The sorting function has four steps, and these are important to understanding the concert of goods flow through the supply chain. The functions involve taking, a heterogeneous supply of products and sorting them into stocks that are homogeneous; bringing together similar stocks from different sources; breaking a homogeneous supply into smaller lots; and finally, building up assortments of small lots for reshipment, usually to retailers.

Warehouses are also needed because production and consumption do not coincide. [4] Canned fruits and vegetables are examples of one extreme in which production occurs during a short period, but sales are spread throughout the year. An example of the other extreme is Cleo Wrap, a large manufacturer of Christmas wrapping, which sells 90 percent of its output during the last 2 months of each year. In both instances, warehouses serve to match different rates of flow. Sometimes, larger quantities of goods are purchased than can be immediately consumed. This may occur to prevent anticipated scarcity or to benefit from a seller's advantageously priced deal. Warehousing space is needed to store the surplus supplies.

Warehouses discussed in a distribution textbook would be viewed as primarily market oriented. However, some warehouses are production or raw material oriented. Manufacturers that stockpile some of the items they need consider their warehouse selection decision as being production oriented.

Integral to many warehouse functions are assembling or light manufacturing processes. Goods are uncrated and tested. Some goods are repackaged and labeled prior to distribution to retail outlets. State tax stamps may be affixed. Minor damage to incoming goods may be repaired (and the carrier or party responsible for the damage billed).

In an era of logistics partnerships, new long-term alliances are being formed between shippers and warehouses. Leveraging is involved in that firms join to use all partners' asset bases, the whole is greater than the sum of the parts. For example, customer service representatives of both the distribution center and the supplier make separate calls on the customer; the value-added part is that the distribution center representative also smoothes the way for the supplier's product.

As the relationship builds, additional services may be shifted to the warehouser, such as order receipt and processing, assembly, light repair, pre-testing electrical equipment before shipment, and the like. These services can add incremental revenue to the warehouser's operations.

Partnerships have also developed between carriers and warehouses. Starting in 1988, the Santa Fe Railway developed a Quality Distribution Center (QDC) program that involved about 30 independent warehouses throughout its territory. A single bill of lading covered the movement on rail into and out of the warehouse and delivery to the consignee by truck. The railroad assumed liability for the entire movement.

The function of the distribution center is integrating supplier resources, customer resources and product resources, it can also saving transportation routes. As it is interpreted in figure 5.1, figure 5.2 and figure 5.3.

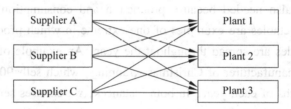

Figure 5.1　The case without distribution center

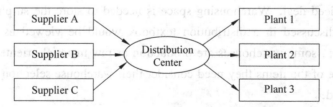

Figure 5.2　The case with distribution center

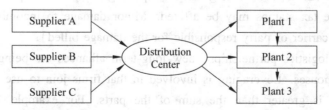

Figure 5.3　The case with distribution center: one route

The Types of Distribution Centers

Distribution centers and warehouses can operate at national or regional level, determined by the supply chain structure and strategic decisions on inventory levels (RDCs). These can use conventional handling and storage systems, or can be designed to use automated or even robotic technology. At a local level there may be "stockrooms" that serve a limited number of retail outlets within a close geographic area. They are stock-holding facilities.

However, a fundamental distinction to make is between stock-holding warehouses and stockless depots, and the latter have been receiving more attention in recent years as enabling fast stock movement and inventory reduction.

Transshipment depots tend to be located to serve specific areas of customer concentration. Orders for customers are picked at a stock-holding depot, typically an NDC, loaded to road trailers in reverse drop sequence and dispatched to the transshipment depot overnight, where the trailer is dropped. The overnight tractor returns to the NDC with the previous day's empty trailer. In the morning, a local tractor unit picks up the overnight trailer, delivers the customer orders and returns the empty trailer to the transshipment depot.

Cross-docking tends to operate out of an "empty" building. Product ordered by product line (SKU) from suppliers in quantities sufficient to meet the next day's total customer orders is delivered to the site and unloaded, often along one (goods receipt) face of the building. It then goes directly to a (manual or mechanized) sorting system, which distributes the required quantities of each product to allocated order locations so that the orders build up, product by product, until the orders are complete. Completed orders are then loaded to outbound delivery vehicles parked along the dispatch face of the building. Dispatch vehicles leave to meet specified departure times to reach customer locations by given deadliness.

New words and terms

wholesale	*n.*	批发
retail outlets	*n.*	零售点
inventory analysis		库存分析
stock	*n.*	存货
concentration	*n.*	集中,集货
storage	*n.*	保管,储存
assemble	*v.*	装配,集配
heterogeneous	*adj.*	不同种类的,不同质的
homogeneous	*adj.*	同类的,同质的

lot	n.	一批,一笔
assortment	n.	分类
reshipment	n.	重新发运,再装运
retailer	n.	零售商
stockpile	n.	堆存
repackage	v.	再包装,重新包装
carrier	n.	承运人
shipper	n.	托运人,发货人
warehouser	n.	仓库经营者,保管人
delivery	n.	交货
consignee	n.	收货人,收件人
turnover	n.	周转,循环

Notes

1. Distribution centers are used to store goods for short amounts of time during their journeys between points of production and to wholesale or retail outlets.

   配送中心通常在短期内储存处于从生产地到批发或零售点之间的货物。

2. They are justified on the basis of cost analysis that a specified level of customer service can be achieved at minimum cost by locating inventories at intermediate locations.

   事实证明,在成本分析的基础上,通过建立一种中途库存能够以最低的成本获得特定的客户服务水平。

3. Storage and sorting features are unique to these facilities. Storage is a somewhat passive function. The sorting function is more dynamic and gets to the basics of logistics and supply chain thinking.

   对于这些设施,储存和分拣特性是统一的,储存是有些被动的功能,分拣功能则更加动态,达到了物流和供应理念的要求。

4. Warehouses are also needed because production and consumption do not coincide.

   因为生产和消费不能同步进行,所以仓库是必需的。

Exercises 5

I. Pair work: Discuss the following questions.

1. What is distribution center?

2. Why is distribution center close to the major market?

3. How do you understand the difference between distribution center and warehouse?

4. What basic function the distribution centers have?

5. How do you understand the cost of distribution?

6. In your opinion, can the distribution costs be reduced?

II. Fill in the blanks with the following words in the boxes, and change the forms if necessary.

automate	focus on	load volume	relationship	advantage
contact	facilitate	fulfill	value-added	transport lane

1. Warehouses _____ minimizing the operating costs to meet shipping requirements.

2. Transportation cost per unit of weight decreases as _____ increases.

3. This short-term storage center is located close to a major market to _____ the rapid processing of orders and shipment of goods to customers.

4. There is a _____ between transport cost and distance.

5. Distribution center is a logistics link to _____ physical distribution as its main function.

6. A _____ refers to movement between origin and destination points.

7. Distribution center performs a great deal of _____ activities, such as packaging, sub-assembly, kitting, labeling, etc.

8. The main _____ of the road transportation is door-to-door delivery.

9. As soon as our store comes in new stock, we'll _____ you without delay.

10. Distribution centers are highly _____ places to receive goods from various plants and suppliers.

III. Translate the following sentences into Chinese.

1. It is not uncommon for transportation cost to account for 20% of the total costs of a commodity.

2. Railway provides terminal-to-terminal service instead of door-to-door service.

3. You must deliver the goods before June, or else we won't be able to catch the shopping season.

4. We ask our suppliers to arrange road or rail transport in time to meet the ship.

5. Transport by air is increasing and for certain types of goods, such as fresh food or flowers as well as valuables; air freight is the best choice.

IV. Translate the following sentences into English.

1. 该配送中心为客户提供高水平、高效率的服务。

2. 距离对运输成本的影响很大。

3. 大部分消费品是由公路运输完成的。

4. 航空承运人通常承运高价值、低重量的产品。

5. 我们将尽力提前装运。

V. Answer the questions according to the text of this chapter.

1. What is a channel of distribution?

2. What is the process of the evolution of marketing channels?

3. What are the functions of distribution centers?

Logistics Situational Dialogues 5

（1）*Mr. Huang, a leader of a food factory, talks with Mr. Green, an importer from America. He is visiting a factory to see whether he can place an order from them.*

H: Welcome, Mr. Green, Please take a seat.

G: Thank you.

H: What do you think about our factory?

G: Quite good, I was deeply impressed by what I saw.

H: We got prize for out products several months ago.

G: Did you? Congratulations! We used to buy your food products through the export corporations. Now we are happy to be able to contact you and deal business with you directly.

H: So are we.

G: First of all, the most important thing we concern is that of the distribution and delivery of the products. And if you can offer us a stable flow of export orders, we won't buy goods from the other sources.

H: No problem if you can conclude a distribution agreement with us, we won't sell goods to other customers in your country.

G: Right, and we will undertake to place others of no less than a fixed amount with you within a fixed time. In this way you needn't worry about the credit of the buyers in this area. You sell only to us and our credit and commercial standing are well known to you.

H: That sounds nice! I hope that it is not a long time, we will establish a concrete business relations with each other.

G: Great, let's get feel of each other's way of doing business first, shall we?

H: Okay, I agree with you.

(2) *Xiao Wang has just been employed by a forwarding company at an airport. It is the first day of his work in the warehouse. His job is to allocate the products to different shelves, waiting for further shipment. At the moment, he is getting himself acquainted with the warehouse facilities with the help of Mr. Chen Weiguo, the assistant to the warehouse manager.*

Chen: Hi, Xiao Wang! Would you please come over here?

Wang: Yes?

Chen: A truck is at the warehouse gate. Go and find what will be discharged.

Wang: (coming back a few minutes later) Mr. Chen, a container chassis is at the gate and workers are discharging it.

Chen: What is being discharged?

Wang: Electronic components in large carton cases. Some of them, they say, are hard disks.

Chen: I see. Now you telephone the customs officers. Ask them to come. These are cargo to be exported to Japan and Singapore. The owners need to go through the customs clearance.

Wang: I saw just now some customs officers at the gate.

Chen: In that case, you don't have to make the call. Instead, have a look at the computer and see where we can put the goods.

Wang: When will the goods be leaving?

Chen: I believe they will go on J211 and W403 flights respectively this afternoon.

Wang: Then we'd better find places near the other end of the warehouse. Yes, there are two shelves available. No. 41 and 43.

Chen: Good. Now you go and direct the handling.

Wang: Who will be moving the goods?

Chen: Oh, I nearly forgot to tell you. Dial No. 201 and call in a forklift.

Dialog Exercise 5

> Two logistics professional college students are talking about the difference between distribution center and traditional warehouse, the main functions of distribution centers. Please finish the dialog and the useful words are as followed.

modern techniques	现代技术
informationization	信息化
intelligentization	智能化
network	网络
mechanization	机械化
conveyor belt	传送带
slideway	滑道
automation control center	自动化控制中心
sorting equipment	分拣设备
distribution processing	流通加工
reduce the number of transactions and circulation	减少交易次数和流通环节
generate scale of economies	产生规模效益

reduce customer inventory, improve level of inventory control
减少客户库存，提高库存控制水平
focus on consolidation and classification for products
集中对商品进行整合以及分类
implement the strategy of total quality management (TQM)
实施全面质量管理策略
meet the customers' requirement of rapid delivery for goods
满足客户快速交付商品的要求

Case Study 5

Seven-Eleven's Distribution System

The Seven-Eleven's Distribution System tightly linked the entire supply chain for all product categories. The distribution centers and information network played a key role in that regard. The major objective was to carefully track sales of items and offer short replenishment cycle times. This allowed a store manager to forecast sales corresponding to each order accurately.

From March 1987, Seven-Eleven offered three-times-a-day store delivery of all rise dishes (which comprised most of the fast-food items sold). Bread and other fresh food were delivered twice a day. The distribution system was flexible enough to alter delivery schedules depending on customer demand. For example, ice cream was delivered daily during the summer but only three times a week at other times. The replenishment cycle time for fresh and fast-food items had been shortened to fewer than 12 hours. A store order for rich ball by 10:00 a. m. was delivered before the dinner rush.

As discussed earlier, the store manager used a graphic order terminal to place an order from all Seven-Eleven store order was separated so the distribution center could easily assign it to appropriate store truck using the order information it already had. The key to store delivery was what Seven-Eleven called the combined delivery system. At the distribution center, delivery of like products from different suppliers (e. g. , milk and sandwiches) was directed into a single temperature-controlled truck: frozen foods, chilled foods , room-temperature processed foods, and warm foods. Each truck made deliveries to multiple retail stores. The number of store per truck depended on the sales volume. All deliveries were made during off-peak hours and were received using the scanner terminals. The system worked on trust and did not require the delivery person to be present when the store personnel scanned in the delivery. That reduced the delivery time spent at each store.

This distribution system enabled Seven-Eleven to reduce the number of vehicle required for daily delivery service to each store, even though the delivery frequency of each item was quite high. In 1974, 70 vehicles visited each store every day. By 2006, only 9 were necessary. This dramatically reduced delivery of a variety of fresh foods.

As of February 2004, Seven-Eleven Japan had a total of 290 dedicated manufacturing plants throughout stores. These items were distribution through 293 dedicated distribution centers (DCs) that ensured rapid, reliable delivery. None of these DCs carried any inventory; they merely transferred inventory from supply trucks to Seven-Eleven distribution trucks. The transportation was provided by Transfleet Ltd. , a company set up by Mitsui and Co. for the exclusive use of Seven-Eleven Japan.

Seven-Eleven in the United States

Seven-Eleven had expanded rapidly around the world (Table 5.1). The major growth was in Asia although the United States continued to be the second largest market for Seven-Eleven. Once Seven-Eleven Japan acquired Southland Corporation, it set about improving operations in the United Stated. In the initial years, several Seven-Eleven stores in the United States were shut down. The number of stores started to grow beginning in 1998.

Table 5.1 Global Store Distribution for Seven-Eleven in January 2011

Country	Stores
Japan	13,049
United States	6,726
Thailand	5,840
South Korea	3,150
China	1,717
Malaysia	1,250
Mexico	1,223
Canada	465
Australia	415
Singapore	549
Philippines	567
Norway	173
Sweden	189
Denmark	129
Indonesia	23
Total	35,465

　　Historically, the distribution structure in the United States was completely different from that in Japan. Direct store delivery (DSD) by some manufacturers, with the remaining products delivered by wholesalers. DSD accounted for about half the total volume, with the rest coming from wholesalers.

　　With the goal of introducing "fresh" products in the Unites States, Seven-Eleven introduced the concept of combined distribution centers (CDCs) around 2000. By 2003, Seven-Eleven had 23CDCs located throughout North America supporting about 80 percent store network. CDCs delivered fresh items such as sandwiches, bakery products, bread, produce, and other perishables once a day. A variety of fresh-food suppliers sent product to the CDCs throughout the day, where they were sorted for delivery to stores at night. Request from store, Fresh-food sales in North America exceeded $450 million in 2003. During this period, DSD by manufacturers and wholesaler delivery to store also continued.

　　This was a period when Seven-Eleven worked very hard to introduce new fresh-food items with a goal of competing more directly with the likes of Starbucks than with traditional gas station food marts. Seven-Eleven in the Unites States had more than 63 percent of its sales from non-gasoline products compared to the rest of the industry, for which this number was closer to 35 percent. The goal was to continue to increase sales in the fresh-food and fast-food categories with a special focus on hot foods.

In 2009, revenue in the United States and Canada totaled $16.0 billion, with about 63 percent coming from merchandise and the rest from the sale of gasoline. The North American inventory turnover rate in 2004 was about 19, compared to more than 50 in Japan. This however, represented a significant improvement in North American performance, where inventory turns in 1992 were around 12.

Please answer the questions after reading the case.

1. Seven-Eleven is attempting to duplicate the supply chain structure that has succeeded in Japan and the United States with the introduction of CDCs. What are the pros and cons of this approach?

2. The United States has food service distributors that also replenish convenience stores. What are the pros and cons to having a distributor replenish convenience stores versus a company like Seven-Eleven managing its own distribution function?

小贴士

物流小常识

　　2004 年 8 月亚马逊公司宣布以 7 500 万美元收购雷军和陈年创办的卓越网,将卓越网收归为亚马逊中国全资子公司,使亚马逊全球领先的网上零售专长与卓越网深厚的中国市场经验相结合,进一步提升了客户体验,并促进了中国电子商务的成长。2007 年将其中国子公司改名为"卓越亚马逊",2011 年改名为"亚马逊中国"。同年宣布开放第三方卖家平台,推出"我要开店"和"卓越亚马逊物流"服务。

　　亚马逊目前有亚马逊自营;第三方卖家销售和发货;第三方卖家销售、亚马逊物流配送三种形式。亚马逊物流配送的商品都放在亚马逊全国各个库房中,配送是亚马逊物流或者合作的第三方物流,商品均由亚马逊库房出库。如果商品在第三方卖家自己处,则自己寻找合作的物流公司配送。

　　亚马逊的物流模式是大规模建设物流中心,截至 2009 年年底,亚马逊在美国本土拥有物流仓储中心约 110 万平方米,在海外则达到 53 万平方米。除了为亚马逊自己的货物提供收发货、仓储周转服务外,也为亚马逊网站上代销的第三方卖家提供物流服务。无论是个人卖家还是中小企业,都可以把货物送到较近的亚马逊物流中心。客户下单后,亚马逊的员工就会负责订单处理、包装、发货、第三方配送及退换货事宜,并按每件货物0.5美元或每磅0.4美元收取订单执行费。目前,由第三方销售的商品占到亚马逊总销量的30%,活跃的卖家有190万,通过亚马逊系统配送的货物达100多万种。通过物流中心,亚马逊将分散的订单需求集中起来(不仅是信息集中,也是货物集中),再对接UPS、基华物流等规模化物流企业,以发挥统筹配送的规模效应。

Supplementary Reading 5

Using Online Sales to Sell Books: Amazon

Book supply chains have been transformed with the advent of online sales and the launching of Amazon. com in July 1995. Since then, Amazon has added many categories to its product offerings, including music, toys, electronics, softwares, and home improvement equipment. Whereas the Internet provided some advantage to Amazon for the sale of physical books, this advantage has magnified with the growth in electronic books(e-books).

Impact of Online Sales on Customer Service in the Book Industry

Online sales have not helped profits for traditional books to the same extent as in the customized PC industry. Unlike the PC industry, in which online sales facilitate direct sales by manufactures, the Internet has not shortened supply chains in the book industry.

For traditional books, Amazon also cannot attract customers who value the ability to leaf through books. The company tries to counter this problem by providing reviews and other information on books to allow customers to get a feel for the book online.

To counter these drawbacks, Amazon has exploited several opportunities on the Internet to attract customers and increase revenues. Amazon attracts many customers by offering a selection of millions of books. Customers can search for hard-to-find books or those special interest. A large physical bookstore, in contrast, can carry fewer than a hundred thousand titles. Amazon also uses the Internet to recommend books to customers based on their purchase history. Customers are sent e-mails informing them of new titles that match their interests. Amazon also provides reviews and comments from other customers on the titles available. New titles are quickly introduced and made available online, whereas in a bricks-and-mortar bookstore chain, all retail stores have to be stocked.

Amazon use the Internet to allow customers to order a book at any time from the comfort of their own home. If customers know the books they want, they can place the order online and the books will be delivered to their door. There is no need to leave the house and spend an hour or two going to a physical bookstore. This fact allows Amazon to attract customers who value this convenience and are willing to wait for delivery.

For e-books, Amazon is able to gain greater advantage using the online channel. For example, customers can download a book in seconds without having to leave home. For people who value time, this experience is superior to buying a traditional book either online or at a bookstore. Product availability is never an issue with e-books, and variety can be added at low marginal cost. In fact, the Internet has allowed the availability of books that are not guaranteed a high enough demand to make them viable for traditional publishers. For very low-volume books, there is no better channel than online as e-books.

Cost Impact of Online Sales on the Book Industry

Amazon also use online sales to lower its inventory and some of its facility costs. For traditional books, transportation costs increase as a result of selling books online. For e-books, however, transportation cost is not a factor given that they can be downloaded efficiently on the Internet.

Inventory Costs

Amazon is able to decrease inventories by aggregating physical inventories in a few geographical locations. A bookstore chain, in contrast, has higher inventories because titles are carried at every store. The reduction of inventories from aggregation is most significant for low-demand books with high demand uncertainty. The benefit is less significant for best sellers with demand that is more predictable. Amazon carriers medium-to-high demand titles in inventory, whereas it purchases low-demand titles from publishers in response to a customer order. In some instances, Amazon also prints very low-volume titles with print-on-demand technology. This allows the Amazon supply chain to further reduce inventories of low-demand titles. For e-books, Amazon incurs no inventory costs because they do not have to be stored physically.

Facility Costs

Its online sales allow Amazon to lower facility costs because it does not need the retail infrastructure that a bookstore chain such as Barnes & Noble must have. Initially, Amazon did not have a warehouse, purchasing all books from distributors. When demand volumes were low, the distributor was a better location to carry inventories because it aggregated demand across other booksellers besides Amazon. As demand has grown, however, Amazon has opened its own warehouses, where it stocks books. Thus, facility costs at Amazon are growing, although they are still much lower than the facility costs for a bookstore chain. For e-books, Amazon needs server capacity to ensure that downloads are quick, but the investment in server capacity is likely to be cheaper than the warehousing required to serve physical demand.

Transportation Costs

The Amazon supply chain incurs higher transportation costs than a bookstore chain selling through retail stores. Local bookstores do not have the cost of individually shipping books to customers. Amazon, in contrast, incurs the cost of shipping books to its customers from warehouses. The shipping cost from an Amazon warehouse represents a significant fraction of the cost of a book (it can be even higher than 100 percent for an inexpensive book). As demand has grown, Amazon has opened several warehouses in an effort to get closer to customers, decrease its transportation costs, and improve response time. Transportation costs at Amazon in 2009 were more than $1.77 billion: after accounting for transportation revenue, the net loss on outbound transportation was $849 million, a very significant amount. In contrast, the cost of delivering e-books and other digital content to customers is negligible in comparison.

Chapter 6

Logistics Information System

Learning Objectives

- Understand the functions of information and communication technology system
- Understand how company can realize order management and customer service through information system

Lesson 6.1   Information and Communication Technology System

What is Information and Communication Technology (ICT) Term

ICT is the use of electronic processing media for the collection, analysis and evaluation of data, and the transfer of information from one point to another. [1]

- Flows of information in logistics and supply chains are as fundamental as the flows of goods and materials and people. Such information flows occur not only internally within companies, but also between external suppliers, contractors, and customers.
- All the flows of physical goods, people and material are triggered by ICT. The whole logistics and supply chain process is kept moving by the supply of information and communication. [2]
- The timing and quality of the information affects the quality of decision-making. Good information enables good decisions to be made. Inadequate or incorrect information leads to poor decisions.

Importance of Information in Logistics Management

According to some examples, timely and accurate information is more critical now than at any time in the history of American business. Three factors have strongly impacted this change in the importance of information. First, satisfying, in fact pleasing, customers have become something of a corporate obsession. Serving the customer in the best, most efficient and effective manner has become critical, and information about issues such as order status, product availability, delivery schedule, and invoices has become a necessary part of the total customer service experience. Second, information is a crucial factor in the managers' abilities to reduce inventory and human resources requirements to a competitive level. Finally, information flows play an essential role in the Strategic Planning for the deployment of resources.

A key notion in the essential nature of the information systems in the development and maintenance of successful logistics is the need for virtually seamless bonds within and between organizations. This means creating inter organizational processes and links to facilitate delivery of seamless information between marketing, sales, purchasing, finance, manufacturing, distribution and transportation internally, as well as inter organizationally to customers, suppliers, carriers, and retailers across the logistics. Perhaps more importantly, it means alteration of perspective at the firm's highest levels. Changes in thinking that become necessary include aligning corporate strategies to the paradigm, providing incentives for functions to achieve common goals through the sharing of information, and implementing the technologies to redesign the movement of goods to maximize channel value and lower cost.

The Demand of the Information

All parts of logistics rely on ICT for planning, organizing, production, administration and all of the management processes involved. This will also include the customer interface, when using any form of electronic communication.

There are different levels of information required in logistics. These different levels and functions can be identified as the strategic, tactical and operational levels.

1. Information at the Strategic Level

The strategic levels are mainly involved with medium-to-long term planning. This level requires information on the following areas, typically for the senior managers in a business.

- Purchasing: information about alternative suppliers
- Production: information to help determine product ranges
- Inventory: information to help decide on format of stockholding
- Warehousing: information to help decide to use an own-account operation or third party contractors
- Transport: information to help decide to buy or lease vehicles

- Marketing: information on demographic patterns

2. Information at the Tactical Level

The operational level is mainly involved with shorter-term to minute-by-minute decisions such as dealing with contingencies and changes. This level requires information for typically the first line management and operatives in a business.

- Purchasing: information to help decide when to place orders with suppliers
- Production: information on release of raw materials from stock
- Inventory: information on scheduling supplier orders
- Warehousing: picking lists
- Transport: delivery notes
- Marketing: order receiving

Clearly in practice, these levels overlap in a business. Additionally, the information flows from top to bottom and also flows internally and externally. For example, a warehouse order picker uses a pick list, which is generated from the (external) customer order. These picking operations, in turn, are part of decisions taken at the tactical warehouse planning level and the tactical inventory planning levels. In turn, these are part of the strategic decisions taken, on the location of the warehouse in the first place.

The information required by anyone at any level is therefore connected and is part of a complex set of data handling and communication. ICT will facilitate all these fundamental triggering, coordinating and controlling functions in logistics.

New words and terms

trig	n.	刹车,触发器
triggered	adj.	引发的,触发的
availability	n.	可用性,实用性
seamless	adj.	无缝的
alteration	n.	变更,改造
tactical	adj.	战术的
incentive	n.	动机
	adj.	激励的

Notes

1. ICT is the use of electronic processing media for the collection, analysis and evaluation of

data, and the transfer of information from one point to another.

信息与通信技术应用电子介质来收集、分析和评估数据,并将信息从一点传输到另一点。

2. All the flows of physical goods, people and material are triggered by ICT. The whole logistics and supply chain process is kept moving by the supply of information and communication.

所有有形产品、人员和物料的流动都是由 ICT 引发。整个物流和供应链的运作流程都是由信息和通信支持的。

Lesson 6.2   Information Technology

Just a few years ago, the Internet was something new that not many people knew much about. Now, it is changing the way we communicate and conduct business. The Internet provides users the opportunity to search for information at any time of the day or night and to communicate instantly with the use of E-mail and electronic forms. Exciting technology-based approaches emerge almost daily. Many of these innovations are well suited to the enhancement of logistics management, including Just-in-time, Quick Response, Efficient Consumer Response, and Continuous Replenishment Program. Some kinds of information technology are described briefly as below:

E-commerce

E-commerce is the term used to describe the wide range of tools and technology utilized to conduct business in paperless environment. The main vehicle of E-commerce remains the Internet and the World Wide Web, but uses of E-mail, fax and telephone are also prevalent. The benefits of E-commerce include facilitation of information-based business processes for reaching and interacting with customers, online order taking, online customer service, etc. E-commerce also reduces costs in managing orders and interacting with a wide range of suppliers and trading partners, areas that typically add significant overheads to the cost of products and services.

E-commerce is a way of marketing and selling your products through the Internet. The Internet enables transactions to take place between your company and customers, and between businesses. Business-to-customer E-commerce is where an actual financial transaction takes place for customers to purchase products. Business-to-business E-commerce is when companies deal with suppliers online. [1] It would be here that your suppliers would take orders, do their billing and get paid online.

E-commerce can be defined as modern business methodology that addresses the needs of the organization, merchants and consumers to cut costs while improving the quality of goods and services and speed of service delivery. [2] E-commerce can allow existing merchants the opportunity to expand their client base. It can also be a cost-effective method of marketing products or services and displaying an inventory of products. Traditionally, merchants had to set up physical show rooms or produce costly catalogues to preview their products. Now, the Internet can provide an electronic vehicle to enhance this marketing strategy. [3]

E-commerce includes the following activities:

- Commercial transactions conducted by Internet, telephone and fax
- Electronic banking and payment systems
- Trade in digitized goods and services
- Electronic purchasing and restocking systems (supply chain management)
- Business-to-business exchange of data
- Delivery of goods and /or services purchased (order fulfillment), and customer service

Electronic Data Interchange

EDI refers to a computer-to-computer exchange of business documents in a standard format. EDI is being utilized to link supply chain members together in terms of order processing, production, inventory, accounting, and transportation. It allows members of the supply chain to reduce paperwork and share information on invoices, orders, payments and inquiries. EDI improves productivity through faster information transmission as well as reduced information entry redundancy. [4]

The benefits of EDI are numerous, including:

- Quick access to information
- Better customer service
- Reduced paperwork
- Increased productivity
- Cost efficiency
- Competitive advantage

Bar Coding and Scanning

Bar coding refers to the placement of computer readable codes on items, cartons, containers, and even railcars. This particular technology application drastically influenced the flows of product and information within the supply chain. In the past, this exchange was conducted manually, with error prone and time-consuming paper-based procedures. Bar coding and electronic scanning are identification technologies that facilitate information collection and exchange, allowing supply chain members to track and communicate movement details quickly with a greatly reduced probability of error. The critical point-of-sale data that organizations such as Wal-Mart provide to their supply chain partners is made possible through the use of bar coding and scanning technology.[5] This technology is critical to transportation companies, such as FedEx, by enabling them to provide their customers with detailed tracking information in a mater of seconds.

The Functions of Logistice Information System

There are many functions about logistics information system including learning support system, career support system, registration system on the Web and so on. As is explained in Figure 6.1. These functions are integrated into a whole logistics system and can be realized in Internet.

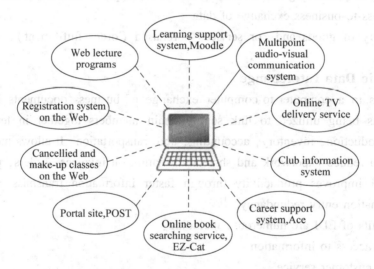

Figure 6.1　The functions of logistics information system

(comes from http://www.chnmc.com)

New words and terms

communicate	*v.*	通信,传达,传送
opportunity	*n.*	机会,时机
emerge	*v.*	出现,浮现,涌现
enhancement	*n.*	增进,增加,提高
just-in-time		准时制

quick response		快速反应
efficient consumer response		有效客户反应
continuous replenishment program		连续补货计划
electronic commerce		电子商务
prevalent	*adj.*	普遍的,流行的
facilitation	*n.*	便利化,简易化
transaction	*n.*	交易
catalogue	*n.*	目录
marketing strategy		市场营销策略
commercial	*adj.*	商业的,贸易的
supply chain management		供应链管理
electronic data interchange(EDI)		电子数据交换
order processing		订单处理
production	*n.*	生产
transmission	*n.*	传送,传递
productivity	*n.*	生产力
efficiency	*n.*	效率,功效
competitive advantage		竞争优势
bar coding and scanning		条形码和扫描
influence	*n.*	影响,势力,改变
time-consuming	*adj.*	耗时的
identification	*n.*	辨认,鉴定
point-of-sale data		销售点数据

Notes

1. Business-to-customer E-commerce is where an actual financial transaction takes place for customers to purchase products. Business-to-business E-commerce is when companies deal with suppliers online.

B2C 电子商务为顾客购买商品提供了实际的金融交易环境;而 B2B 电子商务则应用于公司和供应商的在线交易。

2. E-commerce can be defined as modern business methodology that addresses the needs of the organization, merchants and consumers to cut costs while improving the quality of goods and services and speed of service delivery.

电子商务可以定义为现代企业经营方略,它针对的是组织、商人和消费者的需要,即在减少成本的同时,提高货物和服务质量及服务配送速度。

3. Traditionally, merchants had to set up physical show rooms or produce costly catalogues to preview their products. Now, the Internet can provide an electronic vehicle to enhance this marketing strategy.

传统上,商人不得不设立产品展览室,或者印制高费用的产品目录以展示他们的产品。现在,互联网可以提供一个电子载体来加强这种市场营销策略。

4. EDI improves productivity through faster information transmission as well as reduced information entry redundancy.

电子数据交换通过加快信息传递以及减少冗余的信息输入提高生产力。

5. The critical point-of-sale data that organizations such as Wal-Mart provide to their supply chain partners is made possible through the use of bar coding and scanning technology.

企业,如沃尔玛,向供应链合作伙伴提供的重要销售点数据就是通过条形码和扫描技术实现的。

Lesson 6.3   Order Management and Customer Service through Information System

Order Management

Order management has several definitions, which differ only in the degree of precision with which they are applied. In general terms, order management means how a firm handles incoming orders; more specifically, order management is the activities that take place in the period between the time a firm receives an order and the time a warehouse is notified to ship the goods to fill that order. [1] The order management system represents the principal means by which buyers and sellers communicate information relating to individual orders of product. The order processing system, extremely important to the firm's logistics area, is also one of the most important components of the firm's overall management information system.

Order cycle is a related phrase, also with several meanings, depending on one's perspective. From the seller's standpoint, it is the time from when an order is received from a customer to when the goods arrive at the customer's receiving dock. From the buyer's standpoint, the order cycle is from when the order is sent out to when the goods are received. [2] (This is also known as the replenishment cycle for goods needed on a regular basis.) The shorter and more consistent the order cycle is, the less inventory is needed by one's customers.

Four principle activities, or elements, constitute the order cycle: order placement, order processing, order preparation, and order shipment. Traditionally, the order cycle includes only those activities that occur from the time an order is placed to the time that it is received by the customers. Special activities such as backordering and expediting will affect the overall length of the order cycle. Subsequent customer activities, such as product returns, claims processing, and freight bill handling, are not technically part of the order cycle.

Order placement. Order placement time can vary significantly, from taking days or weeks to being instantaneous. Company experiences indicate that improvements in order placement systems and processes offer some of the greatest opportunities for significantly reducing the length and variability of the overall order cycle. Clearly, significant increases were projected for Internet-facilitated resources such as E-marketplaces, Extranets, and E-mail. Those that were expected to show declines in relative use were electronic data interchange (EDI) and phone/fax.

Order processing. The order processing function usually involves checking customer credit, transferring information to sales records, sending the order to the inventory and shipping areas, and preparing shipping documents. [3] Many of these functions can occur simultaneously though the effective use of available information technologies. Recent improvements in computer and information systems have led to considerable reductions in the times needed to accomplish these activities.

Order preparation. Depending on the commodity being handled and other factors, the order-preparation process sometimes may be very simple and performed manually or, perhaps, may be relatively complex and highly automated. Since the time needed to prepare orders for shipment frequently represents a significant bottleneck in the overall order cycle, advance information concerning the composition of individual shipments has become highly desirable. [4] The availability of real-time information systems has helped significantly to see that this information is available in a timely and functional manner.

Order shipment. Shipment time extends from the moment an order is placed upon the transport vehicle for movement, until the moment it is received and unloaded at the buyer's location. Measuring and controlling order shipment time sometimes can be difficult when using for-hire transportation services. However, most carriers today have developed the ability to provide their customers with this type of information.

One way for receivers of product to increase the likelihood of timely delivery is to ask for advance shipment notification (ASN) from supplier firms. Alternatively, shippers may prefer to receive proof-of-delivery (POD) documentation, preferably electronically, from carriers. This helps to pinpoint the exact time and location of delivery. To improve service to customers, transport firms have moved to the use of Internet-enabled capabilities to provide services such as these to their customers. In addition, carriers have made it easier for customers to track and trace shipments when needed and have provided these same customers with summary reports of shipment time, service level, and so on.

The Definition of Customer Service

While customer service has no single widely used definition, customer service is often viewed in three principle ways. We can think of them as three levels of customer service involvement or awareness:

Customer service as an activity. This level treats customer service as a particular task that a firm must accomplish to satisfy the customer's needs. Order processing, billing and invoicing, product returns, and claims handling are all typical examples of this level of customer service. [5] Customer service departments, which basically handle customer problems and complaints, also represent this level of customer service.

Customer service as performance measures. This level emphasizes customer service in terms of specific performance measures, such as the percentage of orders delivered on time and the number of orders processed within acceptable time limits. [6] Although this level enhances the first one, a firm must look beyond the performance measures themselves to ensure that is service efforts achieve actual customer satisfaction.

Customer service as a philosophy. This level elevates customer service to a firm-wide commitment to providing customer satisfaction through superior customer service. This view of customer service is entirely consistent with many firms' contemporary emphasis on quality and quality management. Rather than narrowly viewing customer service as an activity or as a set of performance measures, this interpretation involves a dedication to customer service that pervades the entire firm and all of its activities.

The least important level of involvement for most companies would be viewing customer service simply as an activity. From this perspective, customer service activities in logistics are at the transactional level. For example, accepting product returns from customers in a retail store adds no value to product since it is merely a transaction to please the customers. With the possible exception of making it extremely convenient for customers to return products, this level of customer service typically offers limited opportunities to add value for the customers.

The focus upon performance measures for customer service is very important, because it provides a method of evaluating how well the logistics system is functioning. Over time, such measures provide benchmarks to gauge improvement, which is especially important when a firm is trying to implement a continuous improvement program. But this level of involvement is not sufficient. The final level, customer service as philosophy, broadens the role of customer service in the firm. However, this still may not be sufficient unless the value-added dimension is included as the goal of the corporate customer service philosophy.

The definition of customer service that is used in this text is: customer service is a process for providing competitive advantage and adding benefits to the supply chain in order to maximize the total value to the ultimate customer. [7]

Performance Measures for Customer Service through Information System

Finding a comprehensive measure to effectively assess logistics customer service performance is quite difficult, considering the many dimensions of service to customers. Total order-cycle time and its variability are probably the best single measures of logistics customer service since they embody so many of the variables that are considered important to customers. Customer service may also be measured in terms of each logistics activity. Some common performance measures include the following:

Order Entry
- Minimum, maximum, and average time for order handling
- Percent of orders handled within target time

Order Documentation Accuracy
- Percent of order document with errors

Transportation
- Percent of deliveries on time
- Percent of orders delivered by data customers request
- Damage and loss claims as a percent of freight costs

Inventory and Product Availability
- Stock-out percentage
- Percent of orders filled completely
- Order fill rate and weighted average fill rate
- Average percent of items on backorder
- Item fill rate

Product damage
- Number of returns to total orders
- Value of returns to total sales

Production / Warehousing Processing Time
- Minimum, maximum, and average time to process orders

Customer relationship management (CRM) is designed to extend the functionality of the ERP sales and delivery applications, as illustrated in figure 6.2. While traditional ERP applications focus on efficiently taking customer orders, firms are finding it necessary to transition from treating customers as income sources to be exploited to treating customers as assets to be nurtured.

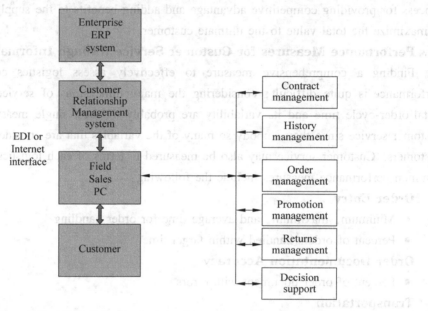

Figure 6.2　Typical customer relationship management extension system

New words and terms

order management	订单管理
order cycle	订单周期
receiving dock	收货装卸平台
replenishment cycle	补货周期
order placement	订单生成
order processing	订单处理
order preparation	订单准备
order shipment	订单装运
backordering	订单延后
expediting	订单加快

product return	产品退回
claims processing	索赔处理
freight bill handling	运输单处理
real-time information system	实时信息系统
for-hire transportation service	租赁运输服务
advance shipment notification（ASN）	提前装运通知
proof-of-delivery（POD）documentation	配送证明文件
track and trace shipment	跟踪和查询运送情况
customer service as an activity	作为活动的客户服务
customer service as performance measure	作为绩效指标的客户服务
customer service as a philosophy	作为经营哲学的客户服务
order entry	订单录入
percent of orders handled within target time	订单在目标时间内处理完毕的比率
order documentation accuracy	订单文件的准确性
percent of deliveries on time	订单准时交货的比率
percent of orders delivered by date customers request	按客户要求的日期交付的比率
inventory and product availability	库存和产品可得率
percent of orders filled completely	完全履行的订单比率
order fill rate and weighted average fill rate	订单满足率和加权平均订单满足率
average percent of items on backorder	出现订单延后的产品比率
item fill rate	单品的订单满足率
number of returns to total orders	退货占订单总数的比率
value of returns to total sales	退货占销售总额的比率
production／warehousing processing time	生产/仓储的作业时间

Notes

1. In general terms, order management means how a firm handles incoming orders. More specifically, order management is the activities that take place in the period between the time a firm receives an order and the time a warehouse is notified to ship the goods to fill that order.

   订单管理通常是指企业如何处理即将到来的订单。更具体地说,订单管理是发生在企业收到订单到仓库被通知运送货物以履行订单之间的活动。

2. From the seller's standpoint, it is the time from when an order is received from a customer to when the goods arrive at the customer's receiving dock. From the buyer's standpoint,

the order cycle is from when the order is send out to when the goods are received.

从卖方的角度来说,订货周期时间是企业从客户处收到订单到货物抵达客户收货装卸平台之间的时间。从买方的角度来说,订货周期是从发出订单到收到产品之间的时间。

3. The order-processing function usually involves checking customer credit, transferring information to sales records, sending the order to the inventory and shipping areas, and preparing shipping documents.

订单处理通常包括检查客户信用、将信息录入销售记录、将订单传至存货和送货部门以及准备装运单据。

4. Since the time needed to prepare orders for shipment frequently represents a significant bottleneck in the overall order cycle, advance information concerning the composition of individual shipments has become highly desirable.

由于为送货而进行的订单准备所需要的时间常常是整个订货周期的重要瓶颈,所以关于单个运送布局的预报就变得十分重要。

5. This level treats customer service as a particular task that a firm must accomplish to satisfy the customer's needs. Order processing, billing and invoicing, product returns, and claims handling are all typical examples of this level of customer service.

这一层次将客户服务作为企业满足客户需求必须完成的特定任务。订单处理、收款和开票、产品返回和索赔处理都是这一层次客户服务的典型例子。

6. This level emphasizes customer service in terms of specific performance measures, such as the percentage of orders delivered on time and the number of orders processed within acceptable time limits.

这一层次就具体绩效指标强调客户服务,如完成订单及时运送的百分比和在可接受的时间限制内订单处理的数量。

7. Customer service is a process for providing competitive advantage and adding benefits to the supply chain in order to maximize the total value to the ultimate customer.

客户服务是指为企业提供竞争优势并增加供应链价值以使最终用户的总价值最大化的过程。

Exercise 6

Ⅰ. Comprehension questions

1. What is the role of information?

2. What's the advantage of the company who has invested in information?

3. What can you get from the cases?
4. Is it possible to build a direct channel to the customer? How can it be done?

II. Cloze test

Information is crucial __1__ supply chain performance because it provides the facts that supply chain managers use to make decisions. Without information, a manager will not know what customers want, how much inventory is __2__ stock, and when more products should be produced and shipped. In short, without information, a manager can only make decisions blindly. __3__, information makes the supply chain visible to a manager. __4__ this visibility, a manager can make decisions to improve the supply chain's performance. Without information, it is impossible for a supply chain to deliver products __5__ to customers. With information, companies have the visibility they need to make decisions that improve company and overall supply chain performance. In this sense, information is the most important of the supply chain drivers because without it, none the other drivers can be used to deliver a high level of performance.

1. a. for	b. to	c. of	d. from
2. a. out of	b. from	c. in	d. at
3. a. whereas	b. therefore	c. however	d. nevertheless
4. a. to be given	b. giving	c. given	d. to give
5. a. effective	b. effectiveness	c. effected	d. effectively

III. Translate the following sentences into Chinese.

1. According to some examples, timely and accurate information is more critical now than at any time in the history of American business.
2. With the goal of reducing total supply chain assets, managers realize that information can be used to reduce inventory and human resource requirements.
3. In this way, information availability can reduce operating and planning uncertainty.
4. Automating and integrating the order process frees time and reduces the likelihood of information delays.
5. In the development and maintenance of the logistics' information systems, both hardware and software must be addressed.
6. The level of customer service a firm offers not only determines whether existing customers will remain customers, but how many potential customers will become customers.
7. Many companies report that most profitable customers are not their largest customers, but their mid-size customer.

8. The role of customer service is to provide "time and place utility" in the transfer of goods and services between buyers and sellers.

9. The basic task of customer service is to analyze customers' needs and set customer service levels.

10. It's estimated that a firm's 80% profit are generated by 20% customers.

11. There are many aspects of customer service, ranging from on-time delivery to after-sales support.

12. Wal-Mart's great success in marketing should be attributed to its superiority in information technology and inventory management.

13. Many international firms operate owned facilities in foreign markets in order to complete effectively on a customer service basis.

14. In general, a firm can provide a higher level of service to its domestic customers than to its foreign customers. This is primarily caused by the distance products must be transported and delays due to customs procedures.

15. The reduction in transportation cost may raise the cost of holding inventory.

Ⅳ. Translate the following sentences into English.

1. 随着全球经济一体化和物流国际化的发展,物流信息化越来越重要。

2. 信息技术在物流系统的经营中起着至关重要的作用。

3. 信息交换/转移的速度当时受制于纸张的传递速度。

4. 设置库存水平,需要来自顾客需求的下游信息。

5. 现代物流就是要求物流、商流、信息流三流合一。

6. 在物流系统中,客户服务是关键活动之一。

7. 出色的顾客服务能够为供应链中的所有成员增值。

8. 客户服务是衡量物流系统有效性的尺度。

9. 众所周知,物流系统的最终目的是使客户满意。

10. 畅通、准确、及时的信息从根本上保证了商流和物流的高质量与高效率。

11. 物流活动贯穿于企业的采购、生产、运输、仓储、分配等各个领域。

12. 公司应该采取相应的措施提高客户服务水平。

13. 你很难解释什么是客户服务,客户服务又做些什么。

14. 很多公司已经建立了以客户为中心的市场战略。

15. 加速物流信息化、标准化建设是物流行业体制创新、技术创新、管理创新的基础。

Ⅴ. Answer the questions according to the text of this chapter.

1. What is Information and Communication Technology Term?

2. Please say something about the importance of information in logistics management.

3. Please give some examples of information technology in logistics management system.

4. How many principle activities or elements constitute the order cycle? And what are they?

5. Please tell three different conceptions about customer service.

6. What is customer service?

7. What is the difference between internal customer and external customer?

8. What is basic service?

9. Why are firms willing to offer add-valued service for certain customers?

10. Customer service is the output of the logistics system, isn't it?

IV. Fill in the blanks with the following words in the boxes, and change the forms if necessary.

available	personal	output	analysis	external customers
retail	demand	place utility	response	convenient

1. Transportation, by moving goods from one place to another place, creates _____ for products.

2. To satisfy customers with special taste, manufactures have to provide _____ services.

3. In the supply chain, _____ may contain wholesalers, retailers and end-users.

4. There is a great _____ for foreign investment in the western part of China.

5. We should make an _____ of products, depending on who use them and how they are used.

6. We must distribute the products to as many places as possible so that our customers find it _____ to get them.

7. Customer service is considered as the _____ of logistics system.

8. The key point in distribution is whether the product is _____ where the customer wishes to consume it.

9. One of the basic tasks of a logistics analyst is to determine customer _____ to service.

10. Generally speaking, soap can be found in a _____ shop.

profit	response	handle	competitive	proximity
offset	basic service	role	coordinate	determine

1. Once their orders are accepted, all customers should be treated equally by receiving _____.

2. It's my job to _____ customer's response to logistics service.

3. Customer service plays a significant _____ in the development of all firms.

4. A firm may have a customer service department or customer service employees that _____ complaints, special orders, damage claims, etc.

5. The mission of logistics management is to plan and _____ all logistics activities to achieve desired level.

6. In today's _____ market, firms find it extremely difficult to create new customers.

7. You can learn about your customer's _____ by analyzing inventory information.

8. Every company ultimate goal is to gain _____, not sales.

9. I think if our warehouses are located in the _____ of customers, we can offer better after-sale service.

10. Good logistics plan _____ the cost of warehousing and transportation of products.

Logistics Situational Dialogues 6

(1) *Mr. Charles just came back from Holland on business. He is talking his experiences to his friend Mike.*

Mike: Hello! Long time no see! Where have you been?

Charles: I have just come back from Rotterdan, I have just concluded a big business on equipments. I have experienced a lot, and I saw something really different!

Mike: Well, what is the difference?

Charles: That is certainly a very good place! Everything goes efficiently.

Mike: What do you mean?

Charles: One of my first concern is information about shipping. You can find every liner service on the North European line, and you can also see the big piles and piles of containers blocked at the gulf of the sea, to be exactly, it is the sea of containers! From Monday to Saturday 24 hours a day the steamers come in and out orderly.

Mike: What do you mean the efficiency?

Charles: For example, one unique item of service is the tracing system. They have installed radio frequency identification equipment on the ships and trucks. This enables us to make real time tracing and reporting of the cargo flow.

Mike: Does it mean the customers can get real time information about their cargo?

Charles: Exactly.

Mike: Can I have to make telephone calls to check on the movement of my cargo at any time?

Charles: Yes, but you needn't have to. The only thing you will do is to connect your computer to the Internet, find the website of companies and login with your company name and the password. You can just enter the number of the container, and you will know where your container is.

Mike: It sounds interesting! Information is really crucial for every business field!

(2) *Judy, a clerk in a Sun Textile Import and Export Co. , Ltd, is complaining about the cargo to Sandy, a logistics company clerk.*

Judy: Hello, may I speak to Sandy?

Sandy: Yes, speaking please.

Judy: This is from Judy in Textile Import and Export Co. , Ltd.

Sandy: How are you? I think the cargo have already reached you. Is there anything else I can do for you?

Judy: Yes. We regret tell you that the goods you sent us are not in conformity with the terms of the contract. On examination, we find a shortage in the delivery.

Sandy: Oh? Please explain in detail.

Judy: As soon as the consignment arrived at our port we had it inspected. To our disappointment, we found a shortage of 2 cartons.

Sandy: 2 cartons?

Judy: Yes. We ordered 20 cartons of garments, but we only received 18 cartons.

Sandy: Did you contact the exporter for the matter?

Judy: Yes. They showed the onboard bill of lading to us. We all consider the carrier should be liable for the shortage. Therefore, we have to raise a claim against your company as the liability with you.

Sandy: We'd like to have your present proof.

Judy: Here is our onboard bill of lading to claim a settlement.

Sandy: Sorry, the evidence you provided is inadequate.

Judy: Wait a moment, here's a survey report issued by the Commodity Inspection Bureau.

Sandy: Have you got any other evidence?

Judy: Not yet.

Sandy: Sorry, we regret being unable to accept your claim because the goods were in perfect condition when the goods were loaded.

Judy：What should we do now?

Sandy：We suggest that you approach the insurance company for settlement as the shortage occurred in transit.

Judy：Which evidence do we provide?

Sandy：The full original set of ocean bills of lading, original policy and the original commercial invoice.

Judy：Thanks a lot, bye.

Sandy：Bye.

Dialog Exercise 6

Lily is a customer manager of a third party logistics company. Susan is her customer who runs an international trade company. Susan wanted to outsource her transportation business considering cutting cost. So Susan asked for Lily to negotiation and cooperation. One day, Susan visited to the third party logistics company, and Lily received her. The objectives of this conversation are understanding the requirements of the customer for Lily and finding out the qualification of the third part logistics for Susan. In the conversations, Lily learned that the international company demands a kind of logistics service with integration, specialization and one-stop, the transportation modes must be personalized such as intermodal. The order management and customer service including business documents flowing and goods location tracking must be finished by information systems in internet or EDI. And then Susan knew that the third party logistics company is a big enterprise that has a good reputation. At last the two sides reached the cooperation in a friendly manner. During the dialog of this scene you may use the useful words which are written as followed：

logistics integration　　　　　　　　　物流一体化

reach the collaboration with each other　相互达成合作意向

customs clearance, inspection, financial settlement, insurance

报关、报检、金融结算、保险

integrate logistics resources　　　　　　整合物流资源

Order fulfillment and order delivery are all through information systems.

订单履行和订单交付均要通过信息系统来完成。

Advanced Reading 6

Logistics service marketing—A new trend of logistics management

Logistics is essentially a service, so logistics service marketing means logistics service is sold to customer as a kind of product through reasonable marketing methods. Nowadays, with the increasing trends of economics globalization, more and more enterprises like to adopt outsourcing in order to improve their efficiency and effectiveness. The professional third party logistics companies even fourth party logistics are becoming more and more popular. These professional logistics companies can provide personalized, integrated, professional and one-stop logistics service to meet the customers' requirements. This is just core content of logistics service marketing in logistics enterprises.

The reason arise of the new trend of logistics service marketing

1. Globalization

Companies now compete for worldwide markets, no longer satisfied with local markets. As sourcing managers expand their search for the best value, they cast their nets in ever widening patterns and are rewarded with attractive sources in non-traditional locations. Logistics managers must transport those materials to global manufacturing locations and then to worldwide customers, achieving time, place and availability goals.

2. Supply chain integration

Many researches have shown that logistics management evolves through five stages, which are transportation and warehousing, physical distribution management, logistics management, supply chain management, global supply chain management, each characterized by unique management approaches. World class companies are integrated internally along horizontal processes, and externally with customers and suppliers worldwide. Integration is achieved through application of technologies, such as ERP and physical integration of joint management processes such as the current collaborative initiatives.

3. Flexibility and speed

The best supply chains are ultimately the most responsive. They are able to recover quickly from unexpected changes in demand or supply. Internal processes of leading companies are not only integrated, but are focused on their customer's need for speed and flexibility in order fulfillment. These goals are achieved by streamlining internal processes, modifying policies and integrating ordering and fulfillment processes with customers. E-commerce trends are also having an impact. Buyers are ordering in smaller quantities and expecting more rapid order processing. Logistics managers must provide for these new requirements. On the other side, the closer the manufacturer to consumer, the less impact intermediaries have on inventory buildup and service failure.

4. Collaborative logistics

Leading companies are employing similar collaborative approaches to assuring transportation and facility capacity is available to meet changing needs, and to further reduce their acquisition costs. In transportation this means real-time information sharing with carriers, to match upcoming requirements with the most effectively positioned equipment. It may also mean sharing of logistics resources with other companies with complementary shipping characteristics. Companies with these relationships are able to further reduce costs by taking advantage of other companies shipping volumes.

The characteristics of logistics services marketing

The essence of modern logistics is to provide logistics service to customers efficiently and effectively based on the weighting of the service costs under the premise of customers' satisfaction. The characteristics of logistics services marketing are as followed:

- Contract-oriented logistics service
- Based on the new customer relationships
- Personalized logistics service
- Supported by the modern information technology
- Having the obvious content of resources integration
- Having the extension of service communication and the extension of service evaluation because of the strategic alliance along with the logistics service supply chain (shown on the figure 6.3)

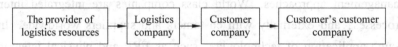

Figure 6.3   The strategic alliance along with the logistics service supply

The processing of logistics service marketing

As we all know that logistics service is kind of product which the third party logistics provides to the customer. So we must pay attention to the requirements and expectations of our customers in order to the product of logistics service can meet the customer's needs. The link of logistics market segmentation and customer survey is necessary. In addition to this, the integration logistics resources are also important because there are no warehouses, teams of transportation or distribution centers in the third party logistics companies. The processing of logistics service marketing is well expressed by the figure 6.4.

Figure 6.4　The processing of logistics service marketing

小贴士

物流小常识（1）

京东快物流运营体系的内核——青龙系统

京东"青龙"物流配送系统通过构建更合理业务流程，建造更高效的信息管理系统，实现海量信息处理能力，提升配送人员的工作效率。上市一周年的京东，在 2015 年年初就开始倾注重要战略布局：启动京东到家 O2O 平台，布局京东到家 O2O 物流服务。负责 O2O 战略的京东副总裁邓天卓曾透露："京东到家会让京东和京东物流产生颠覆性的改变。"邓总的这句话很有内涵，这种颠覆性的变化是让京东传统的物流升级到快物流服务，而快物流后台的核心就是京东物流的内核——青龙系统。

京东副总裁邓天卓给出了一个这样的场景体验，京东根据用户的大数据分析，能够预测核心城市各片区的主流单品的销量需求，提前在各个地区物流分站预先发货，客户下单后会在 2 小时左右的时间享受到惊喜的物流服务。这远远超出了原来的 211 限时达、次日达等服务了。这背后是用户大数据＋青龙系统＋O2O 运营体系的有效支撑。

小贴士

物流小常识（2）

顺丰物流信息系统先进在哪里？

顺丰可以提供全国 31 个省、直辖市、港澳台地区的高水准门到门快递服务。采用标准定价、标准操作流程，各环节均以最快速度进行发运、中转、派送，并对客户进行相对标准承诺。顺丰物流信息系统的先进主要体现在以下几点：第一，信息录入的及时性，不管是收件还是派件，顺丰快递员手上都有扫描仪，这是与网络联网的，扫描后几分钟就可以在网上查到了。第二，顺丰的空运是其他所有的快递没有办法跟上的，顺丰公司有 12 架货机，且与多家航空公司签有协议，空运一定是排完顺丰后，才会有其他快递公司的机会的。第三，顺丰的服务是快递行业最好的，其他没有一家可以比的。只要发过一次快递，顺丰都会有记录的。

Supplementary Reading 6

Customer Service

The only thing harder than delivering excellent customer service consistently is to motivate someone else to deliver excellent customer service consistently. Customers are more demanding than ever. Professionals are more difficult to hire and retain than ever. Splitting an atom might be easier than rallying an entire organization to satisfy customers. Yet, some organizations succeed. Four motivation strategies can help your organizations succeed, too. Get excited.

As managers, the first professionals to motivate are ourselves. If we lack motivation, employees will lack motivation. Motivation occurs from the inside out. If we want to motivate someone, we have to communicate to their insides. Emotions communicate on a deep level from inside to inside. This is why one bad apple spoils the bunch. It's also why one excited manager can mobilize a team to move mountains. Dig deep. Feigning excitement is impossible because people's insides come equipped with an infallible phony-detection system that is always on and has an amazing range of reception. Are you genuinely excited about the work your team produces?

Whether we can manage the custodial staff, we need to fall in love with out team's contribution. Hire Motivated Professionals. It's easier to hire motivated professionals than it is to motivate professionals. Experts assert, "Hire smart or manage tough." Do you believe that professionals would revel in the kind of work your team produces? The answer is … they do exist. However, if we are not excited about the work our team produces, we will never attract and hire people who are excited to do it because like attracts like and birds of a feather flock together. Consider that Disney esteems cleanliness. They hire only street sweepers and house cleaners who delight in cleaning. Result: Disney parks and resorts are immaculate.

Answer the following questions briefly according to the passage you have just read.

1. Why is it difficult to motivate the customer service staff?
2. What are the four motivational strategies mentioned in the passage that can help your organization to succeed?
3. How could a manager likely be able to mobilize his team?
4. What is the meaning of dig deep?
5. Why should the managers be excited about the work their team production?

Chapter 7

Supply Chain Management

Lesson 7.1   Origin and Definition

The term "supply chain management" entered the public domain when Keith Oliver, a consultant at Booz Allen Hamilton, used it in an interview for the Financial Times in 1982. The term was slow to take hold. It gained currency in the mid-1990s, when a flurry of articles and books came out on the subject. One of the first to formally define supply chains as encompassing all activities associated with the flow and transformation of goods from raw materials through to the end user, as well as the associated information flows. Supply chain management was thus defined as the integration of these activities through improved supply chain relationships to achieve a competitive advantage.

A dominant logistics philosophy throughout the 1980s and into the early 1990s involved the integration of logistics with other functions in an organization in an effort to achieve the enterprise's overall success. [1] The early to mid-1990s witnessed a growing recognition that there could be value in coordinating the various business functions not only within organizations but across organizations as well, what can be referred to as a supply chain management (SCM) philosophy.

A supply chain "encompasses all activities associated with the flow and transformation of goods from the raw materials stage (extraction), through to the end user, as well as the associated information flows". [2]

There are five components in the supply chain involving supplier, producer, wholesaler, retailer and customer (as the Figure 7.1). Each of the components is called member enterprise of supply chain. The member enterprises must cooperate with each other in order to make the effectiveness maximum in the supply chain management.

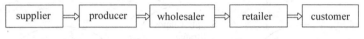

Figure 7.1   Components of supply chain

Supply chain management can be defined as "the pipeline for the efficient and effective flow of products/ materials, services, information, and financials from the supplier's suppliers through the various intermediate organizations/ companies out to the customer's customers or the system of connected logistics networks between the original vendors and the ultimate final consumer". [3] The extended enterprise perspective of supply chain management represents a logical extension of the logistics concept.

Successful supply chain management requires companies to apply the systems approach across all organizations in the supply chain. When applied to supply chains, the systems approach suggests that companies must recognize the interdependencies of major functional areas within, across, and between firms. In turn, the goals and objectives of individual supply chain participants should be compatible with the goals and objectives of other participants in the supply chain. For example, a company that is committed to a high level of customer service might be out of place in a supply chain comprised of companies whose primary value proposition involves cost containment.

One widely used model of supply chain management, the SCOR (supply chain operations reference) model, currently identifies five key processes-plan, source, make, deliver, return-associated with supply chain management. [4] Earlier versions of the SCOR model did not include the return process: as a result, the current model explicitly recognizes that returns should be considered in the design (and management) of supply chains.

Moreover, closer analysis of the five key processes, and their definitions, indicates the important role of logistics in supply chain management. It can be argued that logistics has some involvement in both sourcing and making, for example, with respect to making, the concept of postponement resulting in value-added activities being performed in warehousing facilities. Alternatively, logistics can be heavily involved in delivering and returning; the definition of delivery specifically mentions the key logistics components of order management, transportation management, and distribution management.

There are many contents in supply chain management such as supply chain planning, supply chain enterprise applications, supply chain operations, procurement product lifecycle management, logistics and supply chain strategy. As is explained in figure 7.2. We can see from the figure that logistics is a part of supply chain management.

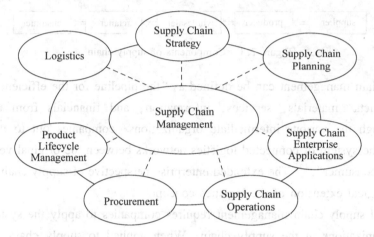

Figure 7.2　The contents included in supply chain management

(comes from http://www.chinascm.net)

New words and terms

supply chain management (SCM)　　　　　　　供应链管理
supply chain operations reference (SCOR) model　供应链作业参考模型

Notes

1. A dominant logistics philosophy throughout the 1980s and into the early 1990s involved the integration of logistics with other functions in an organization in an effort to achieve the enterprise's overall success.

   从20世纪80年代到20世纪90年代早期,占主导地位的物流学原理包括物流与组织内其他功能的整合以达到企业整体的成功。

2. A supply chain "encompasses all activities associated with the flow and transformation of goods from the raw materials stage (extraction), through to the end user, as well as the associated information flows."

供应链包括了货物从原材料阶段直到终端用户手中的全过程,包括商品的流动、转换及相关的信息流。

3. Supply chain management can be defined as "the pipeline for the efficient and effective flow of products/ materials, services, information, and financials from the supplier's suppliers through the various intermediate organizations/ companies out to the customer's customers or the system of connected logistics networks between the original vendors and the ultimate final consumer."

供应链管理被定义为通过各种中介公司有效地将供应商的产品流或者物资流、服务流、信息流、资金流输送到用户的渠道,或者连接卖方和最终用户的物流网络系统。

4. One widely used model of supply chain management, the SCOR (supply chain operations reference) model, currently identifies five key processes—plan, source, make, deliver, return—associated with supply chain management.

一个广泛运用的供应链管理模型是 SCOR(供应链作业参考模型),它指出了五个与供应链管理密切相关的关键过程: 计划、资源、制造、配送、退货。

Lesson 7.2　Barriers to Supply Chain Management

While supply chain management may sound attractive from a conceptual perspective, a number of barriers block its effective implementation.

Regulatory and Political Considerations

Several decades ago, many of the supply chain arrangements in use today would have been considered illegal under certain regulatory statutes. In the United States, for example, cross-business coordination was fostered by the passage of the National cooperative Research and Development Act of 1984. Long-term commitments, which are one of the bedrocks of supply chain management, may stifle competition to the extent that they make it more difficult for others to enter particular markets. While the overall global climate for business has shifted toward allowing more cooperation among firms, it still would be wise to have sound legal advice before entering into future supply chain arrangements.

Political considerations such as war and governmental stability can also act as a barrier to supply chain management. With respect to war, the early years of the 21 century have witnessed increased tensions in the Middle East, as well as between Pakistan and India (both with nuclear weapon capabilities). These political uncertainties might cause some organizations to shy away from joining or developing supply chains that rely on companies located in warring countries. Governmental stability is also a key consideration, because supply chain management is so dependent on inter-organizational coordination. Governmental policies that either discourage such coordination or discourage doing business with certain countries would obviously have a negative impact on supply chain efficiency.

Lack of Top Management Commitment

Top management commitment is regularly cited as an important component when individual companies attempt to initiate and implement new initiatives, programs, and products. [1] For example, the topic of reverse logistics has become increasingly important in recent years, and its importance should continue to increase in the future. Recent research suggests that the relevant reverse logistics goals are more likely to be achieved when there is a high degree of management commitment to them.

Because of supply chain management's inter-organizational focus, top management commitment is absolutely essential if supply chain efforts are to have any chance of success. Unfortunately, top management is sometimes hesitant to fully commit to supply chain management because it is uncomfortable with (or does not understand) one or more of its underpinnings. For example, some companies may be uncomfortable with the concept of customer power in supply chain. Alternatively, other companies may be hesitate to enter into long-term relationships because such relationships might be perceived as limiting their operational flexibility.

Reluctance to Share, or Use, Relevant Data

As pointed out previously, the business bromide "Information is power" can make information (data) sharing somewhat problematic, particularly with data that companies might regard as proprietary. [2] However, a reluctance to share data likely decreases the overall effectiveness and efficiency of supply chains because other members may be making decisions based on erroneous data and / or assumptions.

Furthermore, advances in computer hardware and software now permit copious amounts of data to be processed and analyzed relatively quickly. To this end, data mining, a technique that looks for patterns and relationships in relevant data. As an example, frequent shopper cards, such as those offered by grocery chains, offer the opportunity to develop highly detailed profiles of individual customers. Some companies, however, are reluctant to fully utilize the information that comes from this data: they believe that the highly detailed data that can be provided by frequent shopper cards-what was purchased, when it was purchased, where it was purchased, how it was purchased-potentially violate the customer's right to privacy.

Incompatible Information Systems

One barrier to inter-organizational coordination in the past was incompatible computer hardware. It's more likely today, by contrast, that software compatibility is the more pressing issue, particularly with the growing popularity of enterprise resource planning (ERP) systems. Although ERP systems offer tremendous potential for increasing organizational effectiveness and efficiency, the installation of ERP systems can cost hundreds of millions of dollars and take several years to complete.

While ERP systems may be strong in terms of financial and billing applications, most tend to be relatively weak when it comes to logistics and supply chain requirements. [3] In order to achieve these requirements, other software packages have to be integrated with the chosen ERP system, and these integrations don't always proceed smoothly. One well-known example involved the attempt by Hershey Foods integrates an ERP system with two other specialized software packages. The growing pains of this integration included unfilled candy orders for Halloween and Christmas, longer delivery times, increased inventory levels, and upset customers.

Incompatible Corporate Cultures

Because supply chain management emphasizes a long-term orientation and partnerships between various participants, it is important that participants be comfortable with the companies that they will be working with. In a broad sense, corporate culture refers to "how we do things around here" and reflects an organization's vision, values, and strategic plans. [4]

The myriad manifestations of a company's culture include, but are not limited to, office decor, company brochures, company rituals, and dress codes. [5] All manifestations of corporate culture may provide important clues about the ability of companies to work together. For instance, one of the more notable supply chain failures in recent years involved the dissolution of the relationship between Office Max and Ryder Integrated Logistics. While a number of reasons explain why this relationship didn't succeed, the two companies had quite different dress codes. Indeed, a Ryder manager has stated it was clear from the first face-to-face meeting that the companies were going to have difficulty working together—in large part because of their vastly different dress codes!

As it was interpreted by figure 7.3, the transmission of demanding quantity along with supply chain is steady if without "niubian effectiveness", while it is magnified when in "niubian effectiveness".

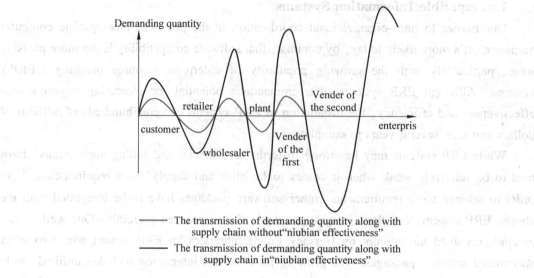

Figure 7.3   The "niubian effectiveness" of supply chain

New words and terms

data mining		数据挖掘
incompatible	*adj.*	不兼容的
partnership	*n.*	伙伴关系
strategic alliances		战略同盟
third-party arrangement		第三方安排
contract logistics		合同物流

Notes

1. Top management commitment is regularly cited as an important component when individual companies attempt to initiate and implement new initiatives, programs, and products.

   私营公司试图发起或实施新的创举或产品计划时,高层管理作为一个重要的部分经常被提及。

2. As pointed out previously, the business bromide "Information is power" can make information (data) sharing somewhat problematic, particularly with data that companies might regard as proprietary.

商业的陈词滥调"信息就是力量"可能会使信息共享不能完全实现,特别是有些公司还把某些数据看作公司的财产。

3. While ERP systems may be strong in terms of financial and billing applications, most tend to be relatively weak when it comes to logistics and supply chain requirements.

企业资源计划系统可能在财务和账单申请方面有优势,而在物流与供应链需求方面比较弱。

4. In a broad sense, corporate culture refers to "how we do things around here" and reflects an organization's vision, values, and strategic plans.

从广义上说,企业文化是指"我们在这里怎么办事",它反映了组织的愿景、价值和战略。

5. The myriad manifestations of a company's culture include, but are not limited to, office decor, company brochures, company rituals, and dress codes.

企业文化的各种表现包括但不限于办公室格调、公司简介材料、公司典礼以及服装式样。

Lesson 7.3　Supply Chain Management and Integration

An individual firm can be involved in multiple supply chains at the same time, and it's important to recognize that expectations and required knowledge can vary across supply chains. For example, food manufacturers may sell to grocery chains, institutional buyers, specialty firms, and industrial users (which might use the product as an ingredient in another product that they manufacture). It seems reasonable that the packaging expectations of specialty firms might be more demanding than those of industrial users.

Supply chains are integrated by having various parities enter into and carry out long-term mutually beneficial agreements. These agreements are known by several names, to include partnerships, strategic alliances, third-party agreement, and contract logistics.[1] Whatever they are called, these agreements should be designed to reward all participants when cooperative ventures are successful, and they should also provide incentives for all parties to work toward success. In a similar fashion, the participants should share the consequences when cooperative ventures are less successful than desired.

When an organization enters into a long-term agreement with a source or customer, the organization must keep in mind how this arrangement could affect the rest of the supply chain. Ideally, all participants in the supply chain will meet at one time and work out whatever agreements are necessary to ensure that the entire supply chain functions in the most desirable manner.

In order to integrate a particular supply chain, the various organizations must recognize the shortcomings of the present system and examine channel arrangements as they currently exist and as they might be. All of this is done within the framework of the organization's overall strategy, as well as any logistics strategies necessary to support the goals and objectives of the firm's top management.

Broadly speaking, organizations can pursue three primary methods when attempting to integrate their supply chains. One method is through vertical integration, where one organization owns multiple participants in the supply chain; indeed, the Ford Motor Company of the 1920s owned forests and steel mills and exercised tight control over its dealers. The most common examples of vertical integration today are some lines of paint and automotive tires. It's important to recognize that there may be regulatory limitations (often in the form of state laws) as to the degree of vertical integration that will be permitted in particular industries.

A second possible method of supply chain coordination involves the use of formal contracts among various participants. One of the more popular uses of contracts is through franchising, which attempts to combine the benefits of tight integration of some functions along with the ability to be very flexible while performing other functions. From a supply chain perspective, a franchiser may exert contractual influence over what products are purchased by a franchisee, acceptable vendors (suppliers) of these products, and the distribution of the product to the franchisee. For example, distribution for many McDonald's franchisees in the United States (e. g. , food , beverage, and store supplies) is provided by the Martin-Brower Company.

A third method of supply chain coordination involves informal agreements among the various organizations to pursue common goals and objectives, with control being exerted by the largest organization in the supply chain. [2] While this method offers supply chain participants flexibility in the sense that organizations can exit unprofitable and/or unproductive arrangements quickly and with relative ease, organizations should be aware of potential shortcomings. For one, the controlling organization may be so powerful that the supply chain becomes more like a dictatorship than a partnership. Moreover, the same flexibility that allows for exiting unprofitable or unproductive arrangements also allows parties the ability to switch supply chains when presented with what appears to be a better deal. The river of supply chain integration is as figure 7. 4.

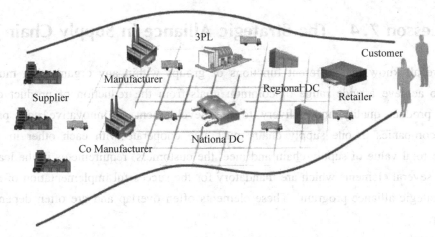

Figure 7.4   The river of supply chain integration

New words and terms

vertical integration		垂直一体化
formal contract		正式合同
franchising	*n.*	特许经营
informal agreement		非正式协议

Notes

1. Supply chains are integrated by having various parities enter into and carry out long-term mutually beneficial agreements. These agreements are known by several names, to include partnerships, strategic alliances, third-party agreement, and contract logistics.

   供应链通过不同参与方的进入并签订长期互利协议而实现一体化。这些协议可以命名为：伙伴关系、战略同盟、第三方协议以及合同物流。

2. A third method of supply chain coordination involves informal agreements among the various organizations to pursue common goals and objectives, with control being exerted by the largest organization in the supply chain.

   协调供应链的第三种办法就是利用不同组织间为寻求共同的目标或目的而签订的非正式协议，这由供应链中最大的组织来控制。

Lesson 7. 4　The Strategic Alliance in Supply Chain

As we all know that different functions or groups within any organization must work together to achieve a wide range of common goals-from the reduction of product cost and improved product quality and delivery to the development of innovative new products. Different companies in one supply chain must also cooperate with each other in order to realize the total value of supply chain and meet the customers' requirements in the least cost. There are several elements which are mandatory for the successful implementation of a supply chain's strategic alliance program. These elements often overlap and are often dependent on each other.

- **Trust**

A primary ingredient in the establishment of a successful relationship between vendor and customer is the element of trust. Without trust, none of the other factors are possible. Trust allows venders to participate and contribute in the new product development cycle, this action is called technical intervention or early supplier involvement. Trust also allows information full shared between suppliers and customers. So we can say that trust is the basic factor of cooperation.

- **Long-term Relationships**

With suppliers taking on a strategic role in a company, it is necessary to develop long-term relationships that permit the sharing of a strategic vision. The term often used in establishing these long-term relationships is evergreen contracts, implying they are automatically renewed as long as the vendors perform as agreed. Long-term relationships can make cooperation less cost of evaluating suppliers, selecting suppliers and trading or operation. Long-term relationships are also benifical to development promotion with each other.

- **Information Sharing**

Successful supply chain management requires the sharing of information between vendors and customers. This information can include everything from new product design specifications to capacity planning and scheduling, and even access to a customer's entire database. This information sharing are built on the basis of strategic alliance. Through this sharing, the customers can know the information about the production or the new products of suppliers at the first time, while the suppliers can also understand the individual requirements or personalized expectations of their customers.

- ### Total Risk, Profit Sharing

Total risk and profit sharing is a real win-win mode. In order to realize this good relationship, companies must have spirit of compromise. For example, the vendors and the customers must try to get the maximum total value instead of maximum individual value.

- ### Individual Strengths of Organizations

If a firm enters into a long-term relationship with a vendor, then it is in that firm's best interest for the vendor to remain in business for a long period of time. Thus a good customer will work with a vendor to ensure that it is profitable and that it remains financially strong. The selection of proper vendors is also important. Thus, in addition to financial strengths, each vendor should have some unique operational or engineering strength with respect to the products it makes and delivers. This permits the firm to incorporate these strengths into its own products, which then provides an added advantage in the marketplace.

New words and terms

innovative	adj.	创新的
mandatory	adj.	强制的
strategic alliance		战略联盟
overlap	v.	重叠
technical intervention		技术介入
early supplier involvement		供应商的早期参与
evergreen contracts		长期有效的合同
total risk and profit sharing		风险共担,利润共享
spirit of compromise		妥协精神
maximum total value		总体价值最大化
maximum individual value		个体价值最大化
incorporate	v.	合并

Exercises 7

Ⅰ. Pair work: Discuss the following questions.

1. What is supply chain?
2. What is the definition of supply chain management?
3. As a consumer, are you a part of supply chain?
4. What are the disadvantages of the traditional supply chain?

3. What are the reasons for developing supply chains?

4. What is the goal of supply chain management?

II. Fill in the blanks with the following words in the boxes, and change the forms if necessary.

competitiveness	utilization	shareholder	optimization	linkage
procurement	throughput	downstream	modeling	margin

1. The river departed from its original course several miles _____.

2. It now provides a _____ to more than 60 home pages of government agencies and related organizations.

3. We'll try to work as _____ agent on behalf of IBM.

4. _____ is also about the quality and creativity of the people.

5. He resigned in the face of mounting pressure from the _____.

6. We expect to increase _____ of the helicopters.

7. Hi-tech industry has been driving the _____ of the economic structure.

8. She would like to be a film actress, but at present she is _____.

9. The general price level declined by small _____.

10. We have the busiest container port in the world and the busiest international air freight _____.

deflation	ultimately	advent	accommodate	turbulence
prominent	configuration	impeccable	collaborate	entail

1. I think I'll be all right as soon as the plane gets out of this _____.

2. People are much better informed since the _____ of television.

3. Vendors could charge between $190 and $375 per computer, depending on _____.

4. Every value they created _____ redounded to his boss.

5. As your company's representative, your phone manners should be _____.

6. Tax became a powerful policy instrument to tackle monetary _____.

7. He is a _____ scholar in the field of linguistics.

8. I would ask you to _____ with us in this work.

9. We must _____ ourselves to circumstances.

10. Her intemperance will _____ the curse of insanity upon her innocent children.

Ⅲ. Translate the following sentences into Chinese.

1. Traditionally, marketing, distribution, planning, manufacturing, and the purchasing organizations along the supply chain operated independently.

2. Supply chain management is "… an integrative philosophy to manage the total flow of a distribution channel from supplier to the ultimate user."

3. The supply chain arrangement links a firm and its distributive and supplier network to end customers.

4. Leading companies are using other tactics in addition to just-in-time and "lean manufacturing" practices.

5. Since World War Ⅱ, with the development of the operations research and management science, there has been an increasing interest in supply chain planning and management.

6. Dynamic markets, characterized by turbulence from changing consumer demands, lower costs and reduced margins means organizations must re-engineer their processes to remain competitive.

7. It requires a great deal of management effort and cooperation to achieve a successful supply chain.

8. The concept of supply chain management is relatively new, however, it is in fact an extension of the logistics.

9. With the numerous advantage of supply chain integration, its management can be a complex challenge.

10. For most manufacturers, the supply chain looks less like a pipeline or chain than an uprooted tree where the branches and roots are the extensive network of customers and suppliers.

Ⅳ. Translate the following sentences into English.

1. 传统供应链中的企业各有其目的且互相矛盾。

2. 物流功能的一个重要目标就是整合供应链管理。

3. 建立供应链企业的战略伙伴关系至关重要。

4. 供应链管理效率最优化的关键在于使顾客满意的同时促进企业的有效增长。

5. 供应链管理软件能够提供解决供应链问题的数学模型。

6. 全球化使得很多企业不得不重新调整其生产或采购网络以使其更合理。

7. 供应链管理使得一些公司发展成真正的全球性公司,一家公司可以在美国开发产品,在印度制造,而在欧洲销售。

8. 供应链管理是以顾客为导向的。

9. 信息技术将极大地提高企业供应链的管理水平。

10. 客户服务能衡量一个企业物流管理的水平。

V. Answer the questions according to the text of this chapter.

1. What is supply chain?

2. How to deal with the barriers to supply chain management?

3. Please say the function of integration in supply chain.

4. What is strategic alliance in supply chain? And what are the most important elements in the cooperation of strategic alliance?

5. What are the most prominent trends in the supply chain industry in the 21st century?

6. Why do some companies close down their operations in Canada or the US and set up or outsource to a company in India, China, Mexico, Africa, etc. ?

7. With the advent of trade liberalization and more countries opening their borders to foreign companies, what will happen?

8. The new competitive frontier is across supply chains, isn't it? Why?

9. What is responsible for the level of customer service in an organization?

10. How to reduce the supply chain cost effectively?

Logistics Situational Dialogues 7

(*In an executive board meeting costs of storage are being discussed. The possibility of creating a supply chain is mentioned. The following is a conversation between Mr. Gao and Mr. Huang.*)

Gao: Our marketing department has developed relations with two American companies which are attracted to our product line for their Christmas market. There's a big problem of storing the products as they come to us from the manufacturers. Mr. Huang, what should we do?

Huang: What size orders do we expect to ship?

Gao: They're each ordering two large containers.

Huang: That's a considerable amount of product. We don't want to lose these orders.

Gao: Yes, and I think we ought to have the product all in one place for final shipping.

Huang: How long will we need to store the product?

Gao: There will be a lead-time of 6-8 weeks between early production and actual shipping.

Huang: And for Christmas we'll need to get it shipped to New York by September 1 at the latest.

Gao: Yes, that means storing the product in the hottest part of the summer. We'll need storage that's well ventilated.

Huang: I suppose our manufacturers are concerned that their capital for raw materials will not be replenished until the order is filled; therefore, their ability to rent space for storage is very limited.

Gao: We need some insurance against losses during the storage period.

Huang: I'm concerned about damage and pilferage during the lead-time.

Gao: We need warehouses that are well managed against damage and that are secure.

Huang: Can the cost of storage be passed along (become part of the retail price) so that the customer actually contributes to it? (An expense of operating a business is shared by each member of the distribution chain.)

Gao: I think we've been absorbing too much of the storage costs on most of our products. The usual plan, as you know, is that this overhead is shared at each step of manufacturing and distribution. You know, manufacturing, warehousing, shipping, wholesaling each adds 1.6% to the price of the production.

Huang: We need some contractual negotiations regarding these handling costs, including storage and some insurance to cover damage and pilferage while the products are stored.

Gao: Didn't you attend training about supply chain advantages and disadvantages?

Huang: Yes, I did. I'll review my notes. The instructor said we could call him for advice if we wished.

Gao: Get your notes together and meet with me in the morning. I'll make some time in the next 48 hours to research what other companies are doing.

Dialog Exercise 7

Jim is a purchasing manager of a car manufacturer. Jim planed to buy a large scale of tires for the production. The most reliable method to select suppliers is to hold the meeting of tender assembly (召开招标大会). There are four tire producer which were participated in this meeting: they are Michelin, Shuangxi, Hankook and Goodyear. If you are Jim, the purchasing manager, please reproduce the situations of this meeting, the useful words are as followed:

evaluation index system	评价指标体系
quality Certification	质量认证
bid	中标

base price	标底
price discounts	价格折扣
preferential procurement	优惠的采购
delivery time	交货期
value-added services	增值性服务
competitive state	竞争性陈述

Case Study 7

Whirlpool Coproration：Evolution of a Supply Chain

Summary

Whirlpool Corporation is the world's leading manufacturer and marketer of major home appliances, with annual sales over $ 19 billion, more than 80,000 employees and more than 60 manufacturing and technology research centers globally. Consumers around the world enjoy Whirlpool's innovative products marketed under Whirlpool, Maytag, KitchenAid, Jenn-Air, Amana, Brastemp, Bauknecht and other major brand names. With this varied inventory, plus a large direct sales force in more than 170 countries and an unpredictable sales cycle, effective supply chain management is critical for continued growth. Whirlpool has not always considered logistics a competitive advantage. However, since naming Penske its lead logistics supplier, Whirlpool experienced cost savings, increased customer satisfaction and found a partner to help integrate the recent acquisition of Maytag.

Challenges

- To effectively leverage its supply chain to maximize cost savings, while also positively influencing the overall Whirlpool customer experience
- To swiftly and efficiently integrate Maytag operations

Solutions / Results

- Through the Penske/Whirlpool LLP relationship, Penske assumed responsibility for execution and management of 3PLs, and provided an enhanced ability to view each supplier's key performance indicators integrated with financials.
- Penske built a new routing tool specifically for Whirlpool that offered overall cost optimization and mode selection.
- Penske helped to integrate Maytag operations through consolidating LDC networks,

optimizing routing of RDC shipments, determining optimal fleet size and operating network, combining collocated Maytag and Whirlpool RDS locations and integrating the Hi/Lo network to improve product availability and fill rates.

Taking a Customer-Centric Approach

Supply chain management was not always a competitive advantage for Whirlpool. Penske initially partnered with Whirlpool as its single logistics provider for the Quality express network. Penske was responsible for the logistics of the entire network, including managing the relationship of the two regions it subcontracted to Kenco. This Penske-Whirlpool partnership replaced Whirlpool's previous logistics solution, comprised of two incumbent third-party logistics providers. The partnership accomplished Whirlpool's early logistics objectives, most notably, to establish effective processes and procedures, allow for more visibility of the company's distribution network and reduce supply chain costs.

Recently, Whirlpool's management took a more customer-centric approach to analyzing its supply chain and began benchmarking its supply chain against other companies to identify "best in class" practices. This exercise prompted Whirlpool to question whether having a single logistics provider was the best structure to exceed customer expectations and maximize cost savings. At the same time, Whirlpool was gearing up for the monumental acquisition of Maytag.

Penske Provides the Solution

"Our business relationship with Whirlpool is one of Penske Logistics' longest-standing and most successful engagements. It's because of that relationship that we are able to quickly understand and evaluate Whirlpool's supply chain and propose solutions to improve efficiency and provide deeper supply chain visibility." Ray Russell, Senior Vice President - Operations, Penske Logistics

After completion of its customer-centric supply chain analysis, Whirlpool knew innovation was necessary to maintain a competitive advantage. After careful consideration, Whirlpool decided to adjust the company's supply chain structure and introduce additional third-party logistics providers (3PLs) into the mix. By taking this step, Whirlpool hoped to further reduce supply chain costs.

However, having multiple 3PLs created the need for an objective resource to keep homogeneity for the consumer, select and manage the 3PLs and analyze the overall supply chain. After reviewing internal options, Whirlpool realized it lacked the capability or resources in-house to manage the 3PL relationships and made the decision not to increase staff to fill this role. This decision crystallized the need to hire a lead logistics provider (LLP).

　　As Whirlpool searched for the right LLP, Penske Logistics continually surfaced as the leader in technology and engineering. Plus, after years of working together, Penske's capabilities were already embedded in Whirlpool's processes and structure. The main concern facing Whirlpool in its decision to appoint Penske as its LLP was that Penske would have to remain objective when reviewing 3PLs. Essentially, Whirlpool was concerned about whether Penske could objectively award or remove business from a 3PL based exclusively on the business requirements and not show any favoritism to Penske 3PL. Penske actually assumed the unofficial role of LLP when the need arose. Penske filled the gaps to re-engineer the Whirlpool network to accommodate the new multiple 3PL structure. By demonstrating its capability ahead of officially being awarded the contract, Penske built the trust of Whirlpool senior management and made the transition easier.

Answer the following questions after reading the case

1. What are the challenges Wirlpool facing in supply chain?
2. What are the solutions provided by Penske for Wirlpool?

Please try to answer these questions after reading the case.

1. What is the new trends or new challenges which HuaWei company must face to now?
2. Please talk about Purchasing integration of HuaWei company.
3. What is collaborative buyer-seller relationships?
4. What is cross-functional sourcing teams? And why HuaWei company adopt this sourcing teams?
5. Please talk about four catalogs of cross-functional sourcing team.
6. What indicators are included in the initial supplier evaluation system of HuaWei? Please try to design a appropriate supplier evaluation system for any company (writing the evaluation result of scores is necessary).

小贴士

物流小常识

　　戴尔的核心能力在于管理好整条供应链,让新产品在最短时间交到客户手上。戴尔的供应链管理可以归纳为:一、减少供货商并将他们集中。将原本下给200多家供货商的订单集中,以就近供货原则交给其中50家,从而使戴尔本身的零件库存不到2小时,接到订单后,再通知供货商送零件来,从进料到组装完出货只要4小时。二、强化供应链上的信息流通速度和透明度。戴尔的供货商,等于转接了戴尔的库存压力,因此必须很清楚戴尔未来的出货计划。三、在研发上,戴尔也选择降低研发和设计比重,放大伙伴价值的做法。此外,在发动价格战争时,供应商也需要扮演极具效率的后勤支持角色。借助供应链的威力,戴尔可以实现顾客下单到出货存货周转天数 4 天、每人每小时的生产效率提升 160%、订单处理效率提高 50%,以及订单错误率降低 50% 的竞争力。

Supplementary Reading 7

Historical Developments of Supply Chain Management

Six major movements can be observed in the evolution of supply chain management studies: creation, integration, and globalization (Movahedi et al., 2009), specialization phases one and two, and SCM 2.0.

Creation Era

The term "supply chain management" was first coined by Keith Oliver in 1982. However, the concept of a supply chain in management was of great importance long before, in the early 20th century, especially with the creation of the assembly line. The characteristics of this era of supply chain management include the need for large-scale changes, re-engineering, downsizing driven by cost reduction programs, and widespread attention to Japanese management practices. However, the term became widely adopted after the publication of the seminal book *Introduction to Supply Chain Management* in 1999 by Robert B. Handfield and Ernest L. Nichols, Jr. which published over 25,000 copies and was translated into Japanese, Korean, Chinese, and Russian.

Integration Era

This era of supply chain management studies was highlighted with the development of electronic data interchange (EDI) systems in the 1960s, and developed through the 1990s by the introduction of enterprise resource planning (ERP) systems. This era has continued to develop into the 21st century with the expansion of Internet-based collaborative systems. This era of supply chain evolution is characterized by both increasing value added and cost reductions through integration.

A supply chain can be classified as a stage 1, 2 or 3 network. In a stage 1 supply chain, systems such as production, storage, distribution, and material control are not linked and are independent of each other. In a stage 2 supply chain, these are integrated under one plan and is ERP enabled. A stage 3 supply chain is one that achieves vertical integration with upstream suppliers and downstream customers. An example of this kind of supply chain is Tesco.

Globalization Era

The third movement of supply chain management development, the globalization era, can be characterized by the attention given to global systems of supplier relationships and the expansion of supply chains beyond national boundaries and into other continents. Although the use of global sources in organisations' supply chains can be traced back several decades (e. g. , in the oil industry), it was not until the late 1980s that a considerable number of organizations started to integrate global sources into their core business. This era is characterized by the globalization of supply chain management in organizations with the goal of increasing their competitive advantage, adding value, and reducing costs through global sourcing.

Specialization Era (phase I): Outsourced Manufacturing and Distribution

In the 1990s, companies began to focus on "core competencies" and specialization. They abandoned vertical integration, sold off non-core operations, and outsourced those functions to other companies. This changed management requirements, by extending the supply chain beyond the company walls and distributing management across specialized supply chain partnerships.

This transition also refocused the fundamental perspectives of each organization. Original equipment manufacturers (OEMs) became brand owners that required visibility deep into their supply base. They had to control the entire supply chain from above, instead of from within. Contract manufacturers had to manage bills of material with different part-numbering schemes from multiple OEMs and support customer requests for work-in-process visibility and vendor-managed inventory (VMI).

The specialization model creates manufacturing and distribution networks composed of several individual supply chains specific to producers, suppliers, and customers that work together to design, manufacture, distribute, market, sell, and service a product. This set of partners may change according to a given market, region, or channel, resulting in a proliferation of trading partner environments, each with its own unique characteristics and demands.

Specialization Era (phase II): Supply Chain Management as a Service

Specialization within the supply chain began in the 1980s with the inception of transportation brokerages, warehouse management (storage and inventory), and non-asset-based carriers, and has matured beyond transportation and logistics into aspects of supply planning, collaboration, execution, and performance management.

Market forces sometimes demand rapid changes from suppliers, logistics providers, locations, or customers in their role as components of supply chain networks. This variability has significant effects on supply chain infrastructure, from the foundation layers of establishing and managing electronic communication between trading partners, to more complex requirements such as the configuration of processes and work flows that are essential to the management of the network itself.

Supply chain specialization enables companies to improve their overall competencies in the same way that outsourced manufacturing and distribution has done; it allows them to focus on their core competencies and assemble networks of specific, best-in-class partners to contribute to the overall value chain itself, thereby increasing overall performance and efficiency. The ability to quickly obtain and deploy this domain-specific supply chain expertise without developing and maintaining an entirely unique and complex competency in house is a leading reason why supply chain specialization is gaining popularity.

Outsourced technology hosting for supply chain solutions debuted in the late 1990s and has taken root primarily in transportation and collaboration categories. This has progressed from the application service provider (ASP) model from roughly 1998 through 2003, to the on-demand model from approximately 2003 through 2006, to the software as a service (SaaS) model currently in focus today.

Supply chain management 2.0 (SCM 2.0)

Building on globalization and specialization, the term "SCM 2.0" has been coined to describe both changes within supply chains themselves as well as the evolution of processes, methods, and tools to manage them in this new "era". The growing popularity of collaborative platforms is highlighted by the rise of Trade Card's supply chain collaboration platform, which connects multiple buyers and suppliers with financial institutions, enabling them to conduct automated supply-chain finance transactions.

Web 2.0 is a trend in the use of the World Wide Web that is meant to increase creativity, information sharing, and collaboration among users. At its core, the common attribute of Web 2.0 is to help navigate the vast information available on the Web in order to find what is being bought. It is the notion of a usable pathway. SCM 2.0 replicates this notion in supply chain operations. It is the pathway to SCM results, a combination of processes, methodologies, tools, and delivery options to guide companies to their results quickly as the complexity and speed of the supply chain increase due to global competition; rapid price fluctuations; changing oil prices; short product life cycles; expanded specialization; near-, far-, and off-shoring; and talent scarcity.

SCM 2.0 leverages solutions designed to rapidly deliver results with the agility to quickly manage future change for continuous flexibility, value, and success. This is delivered through competency networks composed of best-of-breed supply chain expertise to understand which elements, both operationally and organizationally, deliver results, as well as through intimate understanding of how to manage these elements to achieve the desired results. The solutions are delivered in a variety of options, such as no-touch via business process outsourcing, mid-touch via managed services and software as a service (SaaS), or high-touch in the traditional software deployment model.

New Trents of Logistics

New Trends of Logistics

Learning Objectives

- Understand the new trends of logistics
- Understand the interpretations about green logistics, third party logistics and reverse logistics
- Understand the advantages of enterprises cooperation in the supply chain

Lesson 8.1　Green Logistics

Development and Application of Green Logistics

In common with many other areas of human endeavor, "greenness" became a catchword in the transportation industry in the late 1980s and early 1990s. It grew out of the growing awareness of environmental problems, and in particular with well-publicized issues such as acid rain, CFCs and global warming. [1] The World Commission on Environment and Development Report (1987), with its establishment of environmental sustainability as a goal for international action, gave green issues a significant boost in political and economic arenas. The transportation industry is a major contributor to environmental degradation through its modes, infrastructures and traffics. The developing field of logistics was seen by many as an opportunity for the transportation industry to present a more environmentally-friendly face. [2] During the early 1990s there was an outpouring of studies, reports and opinion pieces suggesting how the environment could be incorporated in the logistics industry. [3] It was reported that the next decade would be "the decade of the environment".

Inserting logistics into recycling and the disposal of waste materials of all kinds, including toxic and hazardous goods, has become a major new market. [4] There are several variants. An important segment is customer-driven, where domestic waste is set aside by home-dwellers for recycling. This has achieved wide popularity in many communities, notably because the public became involved in the process. A second type is where non-recyclable waste, including hazardous materials, is transported for disposal to designated sites. As land fills close to urban areas become scarce, waste has to be transported greater distances to disposal centers. A different approach is where reverse distribution is a continuous embedded process in which the organization (manufacturer or distributor) takes responsibility for the delivery of new products as well as their take-back. [5] This would mean environmental considerations through the whole life-cycle of a product (production, distribution, consumption and disposal). For example, BMW is designing a vehicle whose parts will be entirely recyclable.

The Logistics Industry Which Is Still Not Very "Green"

How the logistics industry has responded to the environmental imperatives is not unexpected, given its commercial and economic imperatives, but by virtually overlooking significant issues, such as pollution, congestion, resource depletion, means that the logistics industry is still not very "green". [6]

Murphy et al. (1994) asked members of the Council for Logistics Management what were the most important environmental issues relating to logistics operations. The two leading issues selected were hazardous waste disposal and solid waste disposal. Two thirds of respondents identified these as being of "great" or "maximum" importance. The least important issues identified were congestion and land use, two elements usually considered to be central importance by environmentalists. When asked to identify the future impact of environmental issues on logistical functions, again waste disposal and packaging were chosen as leading factors. Customer service, inventory control, production scheduling-logistical elements-were seen to have negligible environmental implications.

Discussion and Evaluation

Green logistics is still a long way from being achieved. The environment is not a major preoccupation or priority in the industry itself. The exception is where reverse distribution has opened up new market possibilities based upon growing societal concerns over waste disposal and recycling. Here the environmental benefits are derived rather than direct. The transportation industry itself does not present a greener face, indeed in a literal sense reverse logistics adds further to the traffic load. The manufacturers and domestic waste producers are the ones achieving the environmental credit.

The Government and Green Logistics

It is not question of whether or not the logistics industry will have to present a greener face. Pressures are mounting from a number of directions that are moving all actors and sectors in the economy in the direction of increasing regard for the environment. In some sectors this is already manifest, in others, such as the logistics industry, it is latent. The issue is when and in what form it will be realized.

First is that government action will force a green agenda on the industry, in a top-down approach. Although this appeared as the least desirable outcome form the survey of logistics managers (Murphy et al. , 1994), it is already evident that government intervention and legislation are reaching ever more directly over environmental issues. In Europe there is a growing interest in charging for external costs, as the EU moves towards a "fair and efficient" pricing policy. Cooper et al. (1998) estimate that this could bring about a rise of 20% -25% in transport costs. While there is some evidence that price elastic ties are low in the logistics industry, around -0. 1, the extent of the impact is more likely to be determined by how quickly the tax is applied. A sharp increase in costs could have a more serious impact than a more gradual, phased-in tax. In North America there is a growing interest in road pricing, with the re-appearance of tolls on new high ways and bridges built by the private sector, and by congestion pricing, especially in metropolitan areas, the higher road costs are a clear outcome of policy intervention.

Pricing is only one aspect of government intervention. Legislation controlling the movement of hazardous goods, reducing packaging waste, stipulating the recycled content of products, the mandatory collection and recycling of products are already evident in most jurisdictions. Indeed, it is such legislation that has given rise to the reverse logistics industry. Truck safeties, driver education, limits on driver's time at the wheel, are among many types of government action with a potential to impact the logistics industry.

Conclusions

Further government intervention promoting greater environmental regulation appears inevitable. Global, continental, national and local environmental legislation is already taking hold. For the most part this legislation is popular, and while there is considerable industry resistance to increased regulation, the scientific and popular evidence of environmental problems is mounting. Concerns over congestion, land take, environmental degradation are forcing legislators to be seen to be doing something, even if the full impacts remain unclear. [7]

Notes

1. It grew out of the growing awareness of environmental problems, and in particular with well-publicized issues such as acid rain, CFCs and global warming.

   它(指绿色物流)来自对环境问题的认识,特别是对广为宣传的诸如酸雨、氟氯化碳过量和全球变暖等问题的认识。

2. The developing field of logistics was seen by many as an opportunity for the transportation industry to present a more environmentally-friendly face.

   许多人认为,物流的发展使运输业与环境亲和的景象成为可能。

3. During the early 1990s there was an outpouring of studies, reports and opinion pieces suggesting how the environment could be incorporated in the logistics industry.

   20世纪90年代早期,人们做过大量的研究和报告,提出许多建议,内容都是关于环境与物流产业的整合问题。

4. Inserting logistics into recycling and the disposal of waste materials of all kinds, including toxic and hazardous goods, has become a major new market.

   将物流纳入资源再生和各种废弃物(包括各种毒害物资)的处理,形成重要的新兴市场。

5. A different approach is where reverse distribution is a continuous embedded process in which the organization (manufacturer or distributor) takes responsibility for the delivery of new products as well as their take-back.

   不同的方法是:逆向物流中,经营者(生产商和经销商)不仅负责运送新产品,也负责产品的回收。

6. How the logistics industry has responded to the environmental imperatives is not unexpected, given its commercial and economic imperatives, but by virtually overlooking significant issues, such as pollution, congestion, resource depletion, means that the logistics industry is still not very "green".

   考虑到商业和经济的要求,物流业如何应对环境的需求是可以预料的。但是由于现实生活中忽视了诸如大气污染、交通拥堵、资源消耗等重大问题,物流业仍旧不"绿色"。

7. Concerns over congestion, land take, environmental degradation are forcing legislators to be seen to be doing something, even if the full impacts remain unclear.

   人们对交通堵塞、土地侵占及环境恶化的关注,迫使立法者必须有所作为,尽管这个作为的影响有多大还不甚了了。

Lesson 8. 2   Third Party Logistics

Anyone can store inventory and send it out on a truck. When looking to outsource all or part of a company's logistics function it is important to look for a third party logistics provider with proven expertise. To put it simply, third party logistics or "3PL" is the integration of a company's warehousing, transportation, and related logistics services through an outsourced or "third party" partnership. Nexus provides its clients with powerful logistics solutions involving people, technology and location working together to provide integrated, full service supply chain management.

Another definition is: A business model of logistics service provided by the third party except both the supplier of logistics service and the demander. TPL is also referred to as outsourcing or contractual logistics. What is outsourcing? Outsourcing is the operation that the manufacturers or sales focus on their core competition and make a contract with TPL to get logistics service party or entirely.

Third party logistics is no longer a new concept to us nowadays. Many world famous logistics companies such as UPS, MAERSK LOGISTICS, and TPG are trusted names in the 3PL field.

As its name implies, 3PL is a kind of logistics service provider expert in logistics industry and capable of professional handling of goods. 3PL differs from those transportation and warehouse providers in that they can provide a value adding services with the software they have. In the logistics industry, the hardware is basically the same everywhere. The trucks are the same, the forklifts are the same, and the warehouses are the same. However, what really make the difference is the software assets such as the management know-how, personnel training program, information technology, global service network, etc.

Nexus Distribution has provided quality logistics services since 1980 and operates warehousing and distribution facilities in the Midwest, Southeast, and Northeast regions of the United States in: Chicago, IL; Atlanta, GA; Allentown, PA.

With comprehensive 3PL services; supply chain efficiency, customer satisfaction and brand value growth come together to benefit you. When Nexus effectively bridges the gap between your goods and your customers, we call it "The Triple Win. "

Nexus specializes in crafting efficient and cost effective logistics solutions customized to client's specific needs. This allows you to focus on core competencies and receive a logistical advantage over the competition through the use of Nexus professional third party logistics services.

Advantages of Third Party Logistics include：

- Allows flexibility to expand and contract inventory levels
- Enhanced technology and supply chain visibility
- Improved customer service offerings
- Allows companies to focus on core competencies
- A more strategic and scientific approach to logistics challenges
- Lower or eliminate capital expenditures associated with equipment and facilities.

Two Management Challenges

There are two key management challenges that are central to implementing and operationalising the vision. The first addresses the alignment of the organization to supply chain goals. The second addresses enabling technologies.

Organizational Alignment

Beyond the need to distribute governance within the supply chain, supply chain managers and executives also need to align with peer function. This however is a formidable and long-lasting challenge. Consider the role of the sales function in the supply chain. Sales generate orders and the supply chain fulfils them-a clear interdependency that requires effective cooperation for success. However, sales often request special services, promotions and new product introductions without first checking that the supply capabilities are in place. For supply chain executives, this means additional costs of complexity and risks of lower efficiency. Such "surprises" may increase the risk of missing orders due to lack of responsiveness. Again, customer profitability analysis is a way to address this challenge. The supply chain also needs to align with other business functions—IT for enabling technologies, R&D for preparing for market introduction of new products and marketing for segmentation. Customer profitability analysis suggests that customer segmentation cannot solely be based on marketing criteria, because customer ordering behaviour has a major impact on fulfillment and ultimately on profitability. Marketing and logistics functions therefore need to align around segmentation schemes that are informed by logistics considerations.

Table 8.1 proposes key considerations in order to move the focal firm towards a differentiated supply chain strategy that aligns supply capabilities to major market segments. Note that achievement of the "common objectives" of inventory, quality of service and unit cost forces organizational alignment.

Organizational alignment has less to do with supply chain technology and specialist functional expertise. It has much more to do with communication, engagement and management skills. Launching into a technical conversation with sales may be the worst thing to do when the objective is to gain the commitment of a busy sales person. This implies a need to focus on development of effective supply chain managers of the future.

Table 8.1   Organisational Alignment Considerations

Focus on the end-customer	Organisational issues	Common objectives
Understand the needs of the end-customer. Revisit regularly	Enhance knowledge of the supply chain within the organization	Incentivise purchasing, operations and logistics on: • Total inventory • Quality of service to end customer • Unit cost
Define customer segments jointly between marketing and logistics	Develop human capabilities through selection cross training and switching between functions	Incentivise sales, marketing and logistics on forecast accuracy and quality of service
Process integration is driven by quality of service to the end-customer. Forecasting and planning are tools to this end	Redesign business processes for flexibility and visibility	Ask people to take more risk by continuous stock reduction
Extend integrative thinking to tier 1 customers and suppliers through relationship management	Align the organization to major end-customer segments to strengthen horizontal business processes	Combine internal measures to drive efficiency with external measures (especially quality of service) to drive effectiveness

Enabling Technologies

E-business, ERP and RFID are among dominant enabling technologies. None of these will structurally alter the supply chain, they will, however, need to be used to enhance and enable its effectiveness.

The term e-commerce is usually used by the media to mean businesses trading with customers via the Internet, i. e. , business to consumer. The hype surrounding "e-commerce" has resulted in organizations stampeding to have a website and then asking themselves "what do we do next?" If they are managing to sell to customers then there is the sudden realization that the organization's back-office processes and supply chains have to be aligned to meet a new set of customer expectations.

The Practical Logistics

Most businesses or organizations are likely to take only one of these five functions as their main area of interest. The bus or train operating company, for example, is clearly involved in the design, development, management and maintenance of passenger systems. But that does not mean that the other areas are not relevant to it.

The bus or train operator may also be responsible or facilities such as stations and maintenance depots and is certainly interested in the collection and distribution of information about where its vehicles are and when a particular service will arrive.

Furthermore, he also needs to obtain new vehicles form time to time, as well as fuel and spares for those currently being operated, in addition to a wide range of other supplies (for running the office and catering, for example).

Finally, the operator must ensure the availability of services such as electricity and water.

There are seven functions in logistics system: Storage, Transportation, Distribution, Unloading and Uploading, Flowing producing, Packaging, Information processing. They are transform processing, when system factors are input in logistics transform processing systems, the products involving commodity and service will be output, at the same time, three effectiveness will be finished also. This is illustrated by Figure 8.1.

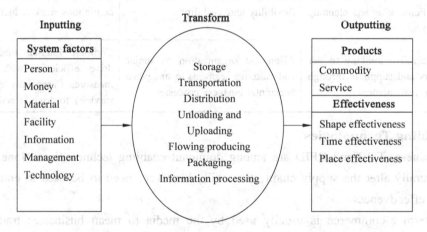

Figure 8.1 The model of inputting and outputting

Lesson 8.3 Reverse Logistics

There are many emerging definitions of reverse logistics. The reason for these varying definitions is that this is one of the fastest developing fields of business logistics, with the result that it continuously changes in scope and significance. We prefer the broad definition below:

Reverse logistics is the management of all the activities involved in goods, demand information, and money flowing in the opposite direction of the primary logistics flow. It involves reducing the generation of waste, as well as managing the collection, transport, disposal, and recycling of both hazardous and non-hazardous waste in a way that minimizes the long-term profitability of the business.

Lesson 8.4 Enterprises Cooperation in the Supply Chain

Cooperation is the essence of supply chain. All members of the supply chain cooperate and band together to create more value than that of each member can do, and to realize the whole value of supply chain, which is far greater than the simple sum of every link value. Cooperative efforts and collaborations between these enterprises make it easier to realize the whole benefit of supply chain and to improve their competitive ability. The relationships among these members or enterprises have direct link to the efficiency and benefit of supply chain. But it is dynamic and unstable, and often causes the instability of supply chain. So it is very important to analyze and management their cooperative relationship. And we have to use game theory to study the cooperative relationship between enterprises on supply chain. By studying the game theory, we try to establish the game model of then-cooperative relationship, and then discuss the existence of equilibrium in this game. We must also resolve two problems: how to establish stable cooperative-relationship and how to make it helpful to supply chain.

Supply chain solutions was told for the sharing of information and set up a "information-sharing systems" model. In order to establish such a system, supply chain enterprises have to integrate network nodes, such as a unified coding. In addition, an important task is to transform the traditional "linear" supply chain model, the establishment of a new Internet-based e-supply chain functions. In this supply chain, a core business at the center of the supply chain, information-sharing platform take on the task, each node can be the core business enterprises to exchange information, to shorten the lead time and improve efficiency. In addition, the integration is also on the traditional supply chain management and new information-sharing model compared to that information-sharing in the supply chain management.

Lesson 8.5   Trends of the Fourth Party Logistics

Fourth Party Logistics is the evolution of supply chain outsourcing. The convergence of technology and the rapid acceleration of e-capabilities have heightened the need for an over-arching integrator for supply chain spanning activities. Fourth party logistics is the shared source of supply chain spanning activity with a client and select teaming partner, under the direction of a 4PLs integrator. In essence, the fourth party logistics provider is a supply chain integrator that assembles and manages the resources, capabilities, and technology of its own organization with those of complementary service providers to deliver a comprehensive supply chain solution.

As conceptually illustrated and examined in the newly released book, Strategic Supply Chain Alignment by John Gattorna, supply chain evolution has occurred, with organizations moving from insourcing to outsourcing to 4PLs arrangements. According to Gattorna, "While outsourcing third party logistics is now accepted by business practice, fourth party logistics is emerging as a breakthrough solution to modern supply chain challenges … to provide maximum overall benefit." The development of 4PLs solutions leverages the capabilities of 3PLs, technology service providers, and business process managers to provide the client organization with greater cross functional integration and broader operational autonomy. Two key distinctions make the concept of 4PLs unique and set it apart from other supply chain outsourcing options available to the market today: 4PLs delivers a comprehensive supply chain solution; and, 4PLs delivers value through the ability to have an impact on the entire supply chain.

A 4PLs supply chain solution should be considered in the broader context of improvements across the entire supply chain, which includes three phases of work: reinvention, transformation, and execution. For a 4PLs to respond effectively to the broad, complicated needs of today's organizations, it needs to deliver comprehensive supply chain solutions that are focused on all elements of supply chain management, yet tailored to specific client needs.

To be successful, a 4PLs leverages a full range of service providers (3PLs, IT providers, contract logistics providers, call centers, etc.) along with the capabilities of the client and its supply chain partners. The 4PLs acts as a single point of interface with the client organization and provides the management of multiple service providers through a teaming partnership or an alliance.

Exercises 8

I. Discuss the following questions.

1. What is the 3PL?
2. What services does the 3PL company often provide?
3. How do you integrate the logistics activities?
4. What is the advantage of 3PL?
5. What is the disadvantage of 3PL?
6. How do you use the advantage of 3PL?

II. Comprehension: True/False/Not Mentioned.

1. The third party logistics provider is a company which provides transportation service only.
2. It costs less to use contract logistics firms than to carry out the same functions in-house.
3. The third party logistics company usually offers consulting service to the firms.
4. The expertise and experience provided by 3PL companies are useful to their clients.
5. The 3PL providers must accomplish all the provided services by themselves.
6. By outsourcing logistics activities, firms can save on capital investments.
7. The use of 3PL is not helpful to building a close customer relationship.
8. Problems will certainly rise in cooperation with the 3PL companies.

III. Fill in the blanks with the following words in the boxes, and change the forms if necessary.

| facilitate | define | outsource | multiple | integrated |
| pursue | in-house | result from | expertise | economies of scale |

1. The Internet has been used to _____ the flow of information between 3PL companies and their clients.
2. Speed and cost are key drivers for our customers seeking to _____ their 3PL logistics activities.
3. The _____ and experience from 3PL providers are vital for some companies which are not familiar with the international regulations.
4. The 3PL companies can achieve substantial cost saving due to _____.
5. A 3PL companies usually can provide _____ logistics services for their clients.
6. Manufacturers usually face decisions whether to make the product _____ or not.

7. Clients generally hope that 3PL suppliers can provide _____ services.

8. Sometimes it is difficult to _____ a term in a few words since it usually has too many things.

9. Cost reduction _____ outsourcing is not so obvious, and it varies from industry to industry.

10. Cost saving is one of the important goals for managers to _____.

Ⅳ. Translate the following sentences into Chinese.

1. The third part logistics industry has entered a period of rapid expansion and transformation.

2. We can increase your profits with our expertise in logistics management.

3. We will keep you up to date on both domestic and international shipping requirements.

4. Third-party logistics providers are commonly classified into the asset-based and the non-asset-based companies.

5. Sometimes the lowest cost is not necessarily the best choice.

Ⅴ. Translate the following sentences into English.

1. 我们的目标是帮助你公司实现顾客满意并提高利润。

2. 合作在第三方物流的应用中非常重要。

3. 进行成本比较时,机会成本也需要考虑在内。

4. 第三方物流有其优点,但并非适合所有的公司。

5. 理解第三方物流的本质对是否使用第三方物流有重要意义。

Ⅵ. Answer the questions according to the text of this chapter.

1. What new trends of logistics are coming in the modern era? Please make some discussion about this topic.

2. What is 4PLs? Please give an example of 4PLs company in your practice.

Logistics Situational Dialogues 8

(*Mr. Wang, the logistics officer in a factory, is talking with Miss Zhang, the customer service representative in an international logistics company.*)

Zhang: Hello, what can I do for you?

Wang: Hello. Our company is growing fast in recent years. So we need a logistics company helping us distribute goods to many countries.

Zhang: Well, that is just our strength. Our company provides comprehensive international logistics services.

Wang: Can you introduce your company in brief?

Zhang: Sure. Our company is one of the leading logistics companies in the world, and our global network can help you manage your goods efficiently.

Wang: What are specific features of your service?

Zhang: Ok. Our shipping service runs 7 days a week, and it is more time guaranteed than any other company.

Wang: How about your tracking service? Our customers sometimes want to know exactly when the goods can reach their warehouse.

Zhang: That's quite simple. You may track your goods anywhere in the world just on our website.

Wang: Since our business is expanding, many international rules are new to us.

Zhang: We can also provide many value-added services. I think it will be very useful to your company.

Wang: What are they?

Zhang: Such as delivery confirmation, delivers the COD package and collects from the consignee.

Wang: Great, we often use this kind of method, since lots of customers are new.

Zhang: Ok. We also provide information based service. It can make your international business easier.

Wang: Really? How it works?

Zhang: We provide trade information about different countries, such as trade agreement, customs regulations, duty rates, etc.

Wang: Yes. They are very important to us.

Zhang: Usually non-compliance with these government regulations can lead to potential fines, or legal actions.

Wang: Exactly.

Zhang: Our strength can help to turn your international trade into a competitive advantage.

Wang: Great. I hope we can have a long-term partnership in future.

Zhang: You can count on us.

Dialog Exercise 8

John is a professor of a university, Tom is a college student. They are talking about the new trends of logistics areas. The useful words which may be involved in the dialog are as follows. Please try to finish the dialog.

the third party logistics service	第三方物流服务
the fourth party logistics	第四方物流
green logistics	绿色物流
integration of supply chain	供应链整合(一体化)
cooperation of strategy	战略合作
reverse logistics	逆向物流
circular economy	循环经济

Case Study 8

Green Logistics the Walmart Way

Why sustainability best practices are part of the retailer's supply chain DNA.

Every once in a while, a company comes along that separates from the herd and differentiates itself through leadership, vision, innovation, and a capacity to change the marketplace. Walmart is one of those companies.

"Early in our journey toward sustainability, it was clear that any efforts we undertook had to make good business sense," explains Jeff Smith, senior director of logistics maintenance and purchasing, Walmart. "We have never been interested in trying to create an image of sustainability just for the sake of the image. Every idea is challenged from a business standpoint, and has to demonstrate that it is a good use of our resources."

In 2009, when Walmart announced it was introducing a sustainability index to evaluate product supplier performance, it pushed the needle forward in a seismic way. Others have innovated more, and some have pushed carbon-less further, but no company has spread the gospel of green quite like Walmart.

Going Green In A Big Way

The five-and-dime thrift shop that Sam Walton built into the world's largest retailer is changing expectations in a big way. Consider that Walmart is succeeding where many governments have failed: legislating behavioral change by raising awareness, facilitating best practices, sharing information, and holding suppliers and partners accountable—all within the framework of sound business principles.

Green is not a contrived part of the business that preys on consumer conscience at the store shelf, then fails to deliver at the loading dock. Business strategy and sustainability go hand-in-hand.

For Elizabeth Fretheim, Walmart's director of business strategy and sustainability, the retailer's ethos is an augmented reality.

"Within the transportation function, for example, we want to accomplish three goals: fill every trailer to capacity; drive those trailers the fewest miles possible; and use the most efficient equipment," she explains. "All these efforts drive sustainability, as well as operational efficiency."

Walmart's green strategy is centrally organized; it has a clear roadmap for where it wants to go. In its quest for a 100-percent renewable energy power supply, for example, the company aims to procure seven billion kilowatt hours of renewable energy globally every year by 2021, and reduce by 20 percent the kilowatt-hour-per-square-foot energy intensity required to power its buildings globally during the same period.

Thriving on Collaboration

With that direction, Walmart has made a concerted effort over the past several years to put in place organizational structures that ensure broad support for various business units, and that each unit has the autonomy to pursue projects that support these goals. Such an approach thrives on collaboration.

"We need to be well-aligned with buyers to ensure we can fill trailers both inbound and outbound," says Fretheim. "Without that collaboration, it is difficult for us to achieve our goals. Even though our metrics are logistics-focused, what we are trying to do affects the entire company."

Smith recalls attending a recent training class for senior directors where they focused on collaboration to help achieve strategic execution.

"Sustainability is an ideal gateway to establishing relationships internally with other business units and externally with business partners," he says. "The sustainability projects I work on drive collaboration, which can then be leveraged in many other areas of the business. "

The organization is filled with examples of this type of collaboration-from the real estate division's efforts in developing renewable energy projects and vetting new technologies, to the logistics department testing and implementing the use of hydrogen fuel cells in the warehouse. Everyone is accountable for Walmart's performance.

"For Walmart to be successful, we rely on associates at every level to help us not only drive the strategy, but also raise new ideas," Fretheim says. "I need people on the DC dock to tell me when trailers are coming in less than full. Even though I have sustainability in my title, a lot of people within Walmart carry that responsibility. "

A Corporate Culture of Green

Walmart's success is no doubt partly attributed to its leadership. CEO Mike Duke, an engineer by trade, relishes detail. Speaking at Walmart's semi-annual Sustainability Milestones meeting in July 2009, Duke stated: "The engineer in me likes data. I like research. I like metrics. More than anything, I love an elegant process for arriving at innovative solutions that are both profitable and sustainable. "

It's not hard to see the impetus for much of what Walmart has endeavored to do. And the company's success demonstrates the importance of having executive-level buy in. Equally important is growing an organizational culture that embraces the CEO's mission. Walmart employees are an integral part of its sustainability program, and the company invests in their development.

For example, the company engineered its My Sustainability Plan program, with the guidance of consultancy BBMG, to provide a framework for individuals and organizations to augment their respective well-being. It provides a tailored scorecard to help users incorporate sustainability into their own lives. It's pragmatic in the sense that developing happier employees reduces costly turnover. But it also contributes to a happier shopping experience for the customer. It's the essence of the iconic Walmart greeter or yellow smiley-face sign.

"As associates bring these sustainable best practices into their personal lives, we believe they'll carry them back to work—if you get into the habit of turning off lights at home, you will do the same when leaving a meeting room," says Fretheim.

In this manner, employees become invested in green. When you consider the breadth of Walmart's global workforce—2. 2 million people in nearly 30 countries—that's a sizable group of disciples living and breathing Walmart's word.

Walmart's mission, though, extends well beyond the enterprise—and that's where the company has earned its reputation. The much-ballyhooed supplier sustainability index introduced in 2009—which measures a product's sustainability using various metrics across nearly 200 product categories and more than 100,000 global suppliers—has some aggressive targets.

By 2017, Walmart expects to buy 70 percent of the goods it sells in U. S. stores and U. S. Sam's Clubs from suppliers that use the index to evaluate and share the sustainability of their products. Taking it one step further, the company hopes to begin using these same standards to influence the design of its U. S. private brand products.

Spreading the Word, Worldwide

The Walmart Foundation has also provided a $2-million grant to help support the launch of The Sustainability Consortium—a group of green-minded global companies—in China, to help provide training and develop partnerships that will improve sustainability in-country.

Those are future aspirations. The returns are equally bold.

In 2012, the EPA Green Power Partnership recognized Walmart as the largest on-site green power generator in the United States, with more than 200 solar projects across the country. Renewable energy now provides 21 percent of Walmart's electricity globally. In 2012, the company delivered 297 million more cases while driving 11 million fewer miles, increasing fleet efficiency by 10 percent in 2012 alone—and by 80 percent since 2005. Walmart also fulfilled its 2009 pledge to reduce greenhouse gas emissions 20 percent by 2012—one year early.

Walmart's achievements resonate internally. But they are more persuasive beyond the organization.

"Few companies have the size and scale to communicate with and potentially influence other companies," says Smith. "We have a platform to show our peers where we see success both as a business and as a responsible corporate citizen, then encourage and challenge them to do the same. "

The sustainability index is the embodiment of this advocacy. It provides a platform for companies to jump from and climb back on as they follow their own unique green journeys. Many companies have already made significant progress pushing sustainability projects, but have no means to benchmark performance.

"Sustainability can be a complex subject," explains Fretheim. "Trying to understand if a process is greener than what you're already doing—when you're trying to drive that down into every level of your business-is difficult. The business understands the business goals. It's more difficult to perform sustainability assessments at every level. "

The index has become a de-facto standard for businesses to follow. If nothing else, it gives partners an idea of the types of questions they should be asking themselves, or areas of the business where they should focus attention—whether it's renewable energies, energy efficiency, or waste reduction.

"The idea is to help suppliers understand how they can improve their logistics functions—not only from their plant to our DC or store, but also back through their supply chain to raw material sources," Fretheim says.

Christopher Schraeder, senior manager of sustainability communications for Walmart, goes one step further, suggesting, "It starts to shift the conversation from 'Should we be doing this?' to 'How do we do this?'"

In time, the expectation is these suppliers will return the favor and say, "Hey Walmart, look at what we're doing."

Owning Green

One challenge organizations encounter as they chase sustainability gains is distilling the true value of their investments so they can demonstrate ROI to the CFO and continue to raise expectations and inject capital in new projects. If business and sustainability strategy aren't aligned, that task is difficult.

At Walmart, the two objectives are firmly knotted. One supports the other. An efficient supply chain is a green one—and vice versa. Everything is measured and benchmarked, and the company goes to great lengths to track ROI on each investment.

"If a sustainable initiative is good for the business in general—and we believe this is true—then each project we implement supports our business, and empowers our efforts to be more sustainable," says Smith.

Making A Positive Impact

There is no downside when it comes to sustainability, provided companies approach it with the right motivations and perspective. "Based on the positive impact our efforts have had on our business, you'd have to question why companies would choose not to engage in this area to improve their performance when the opportunity is before them," says Smith.

Walmart's objective is to make sustainable best practices a standard course of doing business—so companies will eventually have no other option than to follow a new status quo. Bringing customers into the fold will require a similar metamorphosis. Consumers today have a choice. When that decision pits cost against conscience, especially in today's economy, the answer for many is simple—with no regrets.

"We don't think our customers should have to make a choice or trade-off between a product that is sustainable and a product that's not," Schraeder concludes. "We're trying to look at how we conduct our business, work with suppliers, and approach and view our entire supply chain to make sure that every product we put on our shelves is driven by sustainable practices."

Answer the following questions after reading the case

1. What is Walmart's green strategy?

2. Describe the major points of Walmart's corporate culture of Green.

3. How does Walmart spread its green idea worldwide?

4. What kinds of impact has Walmart made on other companies?

小贴士

物流小常识

"商务谈判三部曲"即谈判的步骤应分为申明价值、创造价值和克服障碍三个进程。

1. 申明价值。谈判双方彼此应充分沟通各自的利益需要,申明能够满足对方需要的方法与优势所在。此阶段的关键步骤是弄清对方的真正需求,因此其主要的技巧就是多向对方提出问题,探寻对方的实际需求;与此同时,也要根据情况申明我方的利益所在。

2. 创造价值。谈判双方需要想方设法去寻求更佳的方案,为谈判各方找到最大的利益,这一步骤就是创造价值。

3. 克服障碍。谈判的障碍一般来自于两个方面:一个是谈判双方彼此利益存在冲突;另一个是谈判者自身在决策程序上存在障碍。前一种障碍是需要双方按照公平合理的客观原则来协调利益;后者就需要谈判无障碍的一方主动去帮助另一方能够顺利决策。

Supplementary Reading 8

12 Trends that are Shaping the Future of Logistics

World exports as a percentage of global GDP showed a continuous growth trend from the mid-eighties of the last century, until 2008. Since then the growth stopped.

Another indicator for trade, global capital flows between countries, achieved its highest point seven years ago. But times are changing. Growth will still be there, if you know where to find it.

According to McKinsey, approximately 600 cities are likely to realise 65% of the global GDP growth by the mid-twenties. By then, the growing cities are predicted to add up to $30 trillion to the world economy. Incomes in developing economies never rose faster or at a greater scale in history, and about a billion people are becoming part of consuming classes in roughly ten years' time.

Macro-economic changes and shifts in trade patterns have their impact on global supply chains. They provide opportunities as well as challenges. Let's have a closer look at some developments in logistics that are directly or indirectly caused by changes in trade patterns, in GDP growth or in customer behaviour.

- **Growth Patterns**: Growth in the logistics industry is no longer driven by exports from Asia to North America and from Asia to Europe. It will come from elsewhere, and will be more fragmented, more unpredictable and more volatile. Economic and population growth will be increasingly centred in cities. Infrastructure is becoming a major determinant for growth.
- **Flexibility**: Meeting consumer's requirements at multiple locations with multiple transport modes at different times requires a flexible supply chain that can adapt easily to unexpected changes and circumstances.
- **Globalisation**: International, mature and emerging markets have become a part of the overall business growth strategy for many companies. Going "international" has become the standard and logistic solution providers need to enable that trend.
- **Near Shoring**: As labour costs in Asia and transportation costs rise, increasing amounts of manufacturing are being brought closer to the end user.
- **Multi-channel Sourcing**: End-consumers increasingly source via multiple channels, ranging from brick & mortar shops to e-commerce. The logistics industry needs to support multi-channel strategies of their customers.
- **Information Technology**: The growing complexity and dynamism of supply chains requires increasingly advanced Information Technology solutions.
- **Continuity**: To be able to secure speed to market and to reduce risk of delays, alternative transport modes and routes are required to support the continuing trend of outsourcing of logistics services.
- **Sustainability**: Customers increasingly prefer products that are made and sourced in "the right way"; minimising business' social, economic and environmental impact on society and enhancing positive effects.
- **Compliance**: Anti-bribery and corruption legislation is having an increasing impact on supply chains, since multinational companies demand that no facilitation payments are made during the export of their goods, yet still seek to source from low cost countries, which are often also at the bottom of Transparency International's global

corruption index.

- **Partnerships**: Manufacturers continuously search for supply chain innovations and gains through partnerships with logistic service providers.
- **End-to-end Visibility**: Complete visibility of the entire supply chain aspires to achieve true demand-driven planning, allowing efficient response to changes in sourcing, supply, capacity and demand.
- **Complexity**: Supply chains are becoming increasingly complex and dynamic with sourcing locations being changed increasingly quickly and purchase orders becoming smaller and more frequent.

These developments will have their effect on day-to-day logistics, and companies will need to prepare for "the new normal" in supply chain management. With all these changes, staying up-to-date on the latest trends in logistics is more important than ever.

Part Two
Extra–curricular Readings

Chapter 9

International Logistics

Lesson 9.1   Containerization

Container Transportation(集装箱运输)

With the expansion of international trade, the container service has become popular. The transportation of international trading is nowadays frequently carried out in containers. The usage of containers provides a highly efficient form of transport by road, rail and air though its fullest benefits are felt in shipping, where cost may be reduced by as much as one half. [1]

Sizes of Containers(集装箱的尺寸)

Containers are constructed of metal and are of standards lengths from ten to forty feet. [2] 20-foot container and 40-foot container have become more common. The 20-foot container has become the standard unit of measure quoted in terms of "TEUs" or twenty-foot equivalent units. One 40-foot container equates to two TEUs.

the Advantage of Containers(集装箱的优势)

The advantage of containers from the shipper's point of view is that freight can be loaded and the box sealed before it leaves the warehouse. The goods themselves are not touched again until the customer receives the container and opens it.

- There is no risk of goods getting lost or mislaid in transit.
- Manpower in handling is greatly reduced, with lower costs and less risk of damage.
- Overall transportation cost can be reduced since container shipment offers the economy of mass transportation and minimizes the need for transshipment. [3]
- Usage of container reduces the time ships spend in port and greatly increase the number of sailings.
- Temperature-controlled containers are provided for the types of cargo that need them.

the Disadvantage of Containers(集装箱的劣势)

Containers have a restricted application in inland transportation. Because containers on ships must be stacked, they must be sturdy in construction. [4] In turn, this makes them heavy-too heavy for road transport since they unduly restrict payloads.

the FCL Service(整箱服务)

If the exporter intends to fill a full container load (FCL), the forwarder of shipping line will be prepared to send an empty container to the exporter for loading. The container is sealed with the carrier's seal, this is sometimes done by the shipper.

the LCL Service(拼箱服务)

If the cargo is less than a full container load (LCL), the exporter sends it to the container freight stations (CFSs), where it will be consolidated with the goods of other exporters in a group container.

Inter-modal Transportation(多式联运)

Inter-modal transportation refers to the movement of a shipment from origin to destination utilizing two or more different modes of transport. It involves a variety of shipment, transshipment and warehousing activities. The whole intent of inter-modal transport is to allow the shipper to take advantage of the best characteristics of all modes: the convenience of road, the long-distance movement efficiency of rail, and the capacity of ocean shipping. Therefore, inter-modal transportation offers the opportunity to combine modes and find a less costly alternative than a single transport mode. [5] Numerous technical improvements, such as river/sea shipping and better rail/road integration, have been established to reduce interchange cost, but containerization remains the most significant achievement so far. [6]

New words and terms

container	n.	容器,集装箱
containerization	n.	集装箱化
expansion	n.	扩充,开展
construct	v.	建造,建立
quote	v.	引用,提出,提供
mass	adj.	大规模的,集中的
restrict	v.	限制,约束
application	n.	应用,运用
stack	v.	堆放,堆叠

sturdy	*adj.*	坚固的,坚定的
unduly	*adv.*	过度地,不适当的
fill	*v.*	装满,充满,填充
forwarder	*n.*	货运公司,货运代理商
seal	*n.*	封铅,封条,印;v. 封,密封
consolidate	*v.*	装货,配货
origin	*n.*	出发地,生产地
destination	*n.*	目的地
utilize	*v.*	利用
characteristic	*n.*	特性,特征
convenience	*n.*	便利,方便
efficiency	*n.*	效率,功效
capacity	*n.*	容量,装载量
combine	*v.*	(使)结合
alternative	*n.*	二中择一,可供选择的办法
integration	*n.*	综合
significant	*adj.*	有意义的,重大的
achievement	*n.*	成绩,成就,完成,达到
carry out		履行,执行
standard unit		标箱
TEUs = twenty-foot equivalent units		20 英尺的标箱
equate to		相当于,相等于
temperature-controlled		温控
FCL = a full container load		整箱服务
LCL = less than a full container load		拼箱服务
CFSs = container freight stations		集装箱运输站
inter-modal transportation		多式联运
so far		迄今为止

Notes

1. The usage of containers provides a highly efficient form of transport by road, rail and air though its fullest benefits are felt in shipping, where cost may be reduced by as much as one half.

   集装箱的使用为公路、铁路和航空提供了一种高效的运输方式,虽然它的全部益处在海运中体现得最淋漓尽致,在海运中集装箱的使用可以将成本降低一半。

2. Containers are constructed of metal and are of standards lengths from ten to forty feet.

集装箱由金属制造,包括10英尺到40英尺各种标准尺寸。

3. Overall transportation cost can be reduced since container shipment offers the economy of mass transportation and minimizes the need for transshipment.

由于使用了集装箱运输,提供了运输的规模经济并将转运需求降到最低,全面的运输成本得以降低。

4. Because containers on ships must be stacked, they must be sturdy in construction.

因为在船上集装箱必须叠放,所以必须建造的足够坚固。

5. Therefore, inter-modal transportation offers the opportunity to combine modes and find a less costly alternative than a single transport mode.

因此,与单一运输方式相比,多式联运将适当的运输方式结合在一起为降低成本提供了机会。

6. Numerous technical improvements, such as river/sea shipping and better rail/road integration, have been established to reduce interchange cost, but containerization remains the most significant achievement so far.

许多技术进步,如水运/海运和更完善的铁路/公路的结合,使得运输方式转换时成本降低,但是迄今为止,集装箱化运输仍是意义最重大的进步。

Exercises 9(1)

Ⅰ. **Pair work**：**Discuss the following questions.**

1. What is containerization?

2. What basic sizes containers have?

3. What are the advantages of container transportation?

4. What is the multi-modal transportation?

5. Why a shipper would choose multi-modal transportation?

6. What is the FCL?

7. What is the LCL?

8. Why container is suitable to inter-modal transportation?

Ⅱ. **Close test.**

Containerization

The ___1___ cargo transport volume has been on the rise together with the world's economic growth since the third quarter of last decade. Also we are living in a rapidly ___2___ industry society. There have been a number of major changes in the shipping __3__ , but the one that has the most far-reaching __4__ is the development of the container system.

This is referred to as "containerization", by which various general cargoes are stuffed __5__ big containers for the purpose of quick loading on __6__ ships and unloading from ships both for inbound and __7__ transport. By this measure, loading and unloading time at __8__ is reduced to one tenth of the time length on the average compared with the conventional handling method where general cargoes were, being much diversified in __9__ and size, handled on a two-ton sling unit basis.

Containerization has also implemented quick transit between ships and other modes of transportation, such as road and railway transport. Therefore, container transport is __10__ efficient not only for the marine transportation but also for the inland transportation.

1. a. international   b. bulk   c. inventory   d. domestic

2. a. changing   b. changed   c. changeable   d. exchange

3. a. enterprise   b. company   c. terminal   d. industry

4. a. aftermath   b. influence   c. suggestion   d. impact

5. a. from   b. for   c. into   d. down

6. a. board   b. our   c. bond   d. behind

7. a. side   b. bound   c. outbound   d. bounding

8. a. point   b. berth   c. port   d. terminal

9. a. color   b. type   c. material   d. shape

10. a. high   b. highly   c. far   d. quite

Ⅲ. Translate the following sentences into Chinese.

1. Inter-modal transportation is seen as a solution that could work in certain situations.

2. Temperature-controlled containers are provided for the types of cargo that need them.

3. With the improvement of international trade, the container service has become popular.

4. Before containerization, economies of scale were difficult to achieve with break-bulk cargo.

5. Maersk Sealand is one of the largest liner shipping companies in the world, serving customers all over the globe.

Ⅳ. Translate the following sentences into English.

1. 多式联运提供了降低物流成本的机会。

2. 集装箱的使用极大地提高了运输效率。

3. 迄今为止,集装箱化运输仍是意义最重大的进步。

4. 整箱运输的费率低,你最好整箱运输货物。

5. 集装箱的使用降低了货物损坏的风险。

Dialogue 9(1)   Talking about the Unloading Port

(*The following is a conversation between the Mr. Geng, the clerk in a logistics company and Mike, a customer of the company.*)

Geng: Mike, are you tired today after your visit to the Great Wall yesterday?

Mike: No, not at all. I am very interested in the visit.

Geng: What are you impressions about the Great Wall?

Mike: It's just too great, and it has made an everlasting impression on me.

Geng: Well, do you think now we should talk a bit about the port of discharge?

Mike: I'm all ready.

Geng: Our offer is CIF European main ports. The time of shipment is August. What's your unloading port please?

Mike: Hamburg.

Geng: But as I know, sailings to Europe in August only call at London and Antwerp.

Mike: Our customers are all located near Hamburg. It's not reasonable to have the goods unloaded at London.

Geng: I see.

Mike: We do hope you'll contact the shipping company once again to make sure that the shipment will arrive in Hamburg.

Geng: Sure and I will do that, there is a vessel sailing to Hamburg in July. But I'm afraid it's too late to book the shipping space.

Mike: Please try your best, and I trust that you can make it.

Geng: All right. But the question we have at the moment is whether the manufactures can get the goods ready in July.

Mike: You can contact the factory again to hurry them up. It will be marvelous if the goods can be shipped in July.

Geng: I'll certainly try my best, but if we fail to do that, there will be another chance. The next early available chance will be the Hamburg ships in September. There will be two of them. What do you think if the shipment is effected in September, a month later than the schedule?

Mike: We'd like the shipment to be made in July, but if nothing can be done about it, the goods can be shipped in September. There should be no more changes in the schedule, anyway.

Geng: I'm sure there will be no more changes.

New words and terms

impression	*n.*	印象,感想
everlasting	*adj.*	永恒的,持久地
Hamburg	*n.*	汉堡(欧洲主要港口)
Antwerp	*n.*	安特卫普(欧洲主要港口)
reasonable	*adj.*	合理的
marvelous	*adj.*	令人惊异的,不可思议的
effect	*v.*	实现,达到
schedule	*n.*	确定时间
port of discharge		卸货港
CIF		到岸价(成本,保险加运费)

Notes

1. Our offer is CIF European main ports.
   我们的报价是欧洲主要港口的到岸价。

2. It's not reasonable to have the goods unloaded at London.
   在伦敦港卸货不太合理。

Exercises 9(2)

Ⅰ. **Oral Practice**: Practice the above dialogue with your partner until you can learn the lines by heart.

Ⅱ. **Team work**: Make up a dialogue according to the following situation and practice it with your partner.

Situation:

Jerry is a clerk of a logistics company. Now he is talking with his customer about the loading and unloading port.

Tips:

1. We should talk about the port of loading and discharging.

2. I think Dalian is suitable to us.

3. What's your unloading port please?

4. We'd better have a brief talk about the loading port.

5. We'd like to designate Shanghai as the loading port because it is near the producing area.

6. As most of our clients are near London, we'd like to appoint London as the unloading port.

7. An early reply from you will help us to speed up shipment.

8. You may depend on what I promise you.

Ⅲ. Write an e-mail to your customer, telling them about goods transportation.
Contents：

1. 就货物装运推迟之事进行道歉。

2. 由于恶劣天气造成装运推迟。

3. 保证 3 日内再次发运。

Ⅳ. Read the dialogue and translate into Chinese.

A：Hello. Welcome to Bumbles.

B：Can I speak to James Chen?

A：Speaking.

B：This is Zhaoyang Electronics Co. of Suzhou.

A：Have you received the request from the Shanghai Hongqiao Customs House regarding the survey of your cargo?

B：Yes. But is it a condition to go through the custom clearance procedures?

A：Why, of course. The Customs House must make sure that the goods you sent to be exported conform to what is stated on the airway bill.

B：But the consignment is very small, only 100 kilograms of CDs.

A：It is the rule that each and every consignment for export shall be inspected before leaving China.

B：Can you not put in a word for us? You are our freight forwarder for so many years and …

A：Sorry. But that is not the rules of the game. You had better send someone here as soon as possible. Otherwise, warehousing expense will incur.

B：OK, if I must, I must. Xiao Wang from our export department will be with you this afternoon.

A：I will be in my office then. Bye-bye.

B：Bye-bye.

Lesson 9.2 Main Logistics Documents

Introduction to Logistics Documents(物流单据介绍)

Logistics documents refer to all documents involve in the course of logistics. Generally speaking, logistics documents contain two kinds of documents: cargo documents and transport documents. [1] They are applied for various purposes in the whole process of transport of goods. The following paragraphs are introduction to bill of lading, air waybill, packing list, commercial invoice, insurance policy and certificate of origin.

Bill of Lading(提单)

One of the most important documents in maritime is the bill of lading (abbreviated to B/ L). It is used primarily in international sales of goods where the carriage of goods is by sea. It must be presented at the port of final destination by the importer in order to claim goods. [2] A B/L is nearly always prepared on a pre-printed form. Whatever its form, a B/L may contain some main elements, such as quantity of goods, accurate cargo description and condition, date of the bill of lading, names of shipper and consignee, party to be notified, name of vessel, ports of loading and discharge, terms and conditions of carriage and payment of freight. [3]

The functions of the maritime B/L can be classified into three categories:

- a receipt for the goods shipped
- evidence of the contract of carriage
- document of title for the goods[4]

Air Waybill(空运运单)

An air waybill is a form of B/L used for the air transport of goods. It is an evidence of a transportation contract. The air waybill is approximately equivalent to the sea B/L, but it is not a document of title to goods or a negotiable document. [5]

Each air waybill has three originals and at least 6 copies. [6] The air waybill must be accurately completed, clear forwarding instruction must be given to the airline or agent. The air waybill is used as a receipt of the goods for dispatch and evidence of the contract of carriage between the carrier and the consignor.

Packing List(装箱单)

A packing list is a document prepared by the shipper at the time the goods are shipped, giving details of the invoice, buyer, consignee, country of origin, vessel or flight details, port or airport of loading and discharge, place of delivery, shipping marks, container number, weight and cubic of goods, etc. Its prime purpose is to give an inventory of the shipped goods and is required by the customs clearance.

Commercial Invoice(商业发票)

The commercial invoice is a document offered by the seller to the buyer regarding the sold goods. The commercial invoice is issued by the exporter. It provides details of a transaction between the importer and the exporter. Its main function is a check for the importer against charges and delivery. Besides, it used as determination of value of goods for the assessment of customs duties, preparation for consular documentation, insurance claims and packing purposes.[7]

Insurance Policy(保险单)

An insurance policy is a document confirming insurance of cargo and indicating the type and amount of insurance coverage. This document is usually issued to the party buying the insurance.

Certificate of Origin(原产地证书)

A certificate of origin is a document issued by a certifying authority such as a chamber of commerce in the exporter's country stating the country of origin of the goods. It is usually required by countries to set the appropriate duties for the imports.

New words and terms

cargo	n.	货物
invoice	n.	发票
carriage	n.	运输,运费
destination	n.	目的地
element	n.	要素,成分,元素
description	n.	描述,形容
consignee	n.	收货人,收件人
category	n.	种类,分类
approximately	adv.	近似的,大约
equivalent	adj.	相当于,相等于
negotiable	adj.	可流通的,可转让的
dispatch	n.	派遣,发送
consignor	n.	委托者,发货人,交付人
cubic	n.	体积
transaction	n.	处理,交易

assessment	*n.*	评估,估价
insurance	*n.*	保险,保险业
authority	*n.*	权威,权力机关
appropriate	*adj.*	适当的,恰当的
duty	*n.*	义务,责任,关税
bill of lading(B/L)		提单
air waybill		空运运单
packing list		装箱单
insurance policy		保险单
certificate of origin		原产地
port of loading		装货港
port of destination		目的港
document of title		物权凭证
customs clearance		通关,清关
chamber of commerce		商会

Notes

1. Generally speaking, logistics documents contain two kinds of documents: cargo documents and transport documents.

    通常来讲,物流单据包括两类单据:货物单据和运输单据。

2. It must be presented at the port of final destination by the importer in order to claim goods.

    (提单)是进口商为在目的地港领取货物时提交的单据。

3. Whatever its form, a bill of lading may contain some main elements, such as quantity of goods, accurate cargo description and condition, date of the bill of lading, names of shipper and consignee, party to be notified, name of vessel, ports of loading and discharge, terms and conditions of carriage and payment of freight.

    不论形式如何,提单可能包括一些主要的要素,例如:货物的数量、商品准确的名称和状况、提单的日期、托运人和收货人的名称,通知方、船名、装/卸货港、运输合同的条款和运费的支付方式。

4. document of title for the goods

    货物的物权凭证

5. The air waybill is approximately equivalent to the sea B/L, but it is not a document of title to goods or a negotiable document.

空运运单的内容与海运提单大概相似,但是空运运单不是物权凭证,也不能转让和流通。

6. Each air waybill has three originals and at least 6 copies.

每份空运运单有三份正本以及至少六份副本。

7. Besides, it used as determination of value of goods for the assessment of customs duties, preparation for consular documentation, insurance claims and packing purposes.

除此之外,商业发票还用作货物价值评估、关税估价、准备领事文件、保险索赔以及包装目的。

Exercises 9(3)

I. Team work: Discuss the following questions.

1. How many kinds of shipping documents do you know?

2. What is B/L?

3. What are the functions of B/L?

4. What is air waybill?

5. What is the purpose of packing list?

6. How many types of invoices do you know?

II. Fill in the blanks with the following words in the boxes, and change the forms if necessary.

insurance	receipt	cargo	destination	function
amount	document	transport	negotiable	exporter

1. A certificate of origin is a _____ issued by a certifying authority.

2. The shipping company will tell you when your _____ is loaded on board the ship.

3. Logistics documents contain two kinds of documents: cargo documents and _____ documents.

4. B/L must be presented at the port of final _____ by the importer.

5. B/L is a _____ for the goods shipped.

6. Air waybill is not a _____ document.

7. The bill of lading performs a number of _____.

8. The commercial invoice is issued by the _____.

9. An insurance policy is a document confirming _____ of cargo.

10. An insurance policy is a document indicating the type and _____ of insurance coverage.

III. Translate the following sentences into Chinese.

1. One of the most important documents in maritime trade is the bill of lading.

2. A cargo manifest provides information regarding cargoes on board.

3. The shipping note is a commitment on the shipper to ship the goods and serves as the basis for the preparation of the bill of lading.

4. The main parties on a bill of lading are shipper, consignee, notify party and carrier.

5. A mate's receipt is the receipt issued by the carrier in the acknowledgement of the goods received on board.

IV. Translate the following sentences into English.

1. 所有的正本提单都是可流通的。

2. 提单是运输合同的证明。

3. 在国际物流中需要大量单据。

4. 大幅收据随后被换发为提单。

5. 提货单是由承运人或其代理人签发的。

Dialogue 9(2) Change of Port of Destination

(*Jane is talking to the customer, Wang Jian, who came into the office in a hurry.*)

Jane: Hey, Mr. Wang, what's the matter? Why are you wet through?

Wang: I have something urgent to ask you. But as it is raining so hard, I couldn't find any taxi.

Jane: Then tell quickly so that you can go home and change into dry clothes.

Wang: I have just received a fax from our customer in Germany, who wants us to change destination of our cargo.

Jane: What cargo?

Wang: The dresses to Toulouse. I remember the consignment consists of twenty TEUs. [1]

Jane: Where do you wish the cargo to go now?

Wang: Our customer now wishes to land it at Marseilles. Can you do it?

Jane: Let me see. (After checking his computer) The ship that carries your containers is still at Suez, waiting for the transit of the Suez Canal. It will not pass the canal in 48 hours. We can send a cable to the ship and the port of Marseilles and tell them.

Wang：Thank you very much.

Jane：But I must have the three original Bills of Lading. [2]

Wang：Oh, they are now on their way to the consignee. Why do you want them?

Jane：We want to make sure that no third party will claim the cargo with any of the original B/L.

Wang：Do you accept Letter of Indemnity?

Jane：As a rule. We have to make a commercial decision and take the risk ourselves of we do so. But considering you are our long time customer, we accept it.

Wang：Thank you. I will go back to the company and ask the bank to provide you with a Letter of Indemnity.

Jane：Wait a moment. Who will pay for the extra expense that may incur when the containers are moved?[3]

Wang：Of course we will contact the customer and ask them to pay.

Jane：Well, that is not our business. You'll have to advance the expenses, I'm afraid.

Wang：Of course. All the expense incurred for this purpose will be for our account. [4] Now, see you later.

Jane：See you later.

New words and terms

destination	n.	目的地
Toulouse	n.	图卢兹(法国南部港口)
Marseilles	n.	马赛(法国东南部港口)
consignee	n.	收货人,收件人
incur	v.	引起,导致
TEU		20 英尺的标箱
Suez Canal		苏伊士运河
Letter of Indemnity		补偿信
consignment	n.	委托之货物
transit	n.	通过,通行
original	n.	最初的,正本的

Notes

1. I remember the consignment consists of twenty TEUs.

这批货物包括 20 个标箱。

2. I must have the three original Bills of Lading.

我必须有三份正本提单。

3. Who will pay for the extra expense that may incur when the containers are moved?

谁来支付货物转运引起的额外费用？

4. All the expense incurred for this purpose will be for our account.

所有由此引起的费用从我们账户中支付。

Exercises 9(4)

Ⅰ. **Oral Practice**：**Practice the above dialogue with your partner until you can learn the lines by heart.**

Ⅱ. **Team work**：**Make up a dialogue according to the following situation and practice it with your partner.**

Situation：

Jenny is planning to import the goods. She needs the help of the XinXing International Logistics Co. , Ltd on the customs clearance.

Tips：

1. Nice to meet you.

2. We need to talk about …

3. We can provide all types of services on the international logistics.

4. Our core business is the customs clearance.

5. You can depend on us.

6. We specialize in …

7. You need provide all relative documents.

8. All expenses will be on our account.

Ⅲ. **Write an e-mail to your customer**，**telling them politely and patiently like that**：

Contents：

1. 此批出口货物必须检验，这是海关的规定。

2. 我们可以找检验师检验货物。

3. 在 2 天内做完。

4. 所有的费用由你们支付。

Ⅳ. Read the dialogue and translate into Chinese.

Xiaoyang, business representative of A company, negotiates with Mr. Jackson, business representative of B company, concerning shipment of wrong goods.

Xiaoyang：Upon the examination of your delivery, we find it does not contain the goods we ordered. No doubt, you have made an error.

Jackson：Would you please tell us in detail?

Xiaoyang：We ordered tablecloths, whereas the contents are towels. Evidently, the goods are wrong. We're holding the goods for your disposal in our warehouse.

Jackson：The mistake is entirely on our side. We'll try to bring the case to a speedy close and arrange to send you replacement immediately, but it is preferable if you can dispose of them at your end.

Xiaoyang：Let me think.

Jackson：We are prepared to allow 15% off the invoice price if you would accept the wrong delivery.

Chapter 10

Purchasing

Lesson 10.1　Purchasing

Definition of Purchasing(采购的概念)

Purchasing is not simply buying goods and services, and it is a group of functional activities associated with buying the goods and services required by organizations. These activities include supplier identification and selection, buying, negotiation and contracting, supply market research, supplier measurement and improvement, and purchasing systems development, etc. [1]

The Role of Purchasing(采购的作用)

The most important and traditional role of purchasing is to meet the requirements of internal users. In the past, the emphasis was laid to buy what firms need from the right source, at the right price, in the right quantity, to the right internal customer and at the right specifications. However, with the increase of outsourcing, firms are more and more relying on external suppliers to provide not just materials and products, but also information technology, service, and even logistics. Therefore, to ensure the uninterrupted flow of high-quality goods and services is becoming more critical for modern enterprises.

Purchasing department must develop and maintain close relationships with other functional groups within the organization which may include manufacturing, marketing, technology and finance. Effective communication with these departments is essential and necessary for the whole organization to keep as competitive. For example, if a supplier's components are defective and causing problem for manufacturing, then the purchasing department must work with the supplier to improve their quality.

In order to ensure the current suppliers are competitive, purchasing must identify new suppliers and improve or replace the existing suppliers who are not meeting the requirements. That means the purchasing needs to keep abreast of the newest conditions in supply market. [2]

The Need of Purchasing(采购需求)

Nowadays the need for purchasing to be involved in corporate strategy has received a great deal of attention. The reason is that the amount of money spent on purchasing has increased significantly, and the potential savings from strategic management of purchasing are considerable. Another factor is the trend toward outsourcing, which means firms must manage their suppliers effectively. Now it is believed that suppliers play a critical role in supporting a firm's competitive strategy, whether it is cost leadership, differentiation, or a mixed strategy. [3]

Decision of Purchasing(采购决策)

Purchasing those products and services which firms can not produce is necessary and easily understood, but if they can make or provide these products and services in-house, what will they do? Decisions about whether a producer of goods or services will insource or outsource are also called make-or-buy decisions. [4] Answering such questions is often not as obvious as black and white. To make it clear, management needs to answer the question: What is the difference in relevant costs between the alternatives? Therefore, it is necessary to calculate costs among alternatives and consider its resources and opportunity cost. Finally, some other strategic issues also need to be taken into account. [5]

New words and terms

functional	*adj.*	功能的
internal	*adj.*	内部的
specification	*n.*	规格，规范
outsourcing	*n.*	外包，外购
ensure	*v.*	确保
uninterrupted	*adj.*	不间断的，连续的
enterprise	*n.*	企业，商业机构
finance	*n.*	财务，金融
essential	*adj.*	基本的，必需的
competitive	*adj.*	有竞争力的，竞争的
component	*n.*	零件，部分
defective	*adj.*	有缺陷的
differentiation	*n.*	差异化
relevant	*adj.*	相关的，相应的

alternative	*adj.*	选择性的，二中选一的
	n.	可供选择的事物
strategic	*adj.*	战略上的，关键的
laid to		把……归于
rely on		依赖，依靠
keep abreast of		保持与……并列
cost leadership		成本领先
opportunity cost		机会成本
take into account		重视，考虑

Notes

1. These activities include supplier identification and selection, buying, negotiation and contracting, supply market research, supplier measurement and improvement, and purchasing systems development, etc.

这些活动包括供应商的认定和选择，采购，谈判、合同签订，供应市场调研，供应商的考核和改进，以及采购系统的开发等。

2. That means the purchasing needs to keep abreast of the newest conditions in supply market.

这就意味着采购需要与供应市场的最新情况同步。

3. Suppliers play a critical role in supporting a firm's competitive strategy, whether it is cost leadership, differentiation, or a mixed strategy.

供应商在支持企业的竞争战略上可以扮演极其重要的角色，不管这种战略是成本领先、差异化或是二者的混合。

4. Decisions about whether a producer of goods or services will insource or outsource are also called make-or-buy decisions.

有关一个生产者会自己生产或者外包其产品或服务的决策也称为生产或购买决策。

5. Therefore, it is necessary to calculate costs among alternatives and consider its resources and opportunity cost. Finally, some other strategic issues also need to be taken into account.

因此，有必要在不同的可选项之间计算各自的成本，考虑其资源和机会成本。最后，一些其他的战略因素也需要考虑在内。

Exercises 10(1)

Ⅰ. Pair work: Discuss the following questions.

1. What is purchasing?

2. What are the main tasks for a purchasing manager?

3. Price is the only variable concerned by purchasing managers, isn't it?

4. Can purchasing play a role in supporting a firm's strategic success?

5. What requires that purchasing assume more responsibility?

6. How do you understand the role of purchasing?

7. How to manage the suppliers effectively?

8. How to reduce the purchasing cost?

Ⅱ. Comprehension: True/False/Not Mentioned.

1. Purchasing is simply buying the goods needed by firms or organizations.

2. Meeting the requirements of internal users is the traditional role of purchasing.

3. Nowadays price is not important any more for purchasing.

4. It is necessary to develop and maintain close relationships with other functional groups within the organization.

5. Purchasing needs to know the latest condition in supply market.

6. When a supplier's components are defective, the purchasing department will solve the problems solely.

7. Suppliers cannot play a role in supporting a firm's competitive strategy.

8. Firms will only purchase goods or service which they cannot produce or provide.

9. Make-or-buy decisions are usually obvious and clear to answer for managers.

10. Comparing the difference in relevant cost between the alternatives is helpful to make outsourcing decisions.

Ⅲ. Choose the best answer to each of the following questions.

1. What is the passage mainly about? (   )

   a. How to purchase goods and services.

   b. What is purchasing?

   c. Purchasing is important.

   d. Make-or-buy decisions.

2. How many activities are included in purchasing? (   )

a. supplier selection

b. negotiation

c. supplier measurement

d. all of above

3. With the increase of outsourcing, firms are more relying on external suppliers to provide:
( )

a. materials

b. information technology

c. logistics

d. all of above

4. Nowadays, which of the following is more critical for modern enterprises? ( )

a. buying from the right source

b. buying at the right price

c. buying in the right quantity

d. uninterrupted flow of high-quality goods

5. Outsourcing is: ( )

a. to buy goods or services outside

b. to make goods or service inside

c. to buy materials outside

d. none of above

IV. Translate the following sentences into Chinese.

1. One of the most important duties of purchasing is the right to select suppliers.

2. Most firms include purchasing as a major supply chain activity.

3. The purchasing department performs many activities to ensure it delivers great value to the organization.

4. Suppliers can help differentiate a producer's final good or service.

5. A supplier that performs well can help our organization be more efficient, produce higher quality products or services, reduce costs, and increase profits.

V. Translate the following sentences into English.

1. 采购并不仅仅是购买企业所需要的原材料。

2. 采购已经成为供应链管理的一个重要部分。

3. 低价格已经不再是采购考虑的首要因素。

4. 一些战略上的考虑可能要比成本更重要。

5. 对供应商的管理和评价是非常必要的。

Dialogue 10(1) What Is Purchasing

(Mr. Wang, the purchasing manager in a multinational company, is talking with Miss Li, a new graduated university student.)

Li: Good morning, Mr. Wang. My major is marketing, so I know little about purchasing. Could you tell me more about it?

Wang: Ok. Purchasing is an important function for firms and even non-profit organizations. [1] It is just as important as marketing, and it requires a lot of tactics and rich experience.

Li: Really? I thought purchasing was simply to buy something you need, and it will be easier to do.

Wang: In fact, purchasing consists of many tasks, for example, to identify the internal needs, find the suitable suppliers, negotiate contract, and make sure what you purchase will be delivered on time.

Li: May I say that cost control is the most important for you?

Wang: Yes. Price, together with quality and delivery are the most obvious and important factors for purchasing managers to consider.

Li: Are there any other things related to purchasing?

Wang: Yes. Such as make-or-buy decision, supplier technology, and how purchasing can support the firm's competitive strategy. [2]

Li: Well, I know some of them. But how can purchasing support a firm's competitive strategy?

Wang: You know, the movement toward global sourcing, rapid changes in technology, and increased competition require purchasing to assume more responsibility in the planning and implementation of strategies to support corporate strategy.

Li: It sounds reasonable.

Wang: Now considerable focus is placed on ensuring supply, inventory minimization, quality improvement, supplier development, and the lowest total cost of ownership.

Li: Exactly, all of these are connected with purchasing.

Wang: That means good purchasing can make the corporate more profitable.

Li: I know much about purchasing now. So what is the current situation in most firms?

Wang: Unfortunately, most organizations have not fully understood the role of purchasing.

It is clear that the attitudes of top management and purchasing managers themselves must change before purchasing playing a strategic role in organizations. [3]

Li：It must be a long way.

Wang：Yes. Besides, purchasing skills also need to be developed.

Li：Definitely.

Wang：So have you got the rough picture of purchasing now?

Li：Yes. Now I fully understand what you said. Purchasing is really important.

Wang：We welcome you to join the purchasing profession in the future.

Li：Thank you a lot. I will consider it seriously.

New words and terms

major	*n.*	专业，主修方向
function	*n.*	功能
tactics	*n.*	战术，策略
identify	*v.*	确定
negotiate	*v.*	商议，谈判
assume	*v.*	承担
reasonable	*adj.*	有道理的
role	*n.*	任务，角色
management	*n.*	管理
rough	*adj.*	大致的
profession	*n.*	职业，专业
non-profit		非营利的
consist of		由……组成
make-or-buy		生产或购买
competitive strategy		竞争策略

Notes

1. Purchasing is an important function for firms and even non-profit organizations.
   采购是企业甚至非营利组织的一个重要功能。

2. Such as make-or-buy decision, supplier technology, and how purchasing can support the firm's competitive strategy.
   比如：生产或购买的决策，供应商的技术，以及采购如何支持企业的竞争策略。

3. Unfortunately, most organizations have not fully understood the role of purchasing. It is clear that the attitudes of top management and purchasing managers themselves must change before purchasing playing a strategic role in organizations.

遗憾的是,大多数组织还没有完全理解采购的功能。只有高层管理者以及采购经理的态度发生改变,采购才可能在组织中发挥战略作用。

Exercises 10(2)

Ⅰ. **Oral Practice**: **Practice the above dialogue with your partner until you can learn the lines by heart.**

Ⅱ. **Team work**: **Make up a dialogue according to the following situation and practice it with your partner.**

Situation:

Mary is a retailer of daily necessities. Now some of her goods that sell well are going out of stock, so she is phoning her supplier Mr. Smith asking for more supplies.

Tips:

1. Hi, this is … speaking.

2. Is there anything I can do for you?

3. I need some …

4. There is a great need of …

5. I'm in urgent need of …

6. What else do you need?

7. I'm not sure if you have …

8. How soon can I get it?

9. I'm afraid you have to wait until …

10. Sorry, we don't have the goods you need right now, but we can …

Ⅲ. **Write an e-mail to a website to order goods**, **telling them politely and patiently like that**:

Contents:

1. 向某网站订购你所需要的商品

2. 说明商品的名称和型号

3. 说明送货的时间和地点

IV. Give the English words or phrases according to the meanings provided.

1. _____ the activity of buying things, especially for a company or an organization
2. _____ to find or discover somebody/something
3. _____ the main subject or course of a student at college or university
4. _____ to try to reach an agreement by formal discussion
5. _____ a plan that is intended to achieve a particular purpose
6. _____ that is likely to make money
7. _____ a particular situation or fact that makes you sad or disappointed
8. _____ the people who run and control a business or similar organization
9. _____ fair, practical and sensible
10. _____ a situation in which people or organizations compete against each other

Lesson 10. 2　Purchasing Process

The purchasing process usually consists of six stages:

- Identify user need for product and service
- Evaluate potential suppliers
- Supplier selection
- Purchase approval
- Release and receive purchase requirements
- Measure suppliers' performance

However, these stages may vary in different organizations, depending on whether purchasing is to buy a new or repeat item, and also whether there is a approval process for purchases that exceed a specific amount. [1] New items require that purchasing spend much more time evaluating potential sources. Repeat items usually have approved sources already available.

Identify User Need for Product of Service(确认产品的用户需求)

The purchasing process begins with identifying materials or services needed by an internal user. Material requirements might include equipment, components, raw materials, or even completely finished products. [2] Examples of service can be a need for computer programmers, transportation carriers, or maintenance service providers. Users may use different ways to communicate with purchasing, such as by phone, word-of-mouth, or through the internal computer networks.

Evaluate Potential Suppliers(评估潜在的供应商)

Once a firm identifies potential items to be purchased, it must gather and evaluate information on potential suppliers, and this is the case particularly for a new purchase. A list of potential suppliers can be generated from a variety of resources, including market representatives, trade shows, trade journals, the current suppliers, and the Internet. Although the traditional ways are still widely used and helpful, more and more firms are utilizing the Internet as an aid to search business opportunities since it is effective, efficient and inexpensive. [3]

Supplier Selection(选择供应商)

Selecting suppliers is one of the most important activities performed by companies, since mistakes made during this stage can be damaging and long-lasting. When price is a main criteria and the required item or service has clear specifications, competitive bidding is the commonly used method. Generally the lowest bidder receives the contract; otherwise, the buyer must explain why it did not get the contract. However, when non-price variables exist, then the buyer and seller usually negotiate directly. Finally, the purchasing team will select a supplier based on the bids received or the negotiation result, and then move on to the next stage. [4]

Purchase Approval (采购实施)

After the supplier is selected, purchasing grants an approval to purchase the product or service. This is accomplished through issuing a purchase order (PO), also called a purchase agreement. The purchase order will specify the details agreed by the buyer and seller, such as quantity, price, delivery date, method or delivery, and so on. It should be noted that nowadays more and more firms are using computerized databases to perform these tasks and are moving to a "paperless" office. [5]

Release and Receive Purchase Requirements(发送和接收采购需求)

At this stage, purchasing or other functional groups must monitor the process carefully. Lots of potential conflicts may occur at this period, since the supplier and buyer are two separated groups in traditional sense and their goals may be in conflict. For example, the supplier wants to produce and ship in an economic size, while the buyer's goal is to minimize inventory and expect small orders and short lead time.

Performance Measurements(业绩衡量)

Suppliers' performance is critical to an organization, and evaluation should be conducted on a continuous basis. [6] A supplier that performs well can help organizations be more efficient, produce higher quality products or services, reduce costs, and increase profits.

However, very few companies have developed systems to measure their suppliers' performance.

New words and terms

stage	*n.*	阶段,时期
approval	*n.*	同意,批准
exceed	*v.*	超过
maintenance	*n.*	维护
particularly	*adv.*	特别地,独特地
journal	*n.*	期刊
utilize	*v.*	利用
aid	*n.*	帮助,辅助
effective	*adj.*	有效的
efficient	*adj.*	有效率的
grant	*v.*	同意,准予
accomplish	*v.*	完成,实现
issue	*v.*	发布
monitor	*v.*	监控
conflict	*n.*	冲突
conduct	*v.*	实施,进行
depending on		决定于,视……而定
finished product		成品
word-of-mouth		口头的
trade show		贸易展览
long-lasting		持续长时间的
non-price		非价格
on a continuous basis		持续地

Notes

1. These stages may vary in different organizations, depending on whether purchasing is to buy a new or repeat item, and also whether there is a approval process for purchases that exceed a specific amount.

   在不同的组织中,这些阶段可能会有所不同,取决于是重复还是全新的采购,还有是否规定了超过一定限额的采购需要一个批准程序。

2. Material requirements might include equipment, components, raw materials, or even completely finished products.

物料需求可能包括设备、部件、原材料,甚至是完全的制成品。

3. Although the traditional ways are still widely used and helpful, more and more firms are utilizing the Internet as an aid to search business opportunities since it is effective, efficient and inexpensive.

虽然传统的方法仍然广泛的使用,也很有帮助,但越来越多的组织逐渐使用互联网作为一个辅助来搜寻商业机会,因为它不但有效,而且效率高也不昂贵。

4. Finally, the purchasing team will select a supplier based on the bids received, or the negotiation result, and then move on to the next stage.

最后,采购团队将根据收到的标书,或是谈判的结果来选定一个供应商,然后转向下一个阶段。

5. It should be noted that nowadays more and more firms are using computerized databases to perform these tasks and are moving to a "paperless" office.

应该注意到,今天越来越多的企业开始采用计算机数据库来完成这些工作,逐渐走向一个"无纸化"的办公。

6. Suppliers' performance is critical to an organization, and evaluation should be conducted on a continuous basis.

供应商的表现对一个组织来说极为重要,因此评价应该经常地进行。

Exercises 10(3)

I . Comprehension: True/False/Not Mentioned.

1. For any organization, the purchasing process consists of six stages.

2. Repeat items usually have approved sources already available.

3. The purchasing department communicates with internal users by the internal computer networks only.

4. The purchasing department usually uses the Internet as the main source to search suppliers.

5. Bidding is the commonly used method for buyers.

6. Ninety percent of firms now use computerized databases to perform approval tasks and moving to a "paperless" office.

7. Monitoring the purchasing process is necessary and important.

8. Many companies have developed systems to measure their suppliers' performance.

Ⅱ. Fill in the blanks with the following words in the box, and change the forms if necessary.

identify	maintenance	negotiate	accomplish	goal
performance	efficient	effective	bidding	minimize

1. _____ inventory is one of the goals set by management.

2. Purchasing process begins by _____ internal needs.

3. With today's technology you can affordably _____ the dream of a paperless office.

4. Suppliers' _____ is critical for your organization's success in today's competitive environment.

5. The website uses an automatic system to make _____ more convenient and less time-consuming for buyers.

6. The school pays for heating and the _____ of the buildings.

7. _____ communication skills are essential for success in today's knowledge-based society.

8. I was really impressed by their _____ management system.

9. Our _____ is to develop successful, long-term partnerships where our services integrate with your specific needs.

10. _____ contracts require a lot of skills and rich experience.

Ⅲ. Translate the following sentences into Chinese.

1. Purchasing is slowly but surely receiving greater attention from top management.

2. The purchasing process is a cycle consisting of several stages.

3. The process that buyers use to select suppliers can vary widely depending on the required items.

4. Buyers use different performance criteria when evaluating potential suppliers.

5. Online ordering systems involve direct electronic links from a buyer's system to a seller's system.

Ⅳ. Translate the following sentences into English.

1. 不同的行业往往有不同的采购程序。

2. 采购人员的谈判能力和经验对签订合同非常重要。

3. 一个新的采购项目通常要比日常采购花费更多的时间。

4. 利用互联网进行信息沟通已经成为企业节省成本的一个重要手段。

5. 供应商的出色表现可以为企业提高竞争优势。

Dialogue 10(2)　Ordering Equipment

(*Mr. Li, the purchasing officer in a University is talking with Miss Zhang, the marketing representative in an IT company.*)

Zhang: Good morning. Mr. Li.

Li: Hello. Miss Zhang.

Zhang: We know that the University will build a new computer laboratory. Can you give me some details about that?

Li: Yes. The project will need hundreds of computers, relevant software and accessories. [1]

Zhang: That's great. How do you do that?

Li: Bidding. Companies should provide documents for initial evaluation, such as a copy of financial accounts for the previous three years, etc.

Zhang: I see.

Li: All responses will be fully evaluated according to the agreed criteria, including price, lead-time, quality and suitability of equipment, reputation of supplier, etc.

Zhang: Ok. That must include many documents and tables.

Li: Yes. You can get that in our office, or download from our website.

Zhang: Great. May I ask the payment terms?

Li: Payment will be within 45 days of receipt of invoice and goods, but during this period installation and provision of training must be finished. [2]

Zhang: Ok. When should we submit the tender document?

Li: No later than 12：00 a. m. on 21 July. And you may send it to the address on the invitation in a sealed envelope.

Zhang: That will be no problem for us.

Li: Please note that one printed copy of the tender document must be submitted, together with an electronic one. [3]

Zhang: All right.

Li: You can provide companies or organizations, which have previously purchased the same equipment from you as a reference.

Zhang: That is fine for us. We have sold the similar products to several universities in the past few years.

Li: University contracts offer companies a marketing advantage, as those provide them a showcase to the students, who are potential buyers in the future. [4]

Zhang: That depends. It may or may not work.

Li: Anyway, Please consider this and the University looks forward to receiving a substantial educational discount. [5]

Zhang: Ok. I will talk this to my boss.

Li: For more details, you can see from the documents.

Zhang: Thank you very much. We will work on it and submit it on time.

Li: We look forward to seeing it soon. See you.

Zhang: See you soon.

New words and terms

accessory	*n.*	零件,附件
bidding	*n.*	招标
evaluation	*n.*	评价
criteria	*n.*	标准
receipt	*n.*	收到,收据
invoice	*n.*	商业发票
installation	*n.*	安装
envelope	*n.*	信封,信袋
reference	*n.*	参考,证明
showcase	*n.*	展示
substantial	*adj.*	真实的
discount	*n.*	折扣
financial account		财务报告
tender document		标书

Notes

1. The project will need hundreds of computers, relevant software and accessories.
   该项目需要几百台电脑,以及相关的软件和零配件。

2. Payment will be within 45 days of receipt of invoice and goods, but during this period installation and provision of training must be finished.
   在收到货物和发票之后的 45 天内我们会付款,但在此期间安装培训必须完成。

3. Please note that one printed copy of the tender document must be submitted, together with

an electronic one.

请注意需要上交一份打印的标书,还有一份电子版的。

4. University contracts offer companies a marketing advantage, as those provide them a showcase to the students, who are potential buyers in the future.

大学的合同给公司提供了营销的优势,因为它们提供了一个向学生展示的平台,而这些学生都是将来的潜在购买者。

5. Please consider this and the University looks forward to receiving a substantial educational discount.

请考虑这一点,而且学校期待着实实在在的教育折扣。

Exercises 10(4)

I . Read the dialogue carefully again and discuss the following questions.

1. What did the university plan to purchase?

2. How did the university intend to select suppliers?

3. What was the deadline for submitting the tender?

4. Did the university prefer to get references from companies or organizations which had previously bought the same equipment?

5. Did the university ask for installation and training?

6. Why did the university expect substantial discount from suppliers?

II . Brainstorming: Work with your partner, list things which you may concern if you are a purchasing manager.

| price, installation, _____, _____, _____ |
| delivery, _____, _____, _____ |

III. Write an E-mail to your supplier based on the following information provided.

1. 确定所需要购买的计算机和数量50台;

2. 明确交货时间为两周之内;

3. 付款时间为交货后的一个月之内。

IV. Give the English words or phrases according to the meanings provided.

1. _____ an extra piece of equipment that is useful but not essential

2. _____ connected with money

3. _____ a list of goods that have been sold, showing what you must pay

4. _____ to offer to pay a particular price for something

5. _____ the act of receiving something

6. _____ a thing you say or write that mentions somebody/something else

7. _____ an amount of money that is taken off the usual cost of something

8. _____ the act of fixing equipment or furniture in position

V. Answer these questions after reading.

As the growth of international trade continues, the professional standards of buying overseas rises. In many situations such company involvement has arisen due to force of circumstances and has not resulted from any preconceived policy. The end result is sometimes that the company's resources are not always used cost effectively nor are the strategies well conceived. Hence, senior management must devote adequate time and energy to effective planning and the evolvement of sound realizable strategies.

When a company is committed to a policy of buying overseas, it must earmark adequate resources in terms of personnel, finance and accommodation for production, assembly and storage. Such data will feature in the company's budget. Personnel should be professionally qualified in the area of international business with sound linguistic, negotiating and product knowledge skills. Additionally, the executive must be culturally focused with logistic and high-tech computer skills. Furthermore, the buyer must have a good technical knowledge of the product sought and all the ingredients of the overseas contract embracing finance, import duty and documentation.

The buyer must take a keen interest in the supplier's product and company and technical development to ensure it is competitive in the marketplace and cost effective to buy. Regular visits should be exchanged. Company policy on product sourcing overseas requires continuous review in terms of suppliers, price, technical development, general competitiveness and the market environment. Market research should play a major role. The important area is planning.

Planning is the processing of regulating and coordinating activities on a time basis together with the resources necessary to carry out these activities in order to achieve set objectives. Essentially it is a management function and has a strategic focus. Planning is especially important for the complex and diverse process of international purchasing. It yields a great many benefits.

Directions: Reading the passage and answer the following Yes/No questions.

1. Do the professional standards of buying rise as the growth of international trade continues?

(   )

2. Is the end result sometimes that the company's resources are always used cost effectively and strategically? (   )

3. Must senior management devote some time and energy to effective planning? (   )

4. When a company is committed to a policy of buying overseas, must it earmark adequate resources in terms of personnel, finance and accommodation for production, assembly and storage? (   )

5. Should personnel be professionally qualified in the area of international business with sound linguistic, negotiating and product knowledge skills? (   )

6. The buyer doesn't need to take a keen interest in the supplier's product and company's technical development to ensure it is competitive in the marketplace, does he? (   )

7. Should regular visits be exchanged? (   )

8. Does market research play a major role? (   )

9. Does planning have a strategic focus? (   )

10. Does planning yield some benefits? (   )

Chapter 11

Export Payment and Export Documentation

Lesson 11.1   Payment for Imports and Exports

Credit terms and the method by which payment will be effected are agreed at the time the sales contract is concluded. If the relationship between the buyer and seller is good, then it may have been agreed to trade on "open account" terms. This means simply that the seller will despatch the goods directly to the buyer, send him or her an invoice and await the remittance of payment from the buyer, as in domestic trading.

There are several methods by which the debtor may remit payment to his supplier.

Debtor's Own Cheque

This is not a very satisfactory method from the creditor's point of view. Apart from the usual risk that the cheque may be unpaid, it has to be sent back through banking channels to the buyer's country for collection, thus incurring additional expenses. Cheque clearance cycles vary enormously across the world. Negotiated cheques allow the exporter to obtain the immediate value of the cheque or for a pre-set forward value date in the currency of the cheque. Lock boxes provide a fast and secure method of receiving cheque payments from overseas. Cheques are not sent to the seller but are paid directly by the buyer into the seller's bank via a PO Box number reducing the clearance cycle.

Banker's Draft

This would be a draft drawn by the buyer's bank on its correspondent bank in the exporter's country. As such it is good payment but there is always the danger that the draft may be lost in the post and a bank draft cannot be "stopped". A new draft could only be issued against indemnity.

Mail Transfer（MT）

This is the most common method of payment. The debtor instructs his or her bank to request its correspondent bank in the exporter's country to pay the specific amount to the exporter. The whole procedure is done by entries over banking accounts; the buyer's bank debits his account and credits the account of the correspondent bank which, on receipt of the payment instructions, passes a reciprocal entry over its account with the remitting bank and pays the money over to the exporter. The instructions between the banks may be by ordinary mail telex, swift or air mail.

Telegraphic Transfer（TT）

The procedure is similar to that of MT except that the instructions are sent by tele-transmission. This means that the payment is effected more quickly.

Where "open account" terms have not been agreed, then it is for the exporter to arrange for payment to be collected from the buyer. The usual way in which this is done is by the use of bills of exchange. This is the traditional method of claiming that which is due from the debtor, and has been used as a basis for international trade throughout its history.

Instead of merely sending the documents to the debtor with only the covering invoice, the exporter draws a bill of exchange on the debtor for the sum due and attaches the documents to the bill. This is then sent through banking channels for presentation to the buyer. There are several advantages in the employment of bills:

（1）The bill of exchange is an instrument long recognized by trade custom and by the law; there is in consequence an established code of practice in relation to bills.

（2）The bill is a specific demand on the debtor and, if it is drawn in proper form in respect of debt justly due, the debtor refuses it at his or her peril.

（3）The bill is a useful instrument of finance.

The bill provides a useful mechanism for the granting to an overseas buyer of a pre-arranged period of credit. Thus if an exporter has, for some reason, to offer his or her buyer a period of credit, say 90 days, then the bill can be drawn at 90 days' sight. At the same time, the exporter can maintain a degree of control over the shipping documents by authorizing release of the documents on payment, or acceptance of the bill. The bill does provide an instrument on which action can be taken at law.

It should be noted that the drawing of a bill of exchange on the buyer does not guarantee payment and the seller has lost control of the goods to some extent as they are out of his or her country. Moreover, he or she may have to arrange for storage and insurance or even reshipment.

The procedure for the exporter, having obtained the shipping documents, is to draw the bill and lodge it with his or her bank, together with the documents for collection. When lodging the bill, the exporter must give to his or her bank very precise and complete instructions as to what action to take in certain circumstances: whether to forward the bill by air mail, etc., and ask for proceeds to be remitted by telex/fax or air mail; whether the documents are to be released against payment or acceptance of the bill; whether the bill is to be "protested" if dishonoured; whether the goods should be stored and insured if not taken up by the buyer; whether rebate may be given for early payment; who is the Case of Need to whom the collecting bank may refer in case of dispute (usually the exporter's agent).

The exporter's bank will forward the bill and documents to its correspondent bank in the buyer's country passing on exactly the instructions received from the exporter. The correspondent bank (collecting bank) will present the bill and documents to the buyer, and release the documents to the buyer in accordance with the instructions received. If the arrangement was for payment to be made immediately then the bill of exchange will be drawn at "sight" and the instructions will be to release documents against payment (D/P). If a period of credit has been agreed, then the bill will be drawn at say "90 days' sight" and the instructions will be for the documents to be released against acceptance by the buyer of the bill (D/A). In this case, the buyer signs his or her acceptance across the face of the bill, which now becomes due for payment in 90 days' time and the buyer obtains the documents of title to the goods. The collecting bank will advise the remitting bank of the date of acceptance, and hold the bill until maturity, when the collecting bank will present it to the buyer for payment. In case of dishonour, and if so instructed, the collecting bank will arrange "protest" by a notary. This procedure provides legal proof that the bill was presented to the drawee and was dishonoured, and enables action to be taken in the courts without further preliminaries.

The procedures and responsibilities of the banks and other parties are laid down in the "Uniform Rules for Collection" issued by the International Chamber of Commerce—Publication No 522—1995 Revision, in force as of 1st January 1996 and subscribed to by the major banks throughout the world.

The method of collecting payment described above is based on the documentary bill, but in certain circumstances use may be made of a "clean" bill, that is, a bill to which no documents are attached. Such bills may be drawn for the collection of monies due for services, etc. or for any debt which is not a payment for goods. A "clean" bill may also be used to obtain payment for goods sent on "open account", especially where payment is overdue.

Because they are a traditional and accepted means of obtaining payment in international trade, bills of exchange can be used, with one or two exceptions, throughout the world. In the case of some markets, it would be unwise to operate without the protection a bill can provide. In any trade deal there has to be a balance between making the transaction secure while still making it attractive to the customer or supplier.

Lesson 11. 2　Documentary Credits and Allied Documents

Apart from "cash with order", the documentary credit provides the most satisfactory method of obtaining payment. It provides reassurance to both the importer and exporter. Overall, the documentary credit is an under taking issued by a bank on behalf of the buyer (importer/applicant) to the seller (exporter/beneficiary), to pay for goods and/or services, provided that the seller presents documents which comply fully with the terms and conditions of the documentary credit. The documentary credit is often referred to as a DC, LC Letter of Credit or Credit. All documentary credits should be handled according to the International Chamber of Commerce practice known as the "Uniform Customs and Practice for Documentary Credits". The current code is defined in the 1993 revision, ICC Publication No 500 and commonly referred to as UCP 500. A supplement was issued in 2002 which embraces the evolution from paper to electronic Docymentary Credit. It is termed a UCP—electronic presentation—a supplement to UCP 500. Overall, it accommodates trade which is either completely electronic or where a mixture of electronic and paper documentation is used.

In 2005 the ICC were formulating a new set of rules governing documentary credits to ease the movement of goods across borders while reflecting the need to tighten security without impeding trade. It will be known as the Uniform Customs and Practice for Documentary Credits UCP 600 and displace UCP 500 and may be introduced by 2007.

It provides security of payment to the exporter, and enables the buyer to ensure that he or she receives the goods as ordered and delivered in the way he or she requires. It is an arrangement whereby the buyer instructs his or her bank to establish a credit in favour of the seller. The buyer's bank (issuing bank) undertakes, or authorizes its correspondent bank in the exporter's country, to pay the exporter a sum of money (normally the invoice price of the goods) against presentation of shipping documents which are specified in the credit. It is a mandatory contract and completely independent of the sales contract. It is concerned only with documents and not the goods to which the documents refer. Liability for payment now rests with the issuing bank and not the buyer.

The usual form of these credits is the "irrevocable" credit, which means that it cannot be cancelled or amended without the agreement of the beneficiary (the exporter) and all other parties. Such a credit, opened by a reputable bank in a sound country, means that the exporter can rely on payment being made as soon as he or she has shipped the goods and produced the documents called for in accordance with the terms of the credit. The security provided by an irrevocable credit may be further enhanced if the bank in the exporter's country (advising bank) is requested by the issuing bank to add its "confirmation". The exporter then has a "confirmed irrevocable credit" and he or she need look no further than his or her own local bank for payment. With a credit which is not "confirmed", however, the point of payment is the issuing bank (abroad), although the advising bank would usually be prepared to negotiate with recourse.

The credit will set out in detail a description of the goods: price per unit and packing; name and address of the beneficiary; the voyage, that is, port of shipment and port of destination; whether the price is FOB, CFR or CIF; and whether part shipments and transhipment are allowed. In some cases, the ship will be nominated. Details of insurance (if CIF) and the risks to be covered will also be shown. The credit will specify a latest date for shipment and an expiry date which is the latest date for presentation of documents.

Exporters are reminded to be extremely cautious about shipping goods on receipt of an unsolicited documentary credit or if a documentary credit is received directly from an issuing bank. From time to time forgeries of documentary credit have arisen and there have been instances where exporters have shipped and presented documents against a completely false instrument. If an exporter suspects a fraudulent transaction, the bank should be informed to check the authenticity of the documentary credit immediately.

Additionally, exporters on receipt of the documentary credit, should not only assess the strength of the issuing bank, but also consider any risks that may arise due to the country in which the issuing bank is based. There have been many instances in recent history where events in a particular country have resulted in an issuing bank being unable to honour its obligation under a documentary credit. Dun and Bradstreet—the credit agency—provide a credit rating on a country basis.

Invoice

The amount must not exceed the credit amount. If terms such as "about" or "circa" are used, a tolerance of 10 percent is allowed (in respect of quantity the tolerance is 3 percent).

The description of the goods on the invoice and the packing must be exact and agree with the credit. An essential part of the description includes the marks and numbers on the packages. These must appear on the invoice. The invoice should be in the name of the buyer. The commercial invoice represents the sellers claim for payment to the buyer under the terms of the sales contract and outlined in article 37 UCP 500.

Bills of Lading

This is the document of title to the goods, without which the buyer will not be able to obtain delivery from the shipping company. The credit will call for a full set (they are usually issued in a set of three). They must be clean, that is, bearing no superimposed clauses derogatory to the condition of the goods such as " inadequate packing ", " used drums ", " on deck ", etc. Unless the credit has specifically permitted the circumstances contained in the clause, the negotiating bank will call for an indemnity. The bills of lading must show the goods to be " on board "—" received for shipment " bills are not acceptable. They may, however, have a subsequent notation, dated and signed, which states the goods to be " on board " and they are then acceptable. Under the regulations set out in the " Uniform Customs and Practice for Documentary Credits "—ICC Publication No 500—1993 Revision in force as of 1 January 1994—articles 23-26, the following bills of lading will be accepted:

(1) Through bills issued by shipping companies or their agents even though they cover several modes of transport.

(2) Short form bills of lading which indicate some or all of the conditions of carriage by reference to a source or document other than the bill of lading.

(3) Bills covering unitized cargoes such as those on pallets or in containers.

Charterparty bills of lading which do not contain the full conditions of carriage but are detailed in a separate charterparty agreement are not acceptable unless specifically allowed in the credit under article 25 of UCP 500.

Unless specifically authorized in the credit, bills of the following type will not be accepted:

(1) Bills of lading issued by forwarding agents. [1]

(2) Bills which are issued under and are subject to a charterparty.

(3) Bills covering shipments by sailing vessels.

The bills must be made out " to the order of the shipper " and endorsed in blank. If the sales contract is CIF or CFR, then the bills must be marked " freight paid ". The general description of the goods including marks and numbers must match the invoice. The voyage and ship, if named, must be stated in the credit. Unless transhipment is expressly prohibited in the credit, bills indicating transhipment will be accepted provided the entire voyage is covered by the same bill. Part shipments are permitted unless the credit states otherwise. Besides stating an expiry date for presentation of documents, credits should also stipulate a specified period of time after the issuance of the bills during which the documents must be presented payment. If no such period is stipulated in the credit, banks will refuse documents presented to them later than 21 days after the issuance of the bills of lading.

Sea Waybill

This document has been developed to reduce the problem inherent in short voyage where the documentation is not available at the time of arrival of the vessel. It is also used increasingly by multinational industries and their subsidiaries. However, it is not a document of title. It is a receipt for goods and evidence of carriage and should be handled in a similar manner to an air waybill.

An original document is not required as delivery is made to the named consignee against proof of identity—usually a delivery order on the consignees headed stationery. The shipper can vary the consignee and delivery instructions at any time prior to delivery. To counteract this problem certain carriers will apply control or waiver clauses to the waybills to meet the requirements of buyers, insurers and financiers. Sea waybills cannot be issued "to order" or to order of a named party. The non-negotiable sea waybill provisions are found in article 24 of UCP 500.

Multi-modal Transport Document

When goods are carried by more than one mode of transport (usually in containers), a combined (multi-modal) transport document is recommended as the multi-modal transport operator accepts liability for carriage of the goods throughout the entire journey. Where part of the journey is undertaken by sea, some types of multi-modal transport document can convey title to the goods. The multi-modal transport document provisions are found in article 26 of UCP 500.

Air Waybill or Air Consignment Note

Goods which are transported by air require a waybill to act as a receipt for despatch. It will usually show that the goods are consigned either to the buyer or to the issuing bank and may bear a notified party name and address. Unlike bills of lading, air waybills are not issued in sets and do not convey title to the goods. The copy marked—original 3 (for shipper) should normally be presented under a documentary credit.

The principal requirements for this document under a letter of credit include:

(1) the correct shipper and consignee;

(2) the airports of departure and destination;

(3) the goods description must be consistent with that shown on other documents;[2]

(4) any weights, measures or shipping marks must agree with those shown on other documents;

(5) it must be signed and dated by the actual carrier or by the named agent of a named carrier—for example EFGH Forwarding Ltd as agents for the carrier Air India (if the credit states that a house air waybill is acceptable, the forwarder's signature alone will suffice);

(6) it must state whether freight has been paid or is payable at destination. [3]

If required by the letter of credit, it must also carry a specific notation stating the actual flight date, otherwise the date of despatch will be taken to be the date of issuance of the air waybill. The provisions of the Air Transport document are found in article 27 of UCP 500.

Insurance

The document must be as stated in the credit (policy or certificate) and issued by an insurance company or its agent. [4] Cover notes issued by brokers are not acceptable.

The details on the policy must match those on the bills of lading—voyage, ship, marks and numbers, etc. It must also be in the same currency as the credit and endorsed in blank. The amount covered should be at least the invoice amount; credits usually call for invoice value plus 10 percent. The policy must be dated not later than the date of shipment as evidenced by the bill of lading. The risks covered should be those detailed in the credit. If cover against "all risks" is called for (which is obtainable) a policy which states that it covers all insurable risks will be acceptable. The provisions for insurance are found in articles 34-36 of UCP 500.

According to circumstances, the credit may call for other documents such as a consular certificate; a packing list; a certificate of origin; quality, analysis or health certificate (ensures to buyer that the goods are as ordered); an air waybill; railway (CIM) or road (CMR) consignment notes or Post Office receipt; and pre-shipment inspection documentation including Certificate of Inspection/clean report of findings and courier receipt (small parcels/packets).

The credit may stipulate a last shipment date and the bill of lading must show shipment by that date. Extension of the shipment date automatically extends the expiry date but not vice versa.

It is very important that exporters, when they receive advice of a credit established in their favour, check the details immediately to see that the goods and terms agree with the sales contract, and they can comply with all the terms and provide all the documents required. If any amendment is required, this can then be taken up with the advising bank in good time for action to be taken before expiry.

Besides the basic irrevocable credit (confirmed or not), there are revocable credits which, as the name implies, can be cancelled or amended at any time without notice to the beneficiary. They do not constitute a legally binding undertaking by the banks concerned. Once transmitted and made available at the advising bank, however, its cancellation or modification is only effective when that bank has received notice thereof and any payment made before the receipt of such notice is reimbursable by the issuing bank. The value of these credits as security for payment is plainly doubtful. They are used mainly for parent companies and subsidiaries, where a continuing series of shipments is concerned or as an indication of good intent.

Where a buyer wishes to provide his or her supplier with the security of payment by documentary credit, but at the same time requires a period of credit, he or she may instruct his or her bank to issue a credit calling for a bill of exchange drawn at so many days after sight instead of the usual sight draft; this would, of course, be an irrevocable credit. In this case, the beneficiary, when presenting the documents, would not receive immediate cash as under a sight credit but his or her term bill would be accepted by the bank. It could then be discounted in the money market at the finest rates. Thus the beneficiary would still receive payment, but the buyer would not be called upon to pay until the bill matured.

Methods of Settlement and Availability of Documentary Credits

According to UCP 500 (article 10) documentary credit may be made available in one of four ways as detailed below.

(1) Sight payment. Payment is made to the seller locally upon presentation of conforming documents. A sight draft is usually called for although payment can be made against documents alone. If payment to the seller is made before the account is debited, interest will be charged from the date of payment to the date that the paying bank is reimbursed. If the buyer wishes, he or she can authorize the paying bank to claim payment by tele-transmission and have the seller's account debited upon receipt of the claim.

(2) Deferred payment credit. This type of credit does not require the presentation of a draft. The nominated bank is authorized to debit the issuing bank's account at a future date against presentation of conforming documents. The date for payment is defined in the documentary credit, usually as a specific number of days after the date of despatch of goods or after the date of presentation of the documents. It has become increasingly popular where the buyer does not wish the credit period to be represented by a bill of exchange as usually,

under local law, it attracts stamp duty.

Consequently, when documents are presented "in order" by the seller, the bank does not accept a bill of exchange but instead gives a letter of undertaking to the seller advising him or her when he or she will receive his or her money. The main disadvantage is that, should the exporter wish to receive his or her money immediately, he or she does not have a bill of exchange to have discounted. Hence, if the credit is unconfirmed, the undertaking to effect payment on the due date is that of the issuing bank. Payment will only be effected on the due date by the nominated bank after taking account of the same factors involving sight payments. However, if the credit is confirmed, the undertaking to pay is made by the confirming bank. Payment will then be made on the due date by the nominated bank (if any) or by the confirming bank.

(1) Negotiation sight or usance drafts may be drawn and negotiated by a bank. The credit may be made freely negotiable with any bank or negotiation may be restricted to a bank nominated by the issuing bank. Under this type of credit, the seller is responsible for any negotiation interest unless the negotiating bank is specially authorized by the buyer to charge interest to his or her account.

(2) Acceptance credits. This type of credit requires a presentation of a usance draft drawn on the bank nominated as accepting bank. The draft is accepted by the bank, payable at a future date, usually fixed in the documentary credit as a specific number of days from the date of despatch of goods.

Originally this facility was provided by merchant banks. The bank establishes its own credit in favour of the exporter. The credit provides for bills to be drawn by the exporter on the bank which are accepted by the latter and can then be discounted in the money market at the finest rates. It is usual for such credits to run parallel with the bills drawn by the exporter on his or her overseas buyer and which he or she lodges with the bank for collection. The bills under the credit will be drawn on the same terms as those of the buyers and in due course the payment received for the commercial bills will meet the dues to the bank on its acceptances. Exporters who take advantage of finance from their bank under a documentary credit will be charged interest on the amount advanced. The period for which interest is charged will vary for each transaction.

In situations where the buyer has requested an amendment to the documentary credit, it is important that the exporter in varying the payment terms under the documentary credit does not relinquish control of the goods. When an amendment has been received, the following check list must be followed: (a) have all the relevant points been covered; (b) is the exporter in complete agreement with the new terms; (c) has the amendment been made to a confirmed documentary credit, and if so, has the confirming bank chosen to extend its confirmation to cover the amended terms; (d) does the amendment extend the expiry date of the documentary credit, and is this covered by the bank's confirmation; and (e) if the documentary credit is being amended because of the fault of the buyer, can the exporter ensure that all costs related to the amendment are borne by the buyer, including the advising bank's charges.

New words and terms

debtor	*n.*	债务人,借方
telegraphic transfer		电汇
mail transfer		信汇
D/A		承兑交单
advising bank		通知银行
bills of lading		提单
multi-modal transport		多式联运
sight payment		见单付款
draft	*n.*	汇票
cheque	*n.*	支票
D/P		付款交单
issuing bank		开证银行
invoice	*n.*	发票
sea waybill		海运单
insurance	*n.*	保险
acceptance credits		承兑信用证

Notes

1. Bills of lading issued by forwarding agents.
   由货运代理签发的提单。

2. The goods description must be consistent with that shown on other documents.
   货物描述必须与其他文件所示一致。

3. It must state whether freight has been paid or is payable at destination.
   必须说明是否运费已经支付或在目的地支付。

4. The document must be as stated in the credit and issued by an insurance company or its agent.

该单据必须按照信用证的规定由保险公司或其代理人签发。

Exercises 11

Ⅰ. Translate the following sentences into Chinese.

1. A letter of credit is a document typically issued by a bank or financial institution, which authorizes the recipient of the letter to draw amounts of money up to a specified total, consistent with any terms and conditions set forth in the letter.

2. Complete set of clean "Shipped on Board" Ocean Bills of Lading made out to order of yourselves marked.

3. One set of copies with the notify party as the opener of LC with full address as given below.

4. In consideration of your opening this LC we hereby undertake fulfillment of each and every clause of the terms of the undertaking printed overleaf.

5. A letter of credit could be said to document a bank customer's line of credit, and any terms associated with its use of that line of credit. Letters of credit are most commonly used in association with long-distance and international commercial transactions.

Ⅱ. Translate the following sentences into English.

1. 请注意所有运费将由买方支付,提单上应注明"运费到付"。
2. 剩余金额将以支票方式付入你方账户。
3. 为了避免随后修改信用证,务请注意信用证的规定与合同条款完全一致。
4. 中国出入境检验检疫局的调查表明,货物的损坏系由包装不良导致。
5. 现告知你方,我们的一个客户想要购买中国地毯。

Ⅲ. Answering the following questions.

1. Please answer the methods by which the debtor remit payment to his supplier.
2. Unless specifically authorized in the credit, which types bills of lading will not be accepted?
3. Please answer the definition of Back-to-back credits.
4. Please answer the definition of Transferable credits.
5. Please tell the characteristics of Deferred payment credit.

Ⅳ. Fill in the documents.

Basic Materials:

(1) **Commercial Invoice**

COMMERCIAL INVOICE

Shanghai Jie Xu International Trade Co. , Ltd.

Tower B , 23 San Men Rd.

Shanghai 2000045 , China

TEL: 63567455   **FAX:** 63567345

To: **M/S G. S. GILL SDN BHD**	Invoice No. : **JXFP34626-8**
106 JALAN TRANKU ABDUL , RAHMNAN	Invoice Date: May , 25 , 2006
50100 KUALA LUMPUR	**S/C No. : TX890-8**
MALAYSIA	**S/C Date: Mar , 17 , 2006**

From: **SHANGHAI**	To: **KUALA LUMPUR , MALAYSIA**
L/C No. : CITI998990030782-678	**L/C ISSUING DATE. : APR 28**TH , **2006**
Issued by: CITY BANK KUALA LUMPUR BRANCH	

Marks & Numbers	Quantities and Descriptions		Unit Price	Amount
G. S. GILL	**CLEAN EQUIPMENT**		CIF KUALA LUMPUR	
TX890-8	ART No. :			
KUALA	KP3200	1 , 250 CTNS	US $ 57. 00	US $ 71 , 250. 00
LUMPUR	KP5464	570 CTNS	US $ 49. 00	US $ 27 , 930. 00
C/No. 1-2350	K42239	530 CTNS	US $ 22. 00	US $ 11 , 660. 00

TOTAL PACKAGES: 2350 CARTONS   TOTAL US $ 110 , 840. 00

TOTAL MEAS: 23. 679M^3

ART No.	N. W.	G. W.
KP3200	17kg	19kg
KP5464	15kg	18kg
K42239	15kg	18kg

(2) Part of **Letter of Credit**

L/C NO. : CITI978990030782-678

L/C DATE: APR 28TH , 2006

EXPIRY DATE: JUL 15TH , 2006

BENIFICARY: SHANGHAI JIE XU INTERNATIONAL CO. , LTD.

TOWER B , 23 SAN MEN RD.

SHANGHAI 200045, CHINA

APPLICANT: G. S. GILL SDN BHD

106 JALAN TRANKU ABDUL, RAHMNAN

50100 KUALA LUMPUR

MALAYSIA

SHIPMENT: SHIPMENT BY STEAMER NOT LATER THAN 30 JUN. 2006, FROM

CHINA TO KUALA LUMPUR WITH PARTIAL SHIPMENT

ALLOWED TRANSHIPMENT PROHIBITED

DOCUMENT REQUIRED : COMPLETE SET OF 3/3 CLEAN ON BOARD LINER TERM OCEAN BILL OF LADING MENTIONING THIS CREDIT NO. AND ISSUING DATE MARKED FREIGHT PAID MADE OUT TO THE ORDER OF L/C ISSUING BANK INDICATING BUYERS AS PARTY TO BE NOTIFIED ON DECK BILL OF LADING NOT ACCEPTABLE

Question: Use the Commercial Invoice and Letter of Credit fill in the following documents.

Shipper		consignment No:
		Forwarding agents
Consignee		
Tel:		B/L No.
Notify Party		
Tel:		
Pre carriage by Place of receipt		**Container**
Ocean vessel Voy. No Port of Loading		**consignment note**
Port of Discharge Place of delivery		

Container No. Seal No. No. of containers Or P'kgs Kind of Packages; Description of Goods Gross weight Measurement		
TOTAL NUMBER OF CONTAINER OR PACKAGES (IN WORDE)		

FREIGHT AND CHARGES	Revenue Tons （运费吨）	Rate Per	Prepaid	Collect
Ex Rate	PREPAID AT	PAYABLE AT	PLACE OF ISSUE	
	TOTAL PREPAID	NOOF ORIGINAL B/L	Total Value	

Shipper	**B/L NO.** :
	CHINA OCEAN SHIPPING COMPANY
	Cable：0001 Telex：33200 CSCO CN
	Port-to-Port or Combined Transport
Consignee	**BILL OF LADING *ORIGINAL***
	RECEIVED in external apparent good order and condition. Except otherwise noted the total number of containers or units shown in this Bill of Lading receipt. said by the shipper to contain the goods described above.
Notify Party	Which description the carrier has no reasonable means of checking and is not part of the Bill of Lading. One

Pre-carriage by	Place of Receipt	original Bill of Lading should be surrendered except clause 22 paragraph 5 in exchange for delivery of the shipment. Signed by the consigned or duly endorsed by
Ocean Vessel Voy. No.	Port of Loading	the holder in due course. Whereupon the other original(s) issued shall be void. In accepting this Bill of Lading. The Merchants agree to be bound by all the terms on the
Port of Discharge	Place of Delivery	face and back hereof as if each had personally signed this Bill of Lading.
		Final Destination See Article 7. paragraph(2)

Container No.	Seal No. Marks & Nos.	Kind of Package：Description of Goods	Gross Weight	Measurement
		Final Destination (of the goods- not the ship)		

TOTAL NUMBER OF CONTAINERS OF PACKAGES（IN WORDS）					
FREIGHT &CHARGES	Revenue Tons	Rate	Per	Prepaid	Collect

Ex. Fisto	Prepaid at	Payable at	Place And Date Of Issue
	Total prepaid in	No. of Original B（s）/L	Signed For The Carrier

LADEN ON BOARD THE VESSEL

DATE

By _____

（COSCO STANDARD FORM 07）　（TERMS CONTINUED ON BACK HEREOF）

References

一、相关图书

1. 龙贵先.国际物流与货运代理实务[M].北京：机械工业出版社,2005

2. 姚大伟.国际贸易单证实务[M].北京：中国对外贸易出版社,2005

3. Robert Monczka,Robert Trent,Robert Handfield. Purchasing and Supply Chain Management[M].北京：清华大学出版社,2007

4. 李秀华.货代作业实务[M].北京：机械工业出版社,2008

5. 王艳.物流英语[M].北京：清华大学出版社,2008

6. 陈丕西.报关实务[M].北京：北京大学出版社,2008

7. 陈雅萍.第三方物流[M].北京：清华大学出版社,2008

8. 孙军.物流商务英语[M].大连：大连海事大学出版社,2009

9. 中国国际货运代理协会.国际货运代理专业英语[M].北京：中国商务出版社,2009

10. 王任祥.国际物流[M].杭州：浙江大学出版社,2009

11. 吴健.现代物流专业英语[M].北京：机械工业出版社,2009

12. 沈艳丽.物流英语[M].北京：电子工业出版社,2010

13. 张庆英.物流专业英语教程[M].北京：电子工业出版社,2010

14. Paul Myerson. Lean Supply Chain and Logistics Management[M].McGraw-Hill Education,2012

15. 马丁·克里斯托弗(Martin Christopher).物流与供应链管理[M].北京：电子工业出版社,2012

16. 齐利梅,牛国崎.物流专业英语(第3版)[M].北京：北京理工大学出版社,2014

17. Karida T. Moghadam. Strategic Logistics Management[M]. Createspace,2014

18. S K. Nandi,S L. Ganapathi. Logistics Management[M]. OUP India,2015

19. Yi Wang. Fashion Supply Chain and Logistics Management[M]. Routledge,2016

二、推荐网站：

1. 中国物流网 www.china-logisticsnet.com

2. 中国货代协会网 http://www.cifa.org.cn/index.asp

3. 中国物流与采购网 http://www.chinawuliu.com.cn

4. 国际运输网 http://www.gjwlys.com/

5. 商务部网站：http://www.mofcom.gov.cn/

6. 中华人民共和国交通运输部网：http://www.moc.gov.cn/

7. 中国海关网：http://www.customs.gov.cn/

8. 中华人民共和国铁道部网：http://www.china-mor.gov.cn/

9. 中国物流学会：http://csl.chinawuliu.com.cn/

10. http://cordis.lu

11. http://www.idii.com

12. http://jurisint.org

Appendix

Logistics Terms

A

B

C

free on board（FOB） ·· 装运港船上交货
freeze space ·· 冷冻区
freight unit price ··· 基本运价
fulfillment rate ··· 订单满足率
full container ship ·· 全集装箱船

G

geographical information system（GIS） ························· 地理信息系统
global individual asset identifier（GIAI） ······················ 单个资产标识代码
global location number（GLN） ······························· 全球位置码
global positioning system（GPS） ······························ 全球定位系统
global returnable asset identifier（GRAI） ······················ 全球可回收资产标识代码
global trade item number（GTIN） ···························· 全球贸易项目标识代码
goods ·· 物品,货物
goods coding ··· 货物编码
goods consolidation ··· 集货
goods reserves ·· 物品储备
goods stack ··· 货垛
goods-tracked system ··· 货物跟踪系统
grade labeling ·· 等级标签

H

handling/carrying ··· 搬运
hoisting machinery ·· 起重机械
humidity controlled space ·· 控温储存区

I

identification code for commodity ·································· 商品标识代码
import and export commodity inspection ··························· 进出口商品检验
in bulk ··· 散装化
integrated logistics service ··· 一体化物流服务
integration of military logistics and civil logistics ················· 军地物流一体化
intelligent transportation system（ITS） ······················· 智能交通系统
international airline transport ······································ 国际航空货物运输

M

N

S

T

教学支持说明

▶▶ 课件申请

尊敬的老师：

　　您好！感谢您选用清华大学出版社的教材！为更好地服务教学，我们为采用本书作为教材的老师提供教学辅助资源。该部分资源仅提供给授课教师使用，请您直接用手机扫描下方二维码完成认证及申请。

任课教师扫描二维码
可获取教学辅助资源

▶▶ 样书申请

　　为方便教师选用教材，我们为您提供免费赠送样书服务。授课教师扫描下方二维码即可获取清华大学出版社教材电子书目。在线填写个人信息，经审核认证后即可获取所选教材。我们会第一时间为您寄送样书。

任课教师扫描二维码
可获取教材电子书目

 清华大学出版社

E-mail: tupfuwu@163.com　　　　　　　　　网址：http://www.tup.com.cn/
电话：010-83470158/83470142　　　　　　　传真：8610-83470107
地址：北京市海淀区双清路学研大厦B座509室　邮编：100084